The New World of
James Fenimore Cooper

The New World of
James Fenimore Cooper

Wayne Franklin

The University of Chicago Press
Chicago and London

The University of Chicago Press, Chicago 60637
The University of Chicago Press, Ltd., London

Wayne Franklin is associate professor
of English and American Studies at
the University of Iowa.

Library of Congress Cataloging in Publication Data

Franklin, Wayne.
    The new world of James Fenimore Cooper.

    Includes bibliographical references and index.
    1. Cooper, James Fenimore, 1789–1851—Criticism
and interpretation.   I. Title.
PS1438.F67   813'.2   81-16121
ISBN 0-226-26080-1   AACR2

For Nathaniel

Contents

Acknowledgments

I learned how to read Cooper under the careful guidance of Thomas L. Philbrick, first at Union College and then at the University of Pittsburgh, and it is a pleasure to acknowledge his lasting service to both Cooper and myself. If I have gone astray, it is because, like some of those headstrong "wayfarers" led through the woods by Natty Bumppo, I have doggedly preferred my own path to ones pointed out by more experienced hands. Philbrick has been gentler with my vagaries, I might add, than Natty often is with those that come to his attention. Perhaps what I needed was someone with a healthy scorn for "books!" and a capacity for saying "Anan!" when words, as they are wont, obscure the sense. I should add that I have not forgotten the sea.

Be that as it may, I have sought to be consistent in the pursuit which I set for myself in these pages. I should like to thank those other people who, in reviewing parts of the study, have helped me keep to my purpose. David Chamberlain, a colleague at Iowa, read the first three chapters and offered encouragement of an especially heartening sort. David Morrell, also a colleague at Iowa and an "adventurer" in his own right, kept checking on my progress (and my will) with a conscientiousness that meant more than he probably surmised. And then there were the numerous students who, as they read a Cooper novel or two with me, had little sense that they were contributing to something other than our common work, and contributing to that something other in most pertinent, if indirect, ways. Among the latter group, I should like to give special thanks to John Scheckter and Hugh Egan. John's own study of Australian fiction and its relation to "that great America on the other side of the sphere" (as Melville's Ishmael has it) has been of more help to me than he realizes, as has his reading of the third chapter of this book. Hugh's work on first-person narrative, including that of Cooper, has led him off in other directions than those I have followed, but he, too, has helped focus my ideas by focusing and framing his own. Such are the dividends of the joint-stock company of scholarship. Neither taxed nor taxing, the ideal community thrives on shared insights.

To May Brodbeck, then vice-president for academic affairs at Iowa, and John C. Gerber, then head of the English department, I give my thanks for a summer fellowship which freed me to work on Cooper in 1976.

For my son Nathaniel, who through no fault of his own bears certain mysterious sobriquets he has yet to fathom, I have hopes as well as thanks. The dedication of the book to him speaks of both. And for my wife Karin, fellow New Yorker now living on the "prairie" with Natty and me—indeed, in the "Hawkeye" state!—I have these few words, and at least a mention of all that which words cannot express. She did much of positive aid. And she also never said "Anan!"

Introduction

In subject matter, form, achievement, and sympathies, James Fenimore Cooper was a writer of such range that no single study of his career can hope to account fully for his art. But his radiating imagination, though it led off in innumerable directions, did reach out from a real center. This book attempts to describe and explore that unifying point.

Several assumptions underlie the attempt, and a brief mention of them here at the start will prove useful. The first is that, whatever the accidental or economic causes which may have turned Cooper toward authorship in the first place, he found in storytelling the satisfaction of something more strictly personal. Anyone may write a first novel on a dare or a speculation, both of which Cooper is said to have done. But no person persists in the difficult art without having discovered some sustaining inner drive to do so, at least if what results from the persistence warrants the name of art. This brings me to the second assumption. It is, quite simply, that Cooper was an artist of major proportions, for the measurement of which we generally have not applied the proper tools in the past. Accurate editions of his works are only just now beginning to be prepared; we have had full versions of his letters and journals only since the 1960s; and we have as yet no really thorough and accurate biography. Perhaps more importantly, we have not known how to read Cooper in large and small: we have inherited and not yet outgrown the view that he was a romancer for whom the spinning out of plot, at least in such books as *The Last of the Mohicans*, was the primary act—and an act not especially loaded down with the burdens of thought or the strictures of conscious artistry. Yet it also has been clear since the first labors of Robert E. Spiller in the 1920s that Cooper's engagement with ideas and issues, though for some diehard realists it might not wholly redeem his art, added to his presumed romancing a critical intent not usually associated with adventure. Perhaps the more recent view of Cooper as a *moraliste*, to borrow the term chosen by Donald A. Ringe and supported by other readers, has moved us closest to resolving what now seems like a contradiction in Cooper's career. Such a view has the salient virtue of suggesting the unity of ideologue and tale-spinner. It often is of use in explicating certain individual books or given passages in them, as are the allied insights of Marius Bewley regarding the thematic weight of much of what seems, to a hasty reader, the mere incidents of a Cooper plot.

But my emphasis here falls more on Cooper's imagination than on his ideas. Most of those ideas hardly were original, after all, and it is only the tenacity with which Cooper espoused them in his imaginative works that ought to concern a critic, since thereby they became part of his aesthetic effects. It seems clear, furthermore, that the claim of Cooper's fiction on modern understanding—the issue I really address throughout—does not limit itself in any crucial sense to his conscious, intellectual control of the romance formula, which is, in essence, what the term *moraliste* refers to. I would urge that we try to gauge the shaping power which Cooper possessed, for it was this power that nourished and matured whatever purposes he may have had in mind on a given occasion—or whatever conventional form he may have chosen for achieving them. The lasting significance of Cooper's novels derives from their imaginative energy, which does not always operate at the surface; and that energy itself derives from the spacious impulses and patterns of the man's inner life. To see Cooper as a social critic, or as a moralist, is to limit our response largely to the layer of his art which Cooper's personality arguably controlled. That he was responsible for much more than he himself was aware of is one of my main points here.

Such issues may drift away, however, if they are not tied down. The limits I have imposed on this study aim at securing the issues in the firm particularity of a handful of Cooper's books. But those limits have some warrant, I believe, in the recoverable shape of the man's own imagination. It has seemed to me, as to other readers, that there always was something preciously intense about the memories Cooper bore of the little border world of Otsego County where he grew up—in 1838, he called the feeling "the love of particular places, such as the spots in which we were born, or have passed our lives"—and much of my discussion here centers on those tales of border settlement which Cooper wrote at various points in his career. For these tales he drew not only on his own recollections but also on the printed memoir of his father (and its oral sources), as well as on a body of American sentiment which already was transforming the "pioneer" era, receding in space or time so quickly, into a touchstone of national virtue. There thus was a conjunction of personal and public motivations in Cooper's turn toward the plantation theme. Furthermore, since the pioneer age had tensions not often acknowledged in the nostalgic glance cast toward it by the nation—although they were stressed and overstressed by Cooper himself—this "matter" of settlement gave him the sort of dramatic opportunity which, as a romancer, he clearly needed. We are so familiar with what Cooper initiated, familiar with it through later and often derivative imitations, that we may miss the skill with which he put aside the sentiment and appropriated the essentials of the new form. He found an opportunity and left a tradition.

Since I have raised cultural issues beyond the strict boundaries of literary art, it will be helpful to outline here the relation between Cooper's imaginative world and the larger American scene which it resembles and includes. What we mean when we call Cooper a social critic is that his writings directly record and discuss, rather than just reflect obliquely, the actual environment in which Cooper the man lived. At the furthest extrapolation, I think we are making a comment about Cooper's style: that it is markedly referential rather than "free," that it takes its rise and its object from the talk heard in his own contemporary surroundings. But the issue is not quite this simple. Cooper was drawn toward the subject of the frontier, for example, only in part because he had known a fleeting moment of the real border, and only in part because it was becoming conventional in his period to refer to such classic American origins. Beyond these conscious motives on his side or that of his audience, there lay private reasons which are particularly hard to describe but centrally important nonetheless. If *The Pioneers*, his first settlement tale, was a canny artistic venture whose success in 1823 might have been predicted regardless of who wrote it, it also was a profoundly personal gesture aimed at satisfying an impulse about which Cooper himself would have been hard put to testify. He knew what he was about, but not necessarily why.

This is perhaps the most involved matter raised below. Suffice it to say now that Cooper located in the push of American society westwards a paradigm of his own moral state. For his father, national expansion and personal success were interchangeable; for Cooper himself, however, economic failure made the national link less direct. His conscious allegiance to the banner of American growth was high, and precisely because it was conscious; but his own intercourse with the frontier, especially in his young adulthood, was debilitatingly adverse, as the researches of James Franklin Beard have made clear. Indeed, when Cooper wrote *The Pioneers* his hold on the dwindling family possessions in Otsego was insecure and faltering. Whereas Judge William Cooper could look upon the region with a paternal eye, the novelist was cut off from it when he wrote of its early days. His art clearly gave him a means of returning to the place, returning to it and repossessing it with a power more lasting than that provided in the laws of the state of New York.

Possession understandably became one of the main themes of Cooper's American art, as it was one of the themes of his life even to the end. His personal economic struggle thus allied him with the great underlying anxiety of his age in the United States. The very premise of border plantation, after all, was the insecurity of eastern control over the ever-expanding lands of the West. So, too, the nostalgic backward glance toward the American Revolution—another of Cooper's themes—first was cast in this period, and cast because the literal presence of the past was fading. But Cooper's private use of such public themes was not simply acquisitive, and at last it had motives other than those of his era. He wrote his border tales, as he did many of his other works, to dramatize the failed assumptions of his youth; they were tonics prescribed first and last for their author. The need to recognize reality, a need Cooper struggled to accept as his private world disintegrated in the decade before he became a writer, emerged as a consistent preoccupation of his art—a preoccupation which at his best moments assumed (as Bewley has noted in more general terms) a densely physical form. This is to say that Cooper's gift as a moralist had roots deep in his own experience. The losses he had suffered—both financial and emotional—from 1809 to 1819 set the tone of his imagination for his whole career. In this sense, moralism came to him as much more than a convention from the previous century; it was part of his own vision.

And yet Cooper's moralism does not lead us to the deepest layer of his imagination. In order to go lower, we must come back to the appeal that America itself, as place and subject and ideal, held for him. In its vast and often fugitive spaces, the New World gave Cooper an ample metaphor for the psychic terrain which his art was always attempting to explore. The relation of self and world which formed the center of his themes, along with the consequent stress on the need for "attention" which I discuss below, found its fullest expression in the ambiguities that Cooper perceived in frontier life. The literal border, in other words, supplied him with unceasingly fruitful images of lines and boundaries

more figurative in nature: the most compelling of the latter
being that distinction between the "me" and the "it" which
Ralph Waldo Emerson, in a moment of doubt in the 1830s,
poignantly surveyed. Wrenched as he had been from the
comfortable position bequeathed to him by his father,
Cooper continually saw experience in these antagonistic
terms. Indeed, as the public arguments of his later career
suggest, he positively relished such a vision—so much so that
he sought to create its drama when it did not develop on its
own. His romances, especially those set in the forest, grew
from such a hidden apprehension. What is adventure, after
all, but an energy of "unreal" antagonism, an exaggerated
vision of life in which the alienation of self from world is
both motive and meaning? The convention served Cooper's
own purposes very well.

Cooper did not, as has been claimed, seek an enclosed
and secure world in his art any more than he knew it or
sought it in his life. His stress on the disasters of the border
tells us as much, especially if we are aware of the American
conventions that downplayed, controlled, or dismissed
these untoward events of the wilderness. He did relish, on
the other hand, what I have called below the mood of "discovery"—the momentary wonder evoked by an archetypal
new world commensurate with his memories. But it was an
ingrained part of his moral imagination, if not of his conscious moralism, to recognize that the value of such a feeling
depended precisely on its loss. The characters closest to his
heart were losers rather than winners, Natty Bumppo being
the signal case, and if "discovery" as a peculiarly American
emotion underlay Cooper's creativity—as I believe it did—the
drama of his accomplished works derived instead from his
sense of tragedy and disappointment as specifically American
facts. As a hopeful extension of the past into the landscape
of the future, border settlement caught and held his vision.
For the paradigm of his own life, connected to that of the
nation by the little village named for his father, met in
the design of American history the great correlative which

triggered and sustained his art. He kept returning to the prime moment of a new discovery, but he also kept upsetting its calm with the events of his adventurous plots. Wonder and violence were his linked themes.

This is the central subject addressed in the chapters which follow. But in order to address it adequately, and to suggest its wider importance for Cooper and Cooper's nation, I also have taken up a number of related issues. The two opening chapters thus treat in an extended manner Cooper's difficult relation to America as a place and an idea; they should be understood as an anatomy of his imagination. The four chapters following examine his major tales of frontier settlement—*The Pioneers* (1823), *The Wept of Wish-Ton-Wish* (1829), *Wyandotté* (1843), and *The Crater* (1847)—as separate works and as a larger whole. The final essay, devoted mainly to *The Last of the Mohicans* (1826), seeks to pass beyond the "clearing" where the others are centered, and to assess, by looking at Cooper's most intense forest tale, the place which the wilderness held in his mind and art. Throughout all these chapters, I hope to make good on my claim that the center of Cooper's radiating career can be found in his energetic fascination with the American frontier and with what that literal realm suggested to him. The New World border, to be sure, fit superbly the emerging specifications of popular romantic fiction, especially in its "historical" mode. And Cooper himself was prepared to deal with the topic by virtue of his experience as a boy and a young man. But I have sought to locate the central concerns of his imagination less through literary history or biography naively understood than through an intensive examination of the works themselves. I do not mean to suggest that the influence of Walter Scott, or the somewhat parallel concerns of Robert Montgomery Bird and William Gilmore Simms, ought to be ignored; I mean to suggest only that we need to understand Cooper on his own ground, in at least two senses, before we seek to place him in a broader context. Cooper for his own part acknowledged the debts and the parallels, though more often in a general than a particular sense; and he certainly knew that his own personal background made him especially fit to serve as a romancer of the forest. But the crucial force of his art derived instead from something inward and only rarely seen, something so deep and essential that it schooled his imagination and gave it, in all the reaches of his art, its customary language. That this language had intimate connections with the larger style of Cooper's country is one point I should like to keep before my reader; yet even here I have assumed that a close reading, rather than a ranging allusiveness, is to be desired. For the new world of James Fenimore Cooper, whatever the analogues or the direct links it had with the country, was most profoundly his. This was the space in which he lived as a man and an artist.

1   An American Author

The story begins with another story. It was written just after the turn of the nineteenth century by William Cooper, father of the romantic novelist but himself decidedly the son of the neoclassical era. In the fall of 1785, Cooper had ridden his horse through the solitude of an unsettled tract in the southeastern angle of New York State. A New Jersey merchant, Cooper had embarked on a mission typical in many ways of the period just after the Revolution, when a boom in American real estate and a mass movement toward the newly won West absorbed and pacified energies first aroused during the long struggle with England. Holding title to a large part of the land which he now was viewing for the first time (it earlier had been granted to the frontiersman George Croghan, and then had passed to the loyalist William Franklin, Benjamin's son), Cooper already was forming his plan for the future. His main concern centered on what might be made of this tract. But he had an eye on the vast spaces farther west, and his own purposes thus allied him with the emerging design of national history.

William Cooper recognized this connection when, many years later and at the suggestion of an immigrant friend who hoped to encourage other Europeans to set out for America, he put down on paper the tale begun in 1785. In doing so he helped to shape the career of his novelist son, who would write again and again about such resonantly American careers. Judge Cooper saw clearly the public purpose of his old deeds and the new one which sought to record them. But he also enjoyed the chance allowed him by his friend's request to recall and record the pleasures of his personal past.

His little pamphlet, published in Dublin in 1810 under the perfectly innocuous title of *A Guide in the Wilderness*, was a mixture of promotional information and private indulgence. It was no mere budget of dry advice and dispassionate facts, as it might have been. Its poignant evocation of the age came instead from its attempt to extend to the willing reader—potential immigrant or not—something of the contagious American success known to and cherished by the author.

Cooper inscribed in the piece the first emotions of his New World career. The forested expanse of his land seemed vast to him, vast and empty. His words even two decades later caught the sense of negation he had felt in 1785; in this "rough and hilly country," Cooper remarked, "there existed not an inhabitant, nor any trace of a road; I was alone, three hundred miles from home, without bread, meat, or food of any kind; fire and fishing tackle were my only means of subsistence." He survived then like an American Crusoe, his prose suggesting that English myth of the New World even though it does not mention it directly. Roasting the fish which he managed to catch, and then eating it while his horse fed on grass along the water, he lived off the wild land even while, like Crusoe, he kept distant from it: "I laid me down to sleep in my watch coat," runs the elemental record, "nothing but the melancholy Wilderness around me."

The land was "melancholy," clearly enough, because the man who described it that way was uncertain of his place within it. He knew more decisively about his intentions. "I explored the country," he wrote, "formed my plans for future settlement, and meditated upon the spot where a place of trade or a village should afterwards be established." Through the next few years, as settlers began to arrive in the area, and Cooper himself transplanted his family—including his infant son James—thither from Burlington, the old negations lingered. There was a serious "scarcity of provisions," Cooper recalled; and throughout the mountainous countryside where the Appalachian foothills meet the fertile Mohawk valley "neither roads nor bridges" were to be found: the settlers and whatever they might have to exchange for the precious commodities of frontier life could not pass easily, if at all, through the rough terrain. Isolation and deprivation were the ruling forces of the time.[1]

The dispersed community held together as much through the mutual lack of essentials as through the celebration of common ideals or achievements. The most severe problems arose from the uneven landscape, though others came from a lack of human foresight. Cooper remarked that "the greatest discouragement was in the extreme poverty of the people, none of whom had the means of clearing more than a small spot in the midst of the thick and lofty woods, so that their grain grew chiefly in the shade; their maize did not ripen, their wheat was blasted, and the little they did gather they had no mill to grind within twenty miles distance; not one in twenty had a horse, and the way [to the nearest mill] lay through rapid streams, across swamps or over bogs." Though Cooper left the moral of his tale unemphasized, it is clear throughout these pages: imagining the future and building it were quite different acts. For those who took part in the building, the whole weary effort must have been tense with a struggle between their prior hope and the starkly real world where it—like the maize or the wheat—languished. In the abundant wilderness death and life were close allies.[2]

Cooperstown was no utopian enterprise (even though Cooper had his own larger views), so its fortunes improved by a few modest expedients rather than by any grander means. The large-scale production and exportation of maple sugar and potash, the first drawn from living trees and the second made from felled ones heaped and burned in great piles, brought in some needed funds. An almost providential shoal of herring that ascended the Susquehanna from its mouth in the Chesepeake provided a free substitute for the grain which the pioneers could neither raise nor easily purchase. Caught in great quantities and distributed along with ample supplies of salt for their preservation, the fish brightened an otherwise dismal border diet.

These were turning points, at least for Judge Cooper as he recalled the era, and within a short time Otsego County began to wear a more promising aspect. By the time Cooper wrote his memoir two decades after the start, he could assert confidently that Otsego now "produced everything necessary to the support and comfort of man." His language became suddenly positive and laudatory; the melancholic strain was lost altogether. He proudly asserted that the region "maintains at present eight thousand souls, with schools, academies, churches, meeting-houses, turnpike roads, and a market town. It annually yields to commerce," he continued, "large droves of fine oxen, great quantities of wheat and other grain, abundance of pork, potash in barrels, and other provisions; merchants with large capitals, and all kinds of useful mechanics reside upon it; the waters [are] stocked with fish, the air is salubrious, and the country [is] thriving and happy." The emptiness was wholly filled up by now.[3]

Cooper felt deeply moved by such remarkable changes. They gave a visible meaning to his own personal rise in the world, but in part they also told a wider tale. "When I see these good old settlers meet together," he wrote with a tear in his eye, "and hear them talk of past hardships, of which I bore my share, and compare the misery they then endured with the comforts they now enjoy, my emotions border upon [a] weakness which manhood can scarcely avow." Doubt had thus yielded to sentiment. Hence Cooper could view his past without ambivalence, and could write of it without ambiguity; it was a matter of simple contrasts, of early threats met and overcome and now almost forgotten except as the sauce of current nostalgic delight. His "great primary object" from the outset, Cooper declared, was to make "the Wilderness to bloom and fructify." This was a purpose worthy of any Old Testament patriarch (or poet), and everything around the Otsego scene as Cooper adopted that ancient language seemed to verify his stylistic choices. The shape of his whole life as he relived it in writing the *Guide* was echoed in the emerging success of the little country village: "I began with the disadvantage of a small capital," Cooper admitted, "and the encumbrance of a large family, and yet I have already settled more acres than any man in America.... I am now descending into the vale of life"—a nice figure of speech, conventional as it was, for a man whose "life" began with a literal descent into a literal vale—"and I must acknowledge that I look back with self complacency upon what I have done, and am proud of having been an instrument in reclaiming such large and fruitful tracts from the waste of the creation." The impiety of that last phrase—creation itself as a "waste"?—apparently was lost on this child of the age of reason, but he answered the other impious suggestions quite directly. If the "seeming boast" about his accomplishments seemed "vain," he hoped that what he had written might spread to others the advice that "industry has its reward, and age its pleasures." The little book, Cooper suggested, should encourage them "to persevere and prosper." It was a guide, one might say, to the wilderness of the world.[4]

And it remains today as a classic version of its modest type. The pamphlet records in vivid colloquial prose the westward push of the postwar era, and from a viewpoint appropriately in touch with the matter. For better and for worse, Judge Cooper was the very opposite of the absentee landlord; his considerable vigor and good humor (as well as his political irascibility, almost as large) were absorbed with the fortunes of his domain, and with the well-being of its pioneers. A staunch federalist, Cooper nonetheless believed in the virtue of fee-simple conveyance of land, and he sought to establish on the acres he helped settle a society of independent owners—not the tenantry familiar in the feudal lands of the Hudson. This was an important dash of Jeffersonian values in his makeup. If in fact he tried to coerce his tenants and mortgagees into voting his position at the polls, he was by no means an aristocrat in his economic dealings. He urged on other landowners the same active and principled policy he had pursued, and he reminded his heirs in his will that they should be lenient with the pioneers indebted to the estate.[5]

Such issues were to have their place in the career of his novelist son, who abandoned the federalist legacy and came to respect, admire, and partly accept that of Jefferson himself. But it is the story told by the Judge, rather than any implications it may have, that ought to concern us here. In it lay the most direct model of the novelist's border art; the pamphlet of 1810, and the oral lore it recorded, stood like a folk source of peculiar intensity and importance in the mind and feelings of James. Its vernacular quality derived from the fact that William Cooper was a man of action rather than letters, and from the fact, too, that when he sat down to record his memories he did so in a traditional American form first invented on the seventeenth-century frontier. Like other "settlement" accounts, *A Guide in the Wilderness* aimed not at literary effect but at the satisfaction of personal and public needs. It was improvised according to its local origins, and was as deficient in art as it was sufficient in feeling and advice. Within its pages lay the power of significant action movingly recorded and fervently preached. James would sophisticate its naive motions and motivations; but he would also respect, in his own attention to detail, fact, and myth, the larger cultural meaning entombed in it.

Yet the pamphlet itself had its literary shape, and this also was to emerge in the novels. The same folk tradition on which William drew in telling his tale provided certain limits as to meaning. More complex versions of the form, such as Bradford's *Of Plymouth Plantation*, stressed the irony or outright tragedy of the American experiment—much as the novels of Cooper's son James were to. But the Judge's memoir had more modest precedents. It gave voice to an orthodox understanding traceable to the rigors of the Revolution, a way of glossing over—for the sake of national cele-

bration and national "defense" (in its rhetorical form)—
the vexing problems of the actual frontier. An initial period
of brief uncertainty and weakness, in the *Guide* as in other
examples, gives way to an age of secure possession and
surprising progress. The Judge's tale treats of its author's
initial doubts, one at last concludes, only for the sake of
contrasting them to the brighter pictures of the safe village,
gloriously expanded, at the foot of the lake. And herein
lies its debt to the orthodox scheme. The precious details
fade into an act of contrived witness.

We can only speculate about how James would have
viewed the orthodox recounting of his past if he had continued to enjoy the prerogatives of his father. In much of
what he wrote about America, the son in fact revealed his
innocent relish for the simpler strands of frontier memory.
But he also revealed, at greater length and with greater depth,
a more complicated sense of the American past and its
spaces. Even *The Pioneers*, his first and lightest tale of
border plantation, has its uncertainties and doubts; though
based on family recollections of the sort written down by
the Judge, it introduces elements of the family past (such as
the conflict over mere ownership of the land) left out of
A Guide in the Wilderness. And it treats the "completed"
landscape of Otsego—perhaps necessarily, given Cooper's
decision to set the book in the early 1790s—as a rough and
dubious accomplishment. Why Cooper chose that setting is
part of the intriguing argument he carried on with his father's
orthodox memoir. Indeed, even his updating of his father's
pamphlet, *The Chronicles of Cooperstown* (1838), is a
subdued celebration, generated from piety perhaps, but
filled with many impious suggestions. The village of this
little book hardly is so bright as that of its 1810 precursor.
It is a place of endurance as much as growth, a site clearly
left behind by the now distant forces of American expansion.
How such a change of attitude came about, and what it
meant for the final shape of Cooper's art, is the topic of
what ensues. For even though Cooperstown by the time

The Chronicles was written in fact had been passed by,
James Cooper had his own reasons for accepting and recording the truth. He too found in the history of the place a
sign of his personal fate.

We need to review at this point the multiple failures already
mentioned. Judge Cooper himself died in Albany late in
1809, "as the result of a blow on the head, struck from
behind, by an opponent as they were leaving a political
meeting."[6] He was survived by his wife, Elizabeth Fenimore;
five sons; and one daughter. The latter, Anne, had married
George Pomeroy in 1803 and was then living with her husband in the Cooperstown house built for them by the Judge.
The five sons—Richard, Isaac, William, Samuel, and James—
all had reached adulthood at the time of their father's death.
James, born in 1789, was the youngest, and Richard, born
in 1775, was the oldest; three of them had married by 1809.
To each of the five Judge Cooper's will left a substantial
inheritance: $50,000 in cash, twenty-three farms, and a
one-fifth share of the remainder. Two other children, Hannah
and Hendrick Frey, had died earlier.[7]

The death of Judge Cooper, which ironically occurred
before *A Guide in the Wilderness* saw print, was sudden and
unexpected, but the Coopers who remained seemed as well
provided for as the *Guide* hinted they would be. The outlook
appeared bright enough that several of the sons went about
setting themselves up as country gentlemen; this, presumably, was to be the next step in the family's progress as the
Judge had sketched (and funded) it. Isaac's fine brick house,
"Edgewater," was erected east of the family mansion, on a
small rise overlooking the lake, between 1810 and 1813.
James himself began a new stone house in 1813; completed
four years later, it stood on his farm named "Fenimore,"
northwest of the village. This house probably was less preten-
tious than Isaac's, which was designed in the Adamesque
style, but both dwellings suggested the upward aspirations
of the Judge's heirs. Much as he had replaced the first rough

family mansion with a second and finer one, they were laying claim to a physical and social gentility.

And yet the Coopers were living on borrowed time and even borrowed money. By 1820, when James published his first novel, his mother and all four of his brothers were dead. And the family finances had become a shambles. Extravagant expenditures, difficulties with the Judge's complicated affairs, bad investments (some in frontier land, of all things), and a general economic crisis following on the War of 1812 conspired to reduce a large fortune to a set of worries. James was not someone for whom, at earlier times, money had been a source of anxiety,[8] but by the beginning of his career as a writer he was sorely pressed to make good on his liabilities. And though some of the problems came to him from the family, he bore a direct responsibility for others. In 1818 and 1819, for instance, he had borrowed heavily from a friend in New York City—it was the novelist Catherine Sedgwick's brother Robert—securing the loans with his "Fenimore" lands. When he could not repay all the principle and the usurious interest, the real estate went up for forced sale, but failed to produce the necessary amount. Legal action followed on Sedgwick's part; the affair did not reach settlement until the eve of Cooper's departure for Europe in 1826. Nor was this an isolated instance. The Cooper mansion had to be sold from the estate, and Cooper himself lost other holdings as he sought to meet his obligations. Not until 1834, after his return from Europe, was he to purchase the mansion and then, after an absence of seventeen years from Cooperstown, occupy it himself. By this time his literary earnings had given him a modest independence; but it also was only in 1834 that he had himself appointed executor of his father's still unsettled estate, and went about trying to clear up its lingering problems. This was a full quarter-century after the Judge's death.

The financial troubles reflected and deepened others. The decimation of Cooper's family in the decade following 1809 left him, aside from his older sister Anne, the only

survivor of a large brood—a youngest son forced by circumstances into sudden exposure and prominence. He had
married Susan De Lancey about a year after his father's
death, and in another situation the De Lanceys, an old
Westchester family of loyalist connections, might have
offered him a kind of adoptive protection. But they clearly
became suspicious of James's worsening financial condition,
if not of his basic character as well. When James and Susan
moved back to Westchester in 1817—they had lived there
after their marriage in 1811, but then had gone to Cooperstown in 1813—they occupied a farm given in trust to Mrs.
Cooper by her father. The gift was a generous gesture,
perhaps intended as an inducement for Susan to resettle
near her parents, but it was conveyed in such a way that
James could not encumber it in his by then rather feverish
attempt to recover his independence. Apparently the terms
of the gift strained Cooper's affections for the De Lanceys,
so much so that in the fall of 1822 he and his family—there
were five young children to care for now—left the new house
they had built at "Angevine," the Westchester farm, and
moved to rented quarters in New York City. It was just at
this time that many of his landholdings were being lost.
And it also was at this time that Cooper was finishing work
on *The Pioneers,* the first of his imaginative returns to the
ampler ground of his childhood.

Once settled in New York City, Cooper found himself
beset with new troubles. *The Pioneers,* to be sure, soon
would surpass *The Spy* in acclaim and sales, so that Cooper's
risky new career at least seemed promising. But the past
lingered. It was in July of 1823 that his new but unoccupied
house at "Fenimore" burned, perhaps as the result of arson;
the following month came the death of Cooper's "poor little
boy" Fenimore, also named after the family of the novelist's
mother;[9] that fall the sheriff seized and made an inventory
of the Coopers' household goods at their city lodgings; and
in the year following Sedgwick brought his first suit for the
recovery of the old debts, the unsuccessful sale at "Feni-

more" having intervened. This was not the whole of it. Cooper himself had fallen ill in August, 1823, or perhaps somewhat earlier, and he spent much of the month after Fenimore's death "making short excursions to different watering places &c near the city," as he wrote his friend William B. Shubrick on September 7, "with a hope of improving my own condition and relieving the mind of Mrs. Cooper."[10] Part of his trouble when he wrote that letter came from an attack of sunstroke he suffered on a recent trip back home from Hell-Gate. But his larger illness, James Franklin Beard suggests, was a symptom of his overall anxiety. Soon he would begin to suffer from a nervous digestive disorder which later was to become chronic, and which was associated with his death at the age of sixty-one in 1851. This was to be the most inward and lasting result of the family's collapse: history, as one might put it, was in his flesh.[11]

"That prevention is at all times better than cure."[12] It is the kind of aphorism which Cooper might well have taken as his motto during these troubled years. In fact he took it as the concluding line of his first novel, which he published before the onset of his real illness but which owed much to the metaphoric disease of his fortunes. The debt to his own experience was so great that the economic motives which may have helped impel him into writing—as they impelled him into real estate speculation, or the purchase of a whaleship in 1819—seem less important than the very tonic offered by the moral fantasy of *Precaution*.[13] The notion that one can, by careful forethought, control the troubles and deceits of life: this is the conscious assumption of the work, and though Cooper develops it largely along romantic lines it clearly has subtle links to the author's desired view of the world as a problem both solvable and in need of solution. Had he and his brothers done more to prevent the disasters whose effects James now was feeling, the cure he was attempting to effect might not have been necessary.

Beyond its concern with courtship as a challenge to judgment, *Precaution* is obsessed with money, and therein lies its most obvious connection with Cooper's personal fate. We learn on the second page of the book, for instance, that "a great deal of money is a very good thing in itself" (p. 50)—this from the Reverend Dr. Ives, a sympathetic character. But it is the situation of the main family of characters, the Moseleys, which most obviously signals Cooper's investment of his feelings in the tale. Sir Edward had inherited a large estate from his father, but an estate sorely encumbered as a result of his mother's extravagant tastes.[14] That wealth thus forced a long period of strict economies on the heir gives us the book's first irony: Sir Edward rented out his London townhouse and retreated to his country quarters for a decade and a half, hoping that his deprivations would allow him to provide handsomely for his own children. Money certainly is not to be taken for granted in this world, as it was in the world of Cooper's boyhood.

Yet the predicament of the Moseleys lies essentially in the past of the novel. As the story opens it is the spring of a new year, and new in the most comic sense: for the "temporary eclipse of Sir Edward's fortunes" has ended at last; his "system of economy" has succeeded (p. 61). Later in the book, as a result, the family can return to London to repossess their townhouse, and by the end three of the four children are happily and securely married. One hears the comfortable jingle of coin beyond the peal of wedding bells. One hears as well the wishful sigh of the author. Solved offstage, as it were, the Moseleys' troubles seem like a plotted extension—an extension and a verbal solution—of Cooper's private worries. And it is likely that Cooper himself recognized the resemblance. A comment in the first chapter about Sir Edward's limited personal capacities—the gist of it is that the man could not have retrieved his fortunes if more active efforts had been required—seems like a muted reference to the more daring expedients which Cooper felt himself forced of a character previously obscured and misjudged, stand apart in theme as well as in method. They imply together that the ordinary occasions of social exchange, the model for most of Cooper's scenes in *Precaution*, cannot adequately realize private truths; at some point, a more intense divulgence is necessary. Cooper's literary precedents for *Precaution*, of course, delivered to him the assumption that dialogue and chatter, shared events and interaction, ought to suffice for art if not for life. And at certain points, as with his treatment of the social-climbing Mrs. Jarvis, he could exploit social form with some finesse. Yet here, as later in his career, Cooper was unhappy with what, during his experience of Europe from 1826 to 1833, he would term the "fictitious forms" of Old World society.[17] He was to succeed best as a writer when he abridged dialogue or subordinated it to action—especially the kind of violent action typical, as he saw it, of the American border. The interpolated tales in *Precation* are "American" in their violence if not in their setting—American, too, in their suggestion that experience disperses, isolates, and alters whatever order serves as its point of departure.

The Denbigh story inserted in *Precaution* has further implications. Cooper wrote it with an ear peculiarly attuned to the hidden aspects of human feeling and experience, as if only this assault of narrative energy could force an entry for such things into the social world. It is not the mere presence of the tale that matters, or marks Cooper's departure from the larger conventions of the period; it is instead the function and the effect of the Denbigh story that should concern us. For it seems to come at the reader from an entirely different universe, and its very premises—about language, among other things—upset those of the novel. The Gothic power it releases into a world defined by mannerly assumptions cannot be explained by Cooper, or by anything that world itself shows us. We pass abruptly from the security of a universe apparently ruled by moral tags to one in which private life seems chaotically amoral; from a uni-

to try. Moseley survives by passive means, renting out a property conveniently and securely in his possession; he also achieves his recovery with ease, albeit slowly. Cooper, on the other hand, had to indulge in hasty remedies that required "more of enterprise or calculation": just the kind of thing, *Precaution* tells us, which would have left Sir Edward still laboring "under the difficulties which distressed his more brilliant but less prudent parent" (p. 52). We may take Moseley's situation as a projected simplification of the author's own, an easing of his worries via the magic of fiction. That the novel itself was one of Cooper's risky enterprises adds a bit of circumstantial humor to the affair.

There were other personal deflections in the novel. Though blamable for his lax supervision of his daughters' romances, Sir Edward is a serene man marked by self-control, just the kind of person Cooper might have wished he could be at this time, or could make himself become by his various expedients. The record of Cooper's thoughts never has the fullness one might wish for, and for the period before 1820 it has a woeful thinness. It is clear, however, that the rather carefree and even careless young man who peeks out from the early documents—bright, active, but a prankster and fighter rusticated from Yale—underwent an enforced maturing as the family difficulties gathered more and more closely around him. Of this process his first book was a fragmentary result, a testament of his seriousness and responsibility in its sermonlike insistence. It also was a part of Cooper's attempt to seize control of his life, to remake or at least reform or rediscover himself. The book's primary moral thrust aims directly at Cooper; its imagined view of experience as a battle between facts and principles, wishes and ideas, offers a suggestive portrait of Cooper's mind. If he knew what he was about in painting the Moseley predicament as he did—taking his private life as "material" in a rudimentary sense—in other ways he was not so much creating art as using it, not controlling his tale so much as stating and exorcising his own doubts through it. The work seems so shapelessly verbal and improvisatory because it was largely an expressive outpouring from its author. It was talked rather than written.

And so the book's most personal matter is not its outright moralism—for this was the public demonstration of Cooper's new resolve—but its concern with the question of identity. The question comes up with regard to the Moseleys themselves, but more intriguing is the rather Gothic subplot that involves "George Denbigh," who saves Emily Moseley's life at the risk of his own, then woos and is about to win her until he is erroneously identified as the man who once tried to rape a young Irishwoman in the wartorn landscape of Spain. Denbigh at last is exonerated and revealed to be none other than the much praised but mysterious Earl of Pendennyss—the actual rescuer of the Irishwoman and a paragon on every front, despite his willing deception of Emily on the matter of who he really is. Most of this seems like conventional stuff, rare as it may have been in the novel of manners, Cooper's obvious model in the tale. But Cooper dwells on the theme of hidden identity as if moved by an intense fascination with it. In a work which customarily defines character as a function of social position—Mrs. Jarvis, the dowager Lady Chatterton, Mr. Benfield, and Peter Johnson, as well as the Moseleys, are good examples of the habit—the obscurity surrounding Pendennyss seems especially jolting. The man enters the story in a mysterious manner, abruptly, pseudonymously, and with no immediate explanation. And he has the freedom to reveal his moral nature without serious reference to his origins or his intentions. All of this obviously undercuts the outright view of character which the book preaches as well as practices; but the subversion, I would argue, is precisely the heart of Cooper's own involvement in the tale. For Denbigh-Pendennyss is nothing less than an unconscious portrait of the man who later said, and only half-jokingly, that he had written *Precaution* "to prove that the world did not know

me."[15] A British earl Cooper was not; he was hardly even an American landlord any more. But an author, a man with hidden talents, a member of the aristocracy of merit just then being defined as America's substitute for the other kind—this he might, by the revelation of his energies, demonstrate himself to be. Even Cooper's handling of the manuscript of *Precaution* suggests his connection with the book's secretive nobleman and the larger theme of secrecy embodied by that character. He read it to his friends as if it were the product of another hand than his, wanted to keep his name separate from it in print or in gossip, and seemed to treat it as a onetime jeu d'esprit or a simple literary spoof without further consequence. And yet he fell into a rage at the errors of the printers, threatening to halt publication or even sue for damages, and he was busily at work on his next book long before the first appeared. Publishing offered Cooper a means of revealing what lay within himself: the worth beyond a surface of embarrassments and losses. A mangled text, even though anonymously committed to the world, hardly could accomplish that end.

At the same time, however, the novel revealed exactly the troubles which its appearance might counter. The tangled relationships of the Denbigh family—replete with parental favoritism, a hidden rivalry between the two sons, guilt, exploitation, wasted resources, insanity, and so on—provide a startling contrast to the book's official definition of the family itself as a bastion against what *Precaution* typically refers to as "the world." Cooper wrote this part of the novel, concentrated in chapters 41 through 46, as an explanation after the fact of the Earl's behavior. But the revelations offered in these chapters seem longer and more convoluted than they need be for the purposes of the overall plot. As with the interpolated tale regarding the Spanish situation (which comes in chapter 26),[16] this more extended one is an amateur's exercise in pure narrative, something in which the rest of the book is weak. But both tales, as revelations

verse in which the surface troubles of the children stem from the moral laxness of the parents to one in which, as Pendennyss suggests by his personal rightness, teachable values have far less importance than some kind of mysterious inner worth. The conflict between these two views would have to have been resolved in order to make *Precaution* a better book. But as the work stands, it hints, among other things, at Cooper's perennial distrust of the social occasion as a moment of truth, and hence, perhaps, at his often obtuse handling of dialogue throughout his career. And it hints as well at Cooper's later turn, in his American tales, toward physical action, history, and the landscape as the means by which the self achieves definition.

The transformation of Cooper's art after *Precaution* depended most of all on his discovery that his own needs were linked to the concrete patterns of American life, especially those found on the ambiguous border between society and nature. Herein lay the origins of his practice as an indefatigable adventurer. The discovery came about in stages between 1820 and 1830. It involved not only Cooper's turn toward American subjects in *The Spy* and *The Pioneers*, or the works which followed, but also his growing personal identification with America's past and prospects—an identification which became conscious only during his long sojourn abroad. *Precaution* launched his career, for the book, however stiff it seems now, hardly was a failure in its day; his two following books gave that career a professional air and an American tone; his own intellectual development through the decade gave it direction, intensity, and awareness.

The first source of Cooper's tie to the nation was, of course, the legacy of Cooperstown itself. Lost as it surely had been to Cooper's personal control, the eponymic village nonetheless suggested by its very name his enduring claim on the larger country whose history had been repeated with poignantly recalled detail there on the shores of Lake Otsego. Like his father's, Cooper's own identity was tangled up in the place, so closely in fact that we may see his adoption of his mother's name as his own in 1826 as a retreat of sorts from the oppressive publicity of his actual position. To be a "Fenimore-Cooper," as he essentially had promised his mother even before 1809 he would be—the Judge forbade the change then—was to assert some other connection than the one which came to obsess his imagination. The change once accomplished also seems like an actual instance in Cooper's life of his literary fascination with character as an essentially hidden, unknowable, and therefore misnamed entity. As a boy, Cooper has assumed a middle initial drawn from the last name of Moss Kent, an older Cooperstown resident whom he idolized, and in book after book written in his adulthood he split off parts of himself, as he had done with Denbigh-Pendennyss at the start, and gave them a fictitious independence and a new name. The later arguments about the "Effingham" family and the Coopers had a real basis in Cooper's own imaginative habits. He never wrote with the consistent directness of early Melville, or even the veiled but canny voice of Irving; yet there remained a strong expressive impulse to his works. Cooper was always *in* them.

One thus notes the curious fact that *The Pioneers*, which Cooper claimed he had written solely to please himself, contains no direct representation of the novelist. He clearly saw the American interest in Cooperstown—the thematic resonance, that is, of the local details he recalled—but he felt some need (beyond the novel's literal setting in his own young boyhood) to leave anything like himself out of the picture. How deeply his feelings entered the tale in other ways we shall see below. The point at present is that Cooper accepted the challenge of his typicality, the typicality of what was his own story, with a decided indirectness.

Part of the reason had to do with the contrast Cooper may have sensed even this early between his private experience and the public form into which it would have to fit. His outright subject in *The Pioneers* was not loss—which was what Cooperstown in the main meant for him—but the pageant of expansion which the settlement theme in its naive form presented to view. Thus his own tale if told too directly, with a social plot centered, say, on the speculators and the other villains responsible for his dispossession, and the law as an ally of both, hardly could have tapped as *The Pioneers* assuredly did the growing mood of American nostalgia and celebration. To make the story unflinchingly his own would have forced Cooper beyond 1793, beyond 1809, beyond the happy interval immediately following his father's death—happy, that is, in its independence and sense of arrival.

A similar problem had emerged already in *The Spy*, though largely as an intuition. Cooper brought over into this book from *Precaution* the same Gothic fascination with what was hidden: not only loyalties in this case, but identities again, and the essential loneliness of such an archetypal American as Harvey Birch. It is George Washington, as "Mr. Harper," who seems to import the Pendennyss theme; but it is Birch who lives that theme. For Birch is Pendennyss taken seriously in the incognito game, the stakes being enormously raised and the props of actual aristocracy being utterly removed in favor of the natural sort. Birch has no social position whatever to explain, even partly, his inner commitment to a country that gives him, in reward for his services, only a series of woes. Like the wordy but elusive Natty Bumppo, who inherited from Birch some of the same woe, Harvey is secretive, fleeting, and misgauged by those around him. Both come from humble origins but have high aspirations, and both are discarded by the Americans who have profited from their labors and example. Cooper thus made the first two of his American tales into ironic diagrams of loss and gain; he made the national past problematic as much as celebrated it, and thereby expressed—indirectly, again—his own alliance with the nation. Their tone was the mark of his presence.

The most extraordinary thing about *The Spy*, nonetheless, is the intensity with which the unpracticed author of *Precau-*

tion here threw himself into his "material." Thus one finds the professional note mentioned above, the almost immediate grasp of subject *as* subject—as a given that constrained the ensuing development of the story. The first novel had no such constraint for it had no source except in other books Cooper had read; *The Spy* had, on the contrary, the anecdotes of John Jay, the tales Cooper picked up in the Westchester countryside, and perhaps even the memory of his relatives who had been spies in the war.[18] The novelist recognized that this second book departed markedly from the first, even as he was reading proof for the latter. He wanted *Precaution* "push'd through the press," he wrote his printer Goodrich in mid-1820. "It is so—very—very—inferior to the 'Spy' that I have lost most of my expectations of its success—still, as it is a highly moral Book—(which bye the bye the 'Spy' is not) I believe it will sell."[19] The new book was "moral" in its own way, though: for the "neutral ground" of its action clearly gives us the sort of physical embodiment of values which, with one or two exceptions, the verbal first novel lacked.[20] *Precaution* is all text and exposition; *The Spy* is exemplum, with only vestigal indications here and there of the discarded moralism. The reader is delivered from the very first sentence (where "Harper" is introduced as "a solitary traveller" [p. 11] within a threatening landscape) into an intensely real environment that has no counterpart whatever in the previous book, and that provides the only warrant necessary for any lessons which may emerge. Cooper had found his proper ambience along with his proper matter. His Americanism as a writer entailed shifts of technique as well as shifts in scene.

The swiftness of the changes may suggest already the personal basis of Cooper's art, his discovery in *The Spy* of something beyond "material" pure and simple. Though there is no direct transferral of his feelings here, as there arguably was in his creation of the Englishman Moseley, one discovers in Birch a melodramatic version of the author's felt position. Harvey seems imagined, after all, with an

intensity that little in Cooper's sources could have given to
the character. And the psychic exchange between author and
creature had a long but ironic continuance: by the time
Cooper came back from Europe in 1833, successful as a
writer but widely discredited as the spokesman for America
he had tried to be, he was to assume a fugitive stance vis-à-
vis the public—*his* public, as he might have asserted a short
time earlier—strangely like the one his first American character had to endure, and like that endured by Natty Bumppo
as well.[21] Cooper's own rhetoric as a citizen and an active
supporter of American principles had delivered him, ironically enough, into the fate he had imagined for Birch as the
reward for unwavering patriotism. In *The American Democrat*, his most formal argument with the nation, he tried to
claim that he had returned to the United States with the
eyes of "a foreigner."[22] This was partly a ploy, since indulg-
ing the metaphor would allow Cooper to give his real inward
alienation from American assumptions (not principles) an
exaggerated stress, a kind of outward justification. But the
metaphor echoed, with another kind of meaning, the first
movements of Cooper's American muse. His fame at home
and abroad rested, as he surely knew, on the alignment of
his imagination with the country; yet the alignment as seen
in the portraits of Birch and Bumppo at last had a subversive
energy traceable to the dispossession they shared with the
man who called them into literary life. Cooper expressed
himself through them as surely as he wrote his intellectual
autobiography in describing the ideal "American Democrat"
in his pamphlet of 1838.

Already in *The Spy* Cooper thus had found that American
history (and the American landscape) could give him a
sufficient ground for working out his imaginative impulses.
The discovery came fortuitously here, as it did even in
The Pioneers, despite that book's obvious personal dimensions. There followed in quick and unprogrammatic succession three other American tales, *The Pilot, Lionel Lincoln,*

and *The Last of the Mohicans*; they came so quickly, in fact, that Cooper at times was thinking his next book while still entangled in the previous one. And yet his art was maturing significantly throughout the period from 1821 to 1826. Larger patterns, for one thing, were beginning to emerge. *Lionel Lincoln* appeared as the first of a promised series of "colonial" legends, and though in fact it was the only one, Cooper's promise marked something more than his green ambitiousness. He was thinking far ahead in his career, and thinking as well about the larger relations among his books.

The Last of the Mohicans proved that more than thought was involved here. Though patterns had begun to set them-selves in the earlier books—three of them, after all, dealt with the Revolution—this new novel showed Cooper exactly how he could become his own source and model. The dis-covery may have made it somewhat easier to find new subjects by extending old ones (the next novel after *Mohi-cans*, *The Prairie*, did just that again), but it also enforced on Cooper's generating powers a new constraint. It thus made him a more conscious writer, for the need for consistency from book to book—a need Cooper generally satisfied in the whole Leatherstocking series—made strategy more important than mere tactical skill. As long as one of the novels could be checked against the others, Cooper had to worry himself over the whole when he worked on the parts of a part. Perhaps as a result of what he learned here, he finished the first decade of his career with three more novels based loosely on his own models: *The Red Rover* and *The Water-Witch* grew from *The Pilot*, while *The Wept of Wish-Ton-Wish* based itself on the form established in *The Pioneers*. He was writing fresh books but was consolidating the body of his work. The year that *The Last of the Mohicans* came out, 1826, he sold the rights of his previous American books to his new publishers, Carey and Lea, who were to give his public presence a similar sort of coherence.

It also was in 1826 that Cooper departed with his family for Europe. The motives behind his visit were many. Cooper's

health was one of them; another was his hope that his daughters might benefit from schooling in Europe. Though still
shackled by "poverty,"[23] Cooper also felt that the whole
family would derive great pleasure from residence abroad.
And since he was finding it difficult to secure fair payment
for European editions of his works, Cooper believed that
being on the spot would allow him—while taking the cure,
seeing to his daughters' education, and enjoying the sights—
to negotiate directly and forcefully with English and Con-
tinental publishers. With *The Last of the Mohicans* just issued
and headed toward great popularity, the moment for such
a voyage was propitious. That book was an entrance card to
Old World society—and a trump in the publishing game if
he should need it.

The European sojourn, first intended to last only "a year
or two,"[24] stretched out to seven and a half. The period was
long enough that when he finally came back after several
postponements—or indeed even before then—Cooper had
become a figure of contempt for a certain vocal part of the
American public. One of the charges thrust upon him was
particularly hard to bear: it was that he had abandoned
America, that he had become nothing less than a Europeanized exile unworthy of American principles or American
acclaim. He had sold out, that is, to the opposite side in the
transatlantic debate.

This was as ironic as it was maddening, for if anything
Cooper had discovered more about his native land and his
own deep ties to it while he lingered abroad. The contrasts
between Europe and America which developed for him then
helped to clarify his instinctive sense of America's origins and
destiny, its institutions and its customs, its political life,
even its landscape and its art—as well as his own duties as
an American writer. Though his works before the voyage,
except for *Precaution*, had New World settings and themes,
his residence in Europe made him gradually more conscious
of his loyalties: "it is a point of honor to continue rigidly
an American author," he protested to an English publisher

in 1831; to an American friend a month later he asserted,
"I was born and will live and die a Yankee."[25] Becoming
more strident about America's claims on the world while he
witnessed the political oppression and political upheavals
of Europe, he also became more resolved to put his skills
to use in the service of national ideals and goals. His private
doubts hardly were latent in these years, as we shall see
below in examining the grim tragedy of *The Wept of Wish-
Ton-Wish*. But one cannot miss the alert vigor with which
Cooper perceived the implications of his special position as
an American—and a talented American—abroad. He discovered the homeland during these years in the sense that his
ideas about the country congealed, then hardened, then
became a conscious part of his character, manner, and
outlook. Indeed, one might claim that Cooper acquired in
Europe an ideology rooted in his American past but brought
to maturity by the new sights and events he encountered
while absent from the nation.

Cooper went overseas, in fact, as an official representative
of the country, since he carried the title of U.S. consul at
Lyons. But this role had largely symbolic force. It was
intended to give him a certain freedom of movement which,
as a private citizen, he would not have enjoyed. He never
resided in the city given to his charge, worked through an
assistant (or indeed was replaced by him), and gave up the
position as early as 1828. More important to the artist, in
any event, was Cooper's inner sense of being a "representative" American, a public figure in his own right whose
actions abroad (insofar as they came under scrutiny) might
reflect on the country—and whose demonstrated talents
spoke clearly for the wisdom of a society based on merit
rather than inherited status. He had no immunity, as Americans rarely have had, against the seductive charm of high
society in the Old World. He took pains, in fact, to describe
to some of his American correspondents the social occasions
in which he participated. In a letter to Mary Jay in October,
1826, he thus listed the *dramatis personae* of a formal

banquet where he sat among envoys, nobles, and the famous: "On my left was M. de Ischann, Chargé d'Affaires of Switzerland—next, the Baron de Werther, Envoy and Minister of Prussia—next, Mr. Gallatin, En[voy] & Min[ister] U[nited] States to England...." And so it went, "next" following "next" in a round of position and title. Even this early, though, Cooper toyed with the game; the letter to Jay thus comes back around the table to "your humble servant," and it punctures the formality with which the guests earlier went to table, Cooper cataloging who led whom, with a terse joke—"Your humble servant led the—rear."[26]

On this occasion Cooper was conscious of himself as one of "six Americans all ready for the Strangers."[27] His comments to Jay, however, suggest a larger personal detachment from the proceedings. Throughout his years abroad Cooper was to feel ill at ease in European society, out of the circle and out of sorts. And he expressed the feeling often enough by ridiculing what he could not accept, or what would not accept him. A later letter to Jay tells of attending a public dinner given by the French king—the point of the affair was to let the guests see royalty; they did not eat, nor did the king acknowledge their presence: "We were in the room with the Royal Family, and within twenty feet of them, but by a sort of fiction we were supposed to be in another apartment." Cooper referred Jay to a piece he had published in the New York *Commercial Advertiser* if she wanted more details; there, as it turns out, he wrote ironically that "The state of majesty should not be exhibited in the process of eating.... I shall always draw the image of Charles X. in my mind, eating his soup."[28] He answered the "fiction" with a barb of fact: "The Baroness de Damas," he wrote Jay in that 1826 letter, "is a little *hunch'dback'd*, vulgar looking woman, of some great family, who did nothing but snigger and chat with Monseigneur le Nonce [the papal nuncio], as she called him."[29]

Cooper confessed himself incapable of rendering social scenes of the sort that assaulted him in Europe,[30] but he did well with them as long as he did not take them at face value. One senses throughout the documents of his sojourn the same alienation from "butterfly distinctions" and "tinsel"[31]—and one senses, too, exactly how Cooper's reaction to such things both grew from and contributed to his art. The lack of finesse with dialogue to which reference already has been made, for instance, came as much from Cooper's distrust of social palaver as from a chronically bad ear or a serenely bumbling pen. The distrust most likely derived not from Cooper's inheritance—the Cooper fortune was new money, yet Judge Cooper stood for the old order—but from the subsequent dislocations, and their suggestion of the unreality lurking in any external status. Cooper himself had *achieved* his fame, the drive to do so being central to his career at the beginning, and he began to sense in Europe exactly what the achievement meant. He already had created in Harvey Birch and Natty Bumppo a pair of self-created and self-reliant heroes who owed nothing to position; in the presence of a world where position seemed overimportant, he slowly built on the instinctual base that had sustained those two "Americans" an increasingly conscious ideology. Cooper's feeling of marginality in Europe forced him to articulate his assumptions. And this act in turn gave to the further efforts of his imagination a new tone. Seeing himself as a decided American in the midst of Europe, Cooper took upon himself the costume of America's simplicity.

For the fictitiousness of the Old West indeed implicated important American issues. Cooper might give Jay "a famous dish of gossip. . . . Princes, Dukes, Ministers &c, &c—without end";[32] but other Americans abroad, or at home, lacked his critical eye and his acidic pen. Three years later, he told Jay he was "much amused" by his "recollections of what the travellers used to say at home, of what they had seen of society &c in Europe."[33] In 1831, he wrote the English banker Charles Wilkes, now a New Yorker, that a just comparison of America and Europe would bolster one's faith in the former: "If you should come to Europe and live three years, you would go back, with the best possible opinions not only of our institutions but of the men who are in power." He added that the discoveries to be made on such a voyage were salutary enough to put "an American" in "perfect good humor with himself."[34] In between the message to Jay and that to Wilkes, Cooper similarly speculated in his journal about the contrasts between Thomas Jefferson and Alexander Hamilton, contrasts that led him in the same direction. Though "Hamilton was, at heart, a monarchist," Cooper noted, it seemed likely that, had he "been sent to Europe, and had he taken a near view of those institutions, and that state of society, which he so much admired at a distance, his sagacity would at once have enabled him to separate the ore from the dross, and to have found how little there is of the former." A European journey, in other words, would have Americanized Hamilton— much as, one may add, it had strengthened and made conscious Cooper's attachment to national principles. As for Jefferson, his actual experience of Europe disposed him "to practise an austerity of manner and style"—for "simpler forms" were as right for an American as "ceremony" (usually "perverted") was typical of Europeans.[35]

These were late insights, the mature and conscious fruit of Cooper's lengthening experience. But their seed had been planted even in those first days of amused detachment, wit, and awkwardness. His point in the journal about "simpler forms," for example, harked back to that dinner in 1826, and the hundred other such occasions since; what had been an instinctual reaction then, mixed perhaps with a sense of personal insecurity in the "great" world, was coming forth now as part of a political and cultural credo. Soon there would follow the European trilogy and then the series of travel books—both sets insistently bringing American values and an American eye to bear on the Old World—succeeded by Cooper's portrait of the "American Democrat" as a refined but "simple" person.

That the last of these books aimed at American foibles as well as American principles reminds us, however, of the difficulty of Cooper's personal position. He was satisfied with his ability to navigate European social waters even while he condemned their artificial shoals and the pirates who infested them. "Now all these things are important in Europe," he explained to Jay regarding social niceties for which, even though he understood and noted them, his very language expressed scorn. He had abided by them ("in no instance have I neglected the established forms of society, as they are practised in the several countries visited"), but indeed he saw them *as* forms—saw them externally and saw them as external in themselves. In this sense, perhaps, his negative capability as a writer aided him—though in the last analysis he had less of the Shakespearean about him and more of the satirist's expressed scorn for what he could not, even imaginatively, accept. On the issue of his own behavior in Europe, in any event, it became clear to Cooper during the later years of his life abroad that something other than his own tact was to be the arbiter. If he had to represent the nation to Old World eyes, he also had to bear scrutiny from home; he had placed himself in the middle of a complex and acrimonious debate, and he had to accept the consequences. He thus asserted his exact conformity with Old World manners because certain reports had reached him from the United States regarding his behavior: "I was told yesterday that it is said at home, that I gave myself airs in England, and did not meet civilities, myself, as they should be met."[36]

Thus sounded some of the first notes of his discordant homecoming. He explained to Jay on this occasion that he indeed had "refused invitations that many people [i.e., certain Americans] would be glad to accept." The reasons he cited, however, in fact point in a direction Cooper clearly did not intend. He claimed that his health and his writing "demanded" the refusals: "You know," he told Jay, "that unless I manage my time a little, I have neither bread to eat nor the stomach to digest it—Late hours not only destroy my digestion, but they make sad inroads on my ability to buy any thing to digest." Next came his avowal of general "correctness' in manners; far from snubbing the English, he had sought out contacts, and had always behaved properly. All of this explanation, however, harbored a contradiction. If his refusals had been forced by "my health and my business," why did he throw in that barb about the "many people" who would have been "glad to accept" the spurned invitations? Cooper was caught, in effect, between his pursuit of "simple" habits, his scorn for European "tinsel," his private needs—and, again, the American public. He had no difficulty, he likewise wrote Jay, understanding how the rumors of his "airy" pride "got across the ocean"—"we have many people here, who do us no credit, and who move heaven and earth to get into any sort of society." It was these same "many people," whose "disgraceful meanness" Cooper had denounced, that would have attended the affairs he had (surely not just because of illness or necessity) refused to attend—or so the confusing explanations suggest. The defensiveness of his apologia left him pleading for pity but arguing for taste. "Oh! I could give you some precious anecdotes of our people, here," he told Jay, "and unless they are a little more discreet and honest about me, I will. . . . The meanness that I have witnessed among some of our people has made me sick often."[37]

By this point it was no simple matter to embody American simplicity in Europe. And the troubles went further. What he said to Jay about his health was an evasion but it had a certain larger truth. Beard suggests, for instance, that Cooper's troubles in Paris in 1830 stemmed from a kind of nervous reaction to social life: "Cooper was still subject to fits of indigestion and headache after he appeared in crowds, and he and his family were content to live quietly and entertain their friends privately."[38] He still attended soirees and was hardly reclusive or hermitlike; but he was reacting physically to the strains of society, much as he had reacted with illness to his earlier disasters. That he linked his health with his "business" in writing to Jay may show, in effect, the real tie which obtained: not so much that his art cured him, but that it fed off that part of himself which he kept hidden from social life. Perhaps his truest enactment of American realities in the Old World came not in his defense of American institutions, or in his outright simplicity, but in this very conflict between the mask and the man. When he returned home, in any event, he would bring his alienation with him. He had come to inhabit a New World from which the nation as he rediscovered it continually fell short.

2   Orthodox, If Nothing Else

Without his European trip and what it made
him recognize and accept about American ideals—recognize,
accept, and acclaim—Cooper surely would not have fallen
into the weary disillusionment which attended his homecoming. But his self-conscious Americanism in fact had begun
to exist even before the voyage of 1826. One almost can give
a date to his conversion: September 14, 1824. This was a
pleasant late summer day in New York, where Cooper then
was, and the city was full of expectation. The following
spring would usher in the fiftieth anniversary of Bunker Hill,
and at the urging of Congress President Monroe had invited
the aged Lafayette, one of the few surviving heroes of the
Revolution, across the sea to join in the celebration. The
Frenchman had arrived in New York in August, but since
then had been traveling in New England. Now he was back,
and on the evening of the fourteenth the city planned a
grand open-air party for him at the old fortress renamed
"Castle Garden."

The Lafayette visit represented a solemn moment for
Americans, a "Jubilee of Liberty" (as one of the interminable
public speeches proclaimed) during which the nation recalled
its origins.[1] Lafayette visited all two dozen states before
returning home late in 1825, and even at small frontier
settlements in the west the citizens gathered to see and
honor this Frenchman who symbolized the quintessential
act of the national past. Stopping at Shawneetown, Illinois,
on their way back up the Ohio in May, 1825, Lafayette and
his party walked toward the small rude hotel on a calico
carpet stretched between rows of silent, hatless pioneers,

and then paused on the portico of the building to hear
Judge James Hall—later famous as the chronicler of the
Ohio—express the local sentiments. "We receive you with
filial affection," Hall proclaimed, "as one of the fathers of
the Republic."[2] Wherever he went, not surprisingly, Lafayette merged in the public mind with Washington; he was his
spiritual "son" or even his virtual reincarnation. Though the
"American General" (Lafayette's insistent term for himself)
had come back as a frail old man, his long absence from the
country made the return an apt symbol for the recovery of
republican virtue and the revival of liberty. The most telling
act of his visit thus took place in the tomb at Mount Vernon,
where the Frenchman knelt down to kiss the lead coffin,
accidently bruising his forehead as he did so, while an eagle
soared over the scene.[3]

The fete at Castle Garden was a foretaste of these and
other themes in the long official "progress." An elaborate
decorative scheme which played on the evening darkness
(for the moon rose late) gave the spectators a succession
of visual surprises as they moved from the shore toward the
converted fortress on its artificial island. They passed first
through a framed pyramid decked with lamps and sur-
mounted by a single star—the *novus ordo* motif—and then
crossed through the dimly lit canvas tunnel that led over the
bridge. Once on the other side, they passed under a triumphal
arch erected on pillars made from upended cannon barrels
and adorned by an enormous bust of Washington as well as
a painting of Liberty that welcomed "the Nation's Guest."
Now the partygoers had entered the great tent raised over the
old fort, and here they were assaulted with elaborate and
fanciful decorations. A thousand lamps gleamed brightly:
thirteen chandeliers representing the colonies hung down,
for instance, around the central pillar of the tent, itself
symbolizing the union and bearing the names of the revolutionary heroes. The bright air was full of banners and ar-
morial designs. The thirteen columns around the edge of the
tent each carried the escutcheon of a colony and that of the

nation; from column to column at the top, furthermore, the American flag was draped, while shields placed in the gallery seats near the entrance arch proclaimed the enduring memory of Yorktown, Monmouth, and Brandywine—at the last of which Lafayette had received his wound in the service of American freedom. The pavillion intended for the Frenchman stood between the arch and the central pillar; it was of blue and white cloth, and was flanked at the opening by cannon taken from the British at Yorktown. The center post in this smaller tent represented the state of New York. Overhead a large bright "F" shone forth in respect to France, but the letter was guarded by an emblematic American eagle.

Surrounded by such trappings—a long remove from the calico he would find in Shawneetown—Lafayette might have become merely another decoration for the "Jubilee." And indeed the man almost did become an icon. Henry Clay told a joint session of Congress held in the Frenchman's honor and presence, for example, that many a dead patriot of the revolutionary era would relish the chance given Lafayette "to return to [the] country, and to contemplate the intermediate changes which had taken place—to view the forest felled, the cities built, the mountains levelled, the canals cut, the highways constructed, the progress of the arts, the advancement of learning, and the increase of population." The sentiment was right, but Clay was suggesting, after all, that Lafayette himself almost had come from beyond something more than the Atlantic—a hint not countered when he turned to Lafayette, telling him, "You are in the midst of posterity." The American General graciously demurred: "posterity has not begun for me, since, in the sons of my companions and friends, I find the same public feelings ... in my behalf, which I have had the happiness to experience in their fathers."[4] He was very much alive; so, too, he cannily underscored, was the old spirit of America. If, as Fred Somkin has argued, the real national anxiety in the 1820s centered precisely here—on the fear that the present, furiously developing, might lose touch with the patriot age—Lafayette's presence, and his words, helped assuage the feeling. Clay himself pointed to the fear, one notes; and Lafayette, back in New York for July 4, 1825, spoke the reassurance that clearly was being sought: "At every step of my visit through the twenty four United States," he declared, "I have had to admire wonders of creation and improvement. No where can they be more conspicuous than in the state of New York, in the prodigious progress of this city. Those western parts, which I had left a wilderness, I have found covered with flourishing towns, highly cultivated farms, active factories, and intersected by the admirable [Erie] canal... all in consequence of independence, freedom, and a republican spirit."[5] Saratoga, Valley Forge, and Yorktown were the moral capital, in other words, of the booster age.

The *discordia concors* of that notion ought to have raised doubts—for Cooper it later would—but Lafayette did not raise them himself. His real function throughout the celebration was to act as a foreign voice as well as a voice of the national past: he was an ideal European from the American viewpoint since he answered native declarations (quite literally during his tour) with the firm tones of enlightened Old World approval. He thus came into the national drama as a convenient deus ex machina, venerable because of his associations with the great war, but utterly detached from the domestic political broils which had touched even Washington—and had brought denunciation and ruin on another Euro-American, Tom Paine, who had come back too soon and too ebulliently. Because of his curious detachment, Lafayette could help generate a sense of the American past freed from local or factional rancor. Though he drew attention to the lowering issue of slavery, and even aroused hope in the Indians for a juster dispensation at the hands of the whites, his influence on the whole pacified the public. For more than a year the United States experienced a wave of nostalgia—the first ever on these shores—centered in an idealized heroic past made real by the tinsel decorations of a hundred fetes, as well as by the fatherly presence of a man whose selfless devotion to liberty (and America) was proverbial long before he arrived.[6]

For Cooper, who was to know Lafayette intimately in Europe, the general's return to the United States pointed at first toward the past: "I remember the deep, reverential, I might almost say awful, attention," Cooper had the American "guide" of *Notions of the Americans* say in 1828, "with which a school of some sixty children, on a remote frontier, listened to the tale of [Lafayette's] sufferings in the castle of Olmutz, as it was recounted to us by the instructor, who had been a soldier in his youth, and fought the battles of his country, under the orders of the 'young and gallant Frenchman.'"[7] When Lafayette landed in New York, Cooper already had published two tales of the Revolution, and was then at work on *Lionel Lincoln*, in which Bunker Hill and Lexington and Concord were to be memorialized; the novelist was drawing on, and contributing to, the mood of recollection. And his contributions, once Lafayette arrived, were to be more than literary. A member of the party that accompanied the Frenchman to a fort named in his honor, "Mr. Jas. Cooper" on that occasion offered a toast in homage to "The fortress and its name; the former is durable, but the latter shall be imperishable."[8] Indeed, there is some possibility that Cooper himself wrote the account here quoted, which was published in the New York *American*, run by his friend Charles King.[9] It is certain, in any event, that Cooper did write for the same paper in the following week the long report of the Castle Garden fete on which my description above is based. One of the citizens who undertook to arrange for the party, Cooper had stayed at the affair until after four o'clock in the following morning, then went to King's office and quickly composed his narrative.[10]

Cooper showed his artistic temperament in his comments there on the "succession of fanciful pictures" offered to guests at the party, on the "magical" effect of looking from the gallery down onto the crowds of people dressed in bright finery, and the fairylike mood of the whole scene, as though it partook of some dream. Impressed by the orderliness of this republican assembly (a point noticed by countless commentators on Lafayette's visit—and thrown by them in the face of Old World aristocrats), Cooper ended his report with a boast typical of the public declamations which were to dog the Frenchman across the land: for the fete, with its "gay crowd" and its splendid setting amid the waters off lower Manhattan, together with the "fine taste and lavish expenditure" evident in its "embellishments," challenged comparison with other celebrations held for the famous "throughout the world." One signal proof of the republic's maturity, in other words, was to be found in its artful recognition of Lafayette. Since the New York press had promised beforehand that "the decorations" for Castle Garden would be "on a scale and of a magnificence, that has never been equalled in this country," Cooper's boast clearly reflected a widespread perception. Newfound arts and old sturdy patriotism apparently could coexist.[11]

But where, in all of this, was the note of "simplicity" Cooper and other Americans sounded in trying to derive national manners from national principles? As Somkin points out, the foreign press at the time of Lafayette's visit underscored the inconsistency of welcoming the hero of republican virtue by means of ceremonies rooted, after all, in aristocratic and monarchical habit.[12] Nor was this reminder merely a jab at the Republic; the formality of it all reads, today, like another sign of anxiety, as if it was felt that elaborated form might induce that sense of the living past which was fast slipping away. Cooper himself raised no questions in 1824. Indeed, he seems to have been so caught up in the festivities that his conscious alignment with American ideals later in the decade owed a good deal to the "magic" of Lafayette's visit.

As we shall see, Cooper overstated his own assumptions in lending his pen to America. And the overstatement bore an even more direct relation to the triumphal return of Lafayette. The Frenchman had been gone from America less than a year when Cooper and his family left New York for Europe; they arrived at Cowes, the Isle of Wight, on July 2, 1826— just two days before the fiftieth anniversary of the Declaration of Independence and, as it ominously happened, the deaths of two other old patriots, John Adams and Thomas Jefferson. By the end of that month, the Coopers barely had settled down in Paris, but already Lafayette had written to invite them to La Grange. He warmly recalled his relationship with Cooper during the tour ("Mr. Cooper was one of the first New York friends I Had the gratification to take by the Hand"), and regretted now that he had not had "more opportunities to enjoy His Company," a regret he hoped to counter now with the hospitality of his own country.[13]

Some of Lafayette's warmth on this occasion might be traceable to the surplus of good feeling that still lingered from 1824 and 1825. But it is remarkable that he sought Cooper out so quickly. He knew that the Coopers were expected in Paris the night before he wrote the novelist, and he even knew where precisely to address the letter. As it turned out, too, Lafayette himself visited the family before Cooper (who confessed to an American correspondent, "I have postponed my visit until I can, with propriety do so no longer") went to La Grange in early October.[14] It is hard to imagine that Cooper had any specific reason to avoid the general, or at least to put off his visit. From August until the time he did go to La Grange his daughter Caroline was sick with the scarlet fever, a fact which kept the family close to their quarters. But before she fell ill Cooper had answered Lafayette's welcome by writing that he would be spending several months in the French capital; he therefore begged leave "to postpone, that which is both a duty and pleasure to all of my Country," until he had, as he put it, "established my little family." Written in a formal style vaguely reminiscent of the proclamations tendered to Lafayette in America, the answer seems directed as much to a symbol or an institution as a man; it may be that despite their previous meetings in New York Cooper felt uneasy in the presence of the Frenchman, or even the idea of his presence. Cooper received Lafayette's first note, he wrote, "with lively pleasure, and with the deep veneration that every American entertains for his name." It was as if he was not quite sure whether to take Lafayette's overtures as a personal gesture or a public, ceremonial one. He thus closed on a ceremonial chord himself, passing on Susan's "respect and regard for all the family of Gen La Fayette, and chiefly to its venerable and beloved head." Cooper signed himself "With the greatest Respect And Gratitude."[15]

By year's end such hesitations had passed, and Cooper could close a letter of December 5 far more intimately: "I am, my dear Sir, Your faithful and indebted Friend."[16] Propriety had given way to a relationship based, in part at least, on shared political assumptions. Through the next years the two would discuss the great issues of contemporary Europe, work publicly for mutual goals in France and elsewhere, and jointly lament and assault the Old World prejudices uttered there as true accounts of the America both, in different ways, had served. Lafayette's status as a spiritual American and a literal European gave him a broad authority on this last topic, one which Americans in general—and Cooper in particular—found supportive and reassuring. One meaning of Lafayette's return to the United States had been centered precisely here: for his view of America, the citizens convinced themselves by endless repetition, was the proper and informed one—doubly right because it bore a French stamp and yet fit the mature judgment of independent Americans.

Cooper's friendship with Lafayette, however intimate it became, never really escaped the limits of this American viewpoint.[17] And Lafayette countered the formula with expectations of his own about the American Cooper. Perhaps as soon as Cooper's first visit to La Grange (in October, 1826), or even earlier, the general was urging him to write and publish an account of the American tour, and the urging continued as their relations deepened.[18] In a letter to the banker Wilkes, written in January of 1828, Cooper gave what remains the fullest account of the matter. "I am not writing a Naval History," Cooper told Wilkes in reference to an old and much delayed project, "i.e., I am collecting materials but do not expect to produce the book these three years." Part of the reason for this delay was Cooper's current project; for it had been, he wrote,

> now more than a year since La Fayette manifested a strong desire that I should write some account of his reception in America. The good old man was so frank, and showed, mingled with his acknowledged personal interest, so strong a desire to do credit to the country, that I scarcely knew how to resist him. I am perhaps foolishly romantic enough to think that he has almost the right to command the services of an American author. At all events, be the motive what it might, I finally consented, not however to write a tame and monotonous account of La Fayette's visit, for that would put him at fault, but to attempt a sketch of the U. States which should, from time to time, touch on some of [the visit's] striking incidents.[19]

Wilkes was a close friend and something of an agent for Cooper; this letter to him reveals more than the mere facts of Lafayette's influence over *Notions of the Americans*, the work in question. One finds a certain hint of coercion here, for instance, as if Lafayette himself recognized the "right to command" he might exercise over *any* American author. And one finds, perhaps more suggestively, Cooper's own recognition that Lafayette's "acknowledged personal interest" —"be the motive what it might" is revealingly ambiguous— might convert the desired "account" into a self-serving report. The Lafayette conjured up by such hesitations is hardly the hero of the American jubilee. Still, Cooper himself seems affected as much by the lingering sentiments of that occasion as by his new and more private perceptions. The worshipful glow which had surrounded the *idea* of Lafayette in America—and hence the idea of America itself—came with Cooper to Europe as part of his American viewpoint. If Lafayette was ready to "command," this one New World author was ready to serve.

Yet Cooper served in his own manner. Unusually protective about his privileges as an author, Cooper was willing to accept hints about possible literary projects—*The Spy*, *The Last of the Mohicans*, and *The Wept of Wish-Ton-Wish* all testify on this point in his first decade as a writer—but he often covered his present undertakings in secrecy, even when corresponding with his publishers.[20] This secrecy was partly a matter of economics, or so it reads; but it also seems to have been a matter of supposed prerogative. In any event, Lafayette's "strong desire" for a report on his tour from Cooper's hand ran afoul of Cooper's tendency to guard himself, even if the source of the desire called for extraordinary attention. Though he told Wilkes he had "consented" to the request, what in fact Cooper did was to use Lafayette's tour as the excuse for a book quite different from the one Lafayette wanted. And it was to this book, in his later years, that Cooper traced his undoing in America. By lending support to the one surviving European whose life seemed to speak for the American experiment, Cooper alienated himself from his homeland.

Notions of the Americans owed to the Lafayette visit and to Lafayette himself a certain formal exuberance of tone on the matter of American prospects. In his letter to Wilkes, Cooper recalled his dislike years before for what he now called the "eulogiums of Miss Wright" on the United States; hence he felt uneasy about his own glowing portrait of the country.[21] As Wilkes pointed out in a letter the following fall, after he had read *Notions of the Americans*, Cooper in fact had spoken far more harshly of Fanny Wright's *Views of Society and Manners in America* (1821) than the novelist now remembered: he had called the book a piece of "nauseous flattery" which made him "indignant."[22] It is fair to attribute the softening of Cooper's tone, I think, to his own change of voice and his uncertainty about it. *Notions of the Americans* was Lafayette's book insofar as its pictures of the United States, though they pushed Lafayette the traveler off to the side, endorsed the ideal view of the country for which the Frenchman stood. And Cooper's uneasiness about the volume stemmed from his thus having spoken in it with a voice never quite his own as an artist.

The main problem he faced in writing it was to keep it from becoming, like so many of the Lafayette ceremonies, a mere exercise in western congratulation. Cooper wrote to Wilkes about the temptation he felt toward the latter: "I find so much ignorance here concerning America, so much insolence in their manner of thinking of us, which however natural is not the less false, that at every line [of *Notions*] I am tempted to decorate rather than to describe."[23] Old World ignorance on things American was a topic Cooper liked to investigate on his travels, probably because the pain of finding so much of it had a certain pleasure; this was, after all, another means by which, absent as he was from the country, he could still touch back to it. But the same topic drew Lafayette's attention, too: "I am every day vexed at the European ignorance of the U.S.," he had written Cooper a year before in a letter pressing the novelist to write the American book.[24] If Europe could have openly accepted the United States—one notes Cooper's comment about the "insolence" that went with the "ignorance"—perhaps a work like *Notions of the Americans* could have remained soberly descriptive; but the larger issues were polemical, and description almost had to overstate and "decorate."

Cooper went so far as to say of the book to his American publishers, "I am not without hopes, that the Letters on America will be found orthodox, if nothing else."[25] He meant by this, presumably, that he had written it with a pronouncedly public voice, and had done so consciously; the reception at home thus ought to be as good as that in Europe would be bad. "It will be known as mine, and *nicely* abused here, as such," he wrote the firm, "so you will have all the advantage of my sufferings"—the bad foreign reception actually might increase sales at home.[26] Wilkes said after the book appeared that Cooper and Wright sounded alike ("if hers was a picture of all lights and no shadows, you will hardly escape the same charge"), but Cooper already had estimated the effect of this fact on the fortunes of the work.[27] He suggested to Henry Colburn's agent in Paris, when attempting to interest the English publisher in *Notions*, "The subject is of much interest for your country.... I prefer however, not to commit its nature to paper, but would wish to treat with Mr. Colburne concerning its publication."[28] Here his secretiveness was coming out, but one senses as well that Cooper was trying to bait and trick Colburn.

In between Lafayette, the English public, the rest of Europe, and his own homeland, Cooper could dance such evasive steps. But once *Notions of the Americans* appeared and his authorship of it became known, he was a man committed to what the book said, implied, and passed over. Or rather he was responsible for what its main "character" did in these regards, since Cooper had altered Lafayette's proposal most importantly by inventing a European "Count" whose letters home from America make up the book's matter. In part, one sees a novelist's sense at work in this change; Cooper told Colburn's agent that the book, though its subject was "one of fact," would "be sufficiently embellished by adventure and fiction to give it interest to general readers."[29] Yet one sees here as well Cooper's cautious withdrawal from Lafayette's rather fact-bound proposal. He rejected the "tame and monotonous account"—as he called it in writing Wilkes—that would have come from following Lafayette; he did so because such an account would have put Lafayette "at fault." That a boring recital of facts also would put the author himself in an awkward position cannot have escaped Cooper's mind. As he told his publishers, he expected the fact of his authorship to be known quite quickly. He invented the "Count" and made him the observer of various Lafayette scenes, as well as a vast deal else, in order to particularize and hence enliven the narrative. *Notions of the Americans* was, in fact, the first

of his first-person books; he would return to the form for his
own travel books, and then for a collection of novels in the
early 1840s. Lafayette apparently was looking at first for a
third-person record.[30]

And yet the "Travelling Bachelor" who reports on America in *Notions* is, like Lafayette, an ideal European observer
of the West. Unlike Captain Basil Hall, with whose American
Travels Cooper's travelogue was compared (to Cooper's
detriment) in the *Edinburgh Review* in 1829, the Count is a
man of open eye and open mind. His American guide, John
Cadwallader, leads him about the New World scene with a
felicitous talent for revealing the better side of American
life; Hall, Cooper complained in 1831, showed the European
penchant for viewing America "in a false light"—he was
"constantly in error" on matters of fact, and was misled by
erroneous conceptions.[31] Ignorant of America before his
voyage, as Lafayette decidedly was not, the bachelor in
Notions thus has no personal past to justify by his present
understanding of the United States. He certainly shares the
liberal views of the Frenchman, but Cooper's real purpose
is to take a benevolent European of the current age and
use him as a presumably impartial means for gauging America's condition. Lafayette, as Cooper certainly had learned
by 1828, stood too firmly in the midst of political life in
France to serve the purpose; besides, his fame would clearly
detract from Cooper's larger desire to focus on America, and
Europe's ideas about America, rather than on the particular
events of 1824 and 1825.

In these ways, the book aimed toward the Old World.
But it aimed in other ways toward Cooper's American
audience, and the tie with his homeland which that audience
represented for him. Suffering from a mild alienation in Paris
—he continually sought out other Americans abroad whenever he could and wherever he was staying—Cooper inscribed
in *Notions of the Americans* the symbolic gesture of his
homeward-bound thoughts. Hence the book became the
single most important part of his "discovery" of America

during his absence. Beyond the apparatus of the Count and his guide, one finds a wealth of assertions about the United States for which—despite the cited facts and figures—the final authority is simply the desired memories and hopes of the author. Seeking to dwell on those memories and hopes, Cooper came to perceive an ideal land which he clearly knew was untrue to the complex actuality he had left behind: he clearly knew so, one may assert, because *The Prairie* and *The Wept of Wish-Ton-Wish*, the novels that bracketed *Notions*, show complexity, irony, and even tragedy, at point after point. The needs which accounted for Cooper's simplifications—the last being another thing altogether from his pursuit of simplicity—seem to have embarrassed him into apologizing for *Notions* even as he was writing it and seeing it through the press; he rewrote the beginning of the book, in fact, to soften its strident affirmations.[32] Even in the published version, *Notions* nonetheless retained the visionary capacity for seeing the country, as Cooper said of the celebrants at Castle Garden in 1824, through the "magic" of a special illusion. Like that party in New York, the book also suffered from a surplus of decoration. In many senses, it was Cooper's most daring fiction to date.

Cooper acknowledged as much at the time, and other friends than Wilkes politely reported their doubts about the lack of doubts in the work itself. Even before they published it in the states, Carey, Lea, and Carey told Cooper (here was the pragmatic sense of businessmen) that he was "in error as to the extent of interest the book will excite here." What Americans wanted along this line was a work that would treat the nation with "severity"—especially if the treatment came from a real European.[33] This judgment, shrewdly correct as it may have been in gauging the market, must have rankled Cooper; as an American document, *Notions* sought to demonstrate that the country should set Europe straight, as Cadwallader does the Count, rather than vice versa. The staunch American position Cooper was enacting in Europe was the source of his rhetoric in the book.

American self-effacement was something Cooper never could abide. But the nation had, as a logical balance-weight to this attitude, the kind of boastfulness to which his *Notions of the Americans* came close. Cooper blamed the self-effacing tendency for the fate that *Notions* suffered, or he thought it suffered. To the end of his life he kept defending the 1828 volume by appealing to the moral and factual rightness of what it said.[34] The work thus came to hold in his career a certain mythic position: it was the first sign of the breach that later would widen between himself and the nation. Taking Cooper's character into account, however, a modern reader suspects something hidden here: perhaps a feeling of guilt over the ease with which, even as he pulled back from what Lafayette wanted, he had taken up the "orthodox" boasts of the country. He was bothered by the fact that he had so blatantly accepted and endorsed the popular language of his homeland. He had done so in the first place because he wanted to align himself with the nation; this would allow him to repossess what he had lost, to bury the losses, in other words, in the act of native praise. Yet at the center of his own awareness lay the subversive apprehension that loss was a truth not to be denied. *Notions of the Americans* spoke of the "constantly progressive condition" visible in America; already in *The Pioneers*, however, Cooper had intimated that progress in this simple sense had its moral and other costs—that the national comedy in fact was full of problems.[35] His instinctive distrust of the 1828 eulogy, as well as his linked sense that his later difficulties in America were owing to that book, suggest the profound difference between his imagination and his outward public stance. The drama of Cooper's whole career was in many ways generated by this very conflict.

Notions of the Americans is a large and serial book, loosely unified by its apparatus and its conscious assertion of American worth, but sprawling in its wealth of details and facts. The Count is a string tying the latter together rather than a mind perceiving and shaping the New World scene; and Cadwallader, his American friend, winds up as little more than an orthodox national voice without much personal coloring. Perhaps the most important fact about the book to a critic of Cooper's fiction is the mere fact that it exists, for this tells us a good deal about the force of Cooper's conscious attachment to the country, and the energy which that attachment could release.

As opinion stated rather than vision specified and explored, the book also gives us something more: it offers a superb foil to Cooper's typical practice as an imaginative writer. Its very daylight directness and benign factuality show a mind operating not only with material different from that customary to a novelist, but in a manner markedly different as well. The book has few shadows or doubts because it allows the Count to perceive America from the sort of protective distance which Cooper hardly ever granted to the characters in his adventure tales. Nor is this distinction owing wholly to the discursive nature of *Notions*. Its more important source is the author's stance here as a decidedly public figure, as the surrogate of the nation itself; he was not giving rein to his own fancy as, within the conventions of the novel, he could and did. Perhaps this contrast helps explain Cooper's private worries about the travelogue. It was not true to his own critical sense of experience; as ideology, it had to control rather than probe experience.

We can appreciate the differences here by noting how rigidly *Notions* controls the landscape. In Cooper's border tales, as I shall argue below, landscape typically serves as a vast, complex, and changeable symbol of experience; it is less space than it is time given visibility, history brought into focus. In *Notions of the Americans*, landscape seems almost wholly spatial: it is seen rather than lived through, and time enters it only through ideological means—only, that is, as a "constantly progressive" force. Landscape here is the deduced metaphor for a moral idea present to the author's conscious purpose, rather than the given reality with which (and within which) his characters must struggle.

Thus we find the Count and Cadwallader placed upon the edge of a hill in the fourteenth letter, viewing a particularly lovely and expansive scene laid out below them. All they see subordinates itself to Cooper's controlling idea; the world is not so much world as it is picture, or indeed icon. The scene has importance in the book because it marks the first real experience of inland America accorded to the Count. Prior to this point, he has seen much of New York City during Lafayette's arrival, has undertaken a tour of New England (as the general did), and then returned to New York for the September fete at Castle Garden. Now, he has set out for the western districts of New York and Pennsylvania, and it is in this new section of the book that he first encounters and describes the physical expanse of a recently settled area.[36] He thus has entered that region already claimed by Cooper in *The Pioneers*—and entered it in a quite literal sense, since the hill where he and Cadwallader pause lies only a few miles northeast of Cooperstown, where the rolling Otsego countryside yields to the fertile Mohawk valley. Later in the letter, the Count in fact will tell his Old World correspondent about a night spent in Cooperstown itself. And he will mention at this point a certain former resident of the village, "a gentleman who is the reputed author of a series of tales, which were intended to elucidate the history, manners, usages, and scenery, of his native country." Since that gentleman already has given "sufficiently exact" descriptions of Otsego in one of the tales, the Count adds, he must excuse himself from offering his own words on the topic.[37]

We must leave the Mohawk landscape lying there in its rigid fixity while we consider briefly—for these other issues are crucial here—the peculiar implications of this later passage in the letter. There are two that especially should concern us. The first has to do with what seems like Cooper's self-advertisement. I think it unlikely that Cooper intended the reference that way; if anything, he probably would have seen it as a sly miscue to the reader of *Notions*, a miscue suggesting (in case the thought has arisen in the reader's mind) that Cooper was *not* the author of the book in hand. But the mention of himself has meanings as well as possible motives. It places Cooper the novelist in the objective land-scape of *Notions*—makes of him within the book, that is, precisely what he was as he wrote it. It is an act of self-recognition. And the second point has relations to the first one. For Cooper's explicit definition of what he had been about in the mentioned "tales" makes his art as public as his presence. Cooper's description of *The Pioneers* and his other American novels suggests a program much tidier and more aware than any he had consciously pursued in writing them: this is how, especially given his purpose in 1828, he wanted his career to seem.

That he had been up to other things besides "elucidating" America in those books—putting it down on paper, word for thing—is clear even from *The Spy*. The preface to that novel does address directly, to be sure, the possibilities of an "American" literature, much as the label of *The Pioneers* ("A Descriptive Tale") implies some overriding public pur-pose for that work. But the preface of *The Spy* hardly seems overhopeful in its comments on a native art, and the descrip-tive pictures offered in the other book acquire their meaning less by reference to the real America to which *Notions* gestures (indeed, directs us) than by their place in a larger imaginative whole dictated by the author rather than his expectant public. Cooper drew the pictures in *The Pioneers* with a faithful hand—hence the wonder felt by D. H. Law-rence—but he did not do so merely for the stenographic effects sought by an "elucidator." In the simplest sense, the pictures give weight and substance to the actual themes of the narrative: as when, during the superb night-fishing scene, Ben Pump nearly drowns and is saved by Natty, who uses his longhandled fish-spear to snag the sailor's queue and coat collar and pull him to the surface. Cooper purchases the indulgent languor of his descriptions in this episode, in other words, by putting the deathly spear to such a purpose; the props of the scene give him the symbols of his meaning. We are not to read the passage as a piece of local color ("elucidation") but as an emblem of rebirth, and violent rebirth at that. Ben Pump, we have to remember, suffers a moral reformation of sorts here. He remains a drinker, but it is not as a drunk that he shares Natty's prison cell or the stocks.

That the placid beauty of the nighttime landscape in this part of *The Pioneers* bursts into such complex life—into action and meaning at once—can lead us, by way of contrast, back to the landscape described in *Notions of the Americans*. Here, indeed, the descriptive muse seems dominant. The exchange between character and world in this instance has a genteel intellectual tone. The Count already has told his correspondent, an English baronet named Waller, that this is his first view of how the swarming Americans spread out to "convert mazes of dark forests into populous, wealthy, and industrious counties"[38]—Judge Cooper's orthodox theme in his Otsego pamphlet. The actual landscape the Count surveys bolsters precisely this prior idea. "It was completely an American scene," he writes, "embracing all that admixture of civilization, and of the forest, of the works of man, and of the reign of nature, that one can so easily imagine to belong to this country."[39] And it is all an easy act of imagining, on Cooper's part as well as the Count's; the neatness of the balanced style tells us as much.

Hence the very line of conflict in novel after novel by Cooper—the border rendered in the passage just quoted as a set of antitheses—becomes in the rest of the Count's letter little more than a visual boundary between coalescent facts. The European refers his English friend to, of all things, a French landscape—"completely ... American" as the world before the writer may be! The scene in France, so long settled, is familiar to both the Count and his correspondent.

Its "chequered" pattern of multicolored fields—grain, vine, and grass—is, nonetheless, what the European thinks of as he looks out now over the obvious contrast of field and forest in the American valley. The frontier has become a matter of nicely discriminated shades. In such a world, of course, nothing like Ben Pump's adventure can occur.

The trick of it lies in distance. "The distance diminishes the objects to the eye," the Count writes, "and brings the several parts so much in union, as to lend to the whole the variegated aspect of the sort of plain just mentioned"—the French landscape, that is. The world beneath the Count accordingly has a two-dimensional feel; farmhouses and outbuildings seem "like indicated spots on a crowded map," the sheep are "nearly imperceptible white atoms," and at last, near the horizon, the "power of vision" fails.[40] The landscape thus seems to move away from (perhaps out of) the viewer. It diminishes itself, fades, disperses.

Which is to say that it has no action. The landscapes of Cooper's fiction, on the contrary, typically close up and move in upon those viewing them; or, and this has the same effect, the viewers must enter them as actors themselves, making the seen world a felt environment. (One might add here that the intentional entrance of the settler into the wilderness gave Cooper, in this connection, his surest hints.) How different, then, the scene in *The Spy* which shows us Harvey Birch and Henry Wharton struggling through a benighted and rough country, alert to danger at every step and completely bereft of the Count's wholesome distance. These two wanderers rest at last, to be sure, on the summit of a hill above the Hudson just as day approaches. Yet the coming of light throws the "landscape" into action: "A ray of the rising sun," Cooper writes, "darted upon the slight cloud that hung over the placid river, and at once the whole scene was in motion, changing and assuming new forms, and exhibiting fresh objects in each successive moment." Space is implicit with time; the darkness passes and a new kind of darkness, a complexity of movement, takes over. Cooper's conscious symbol of the event is a British war

vessel down on the water: "Before the fog had begun to
move, the tall spars were seen above it, and from one of them
a long pennant was feebly borne abroad in the current of
night air, that still quivered along the river; but as the smoke
arose, the black hull, the crowded and complicated mass
of rigging, and the heavy yards and booms, spreading their
arms afar, were successively brought into view."[41] Piece by
piece, the ship comes into focus; and it is as a focus for
the whole scene that the vessel functions—appropriately,
in view of the plot, since it offers the British officer Wharton
the hope of escape. In the landscape from *Notions of the
Americans*, on the other hand, there is no real focus, no
one object that rests outside the viewer and that organizes
the scene. Only a subjective idea of American achievement
and progress shapes it. And that idea is present merely by
assertion; we read of it but do not see it actually realizing
itself in what is presented to view.

It is worth reiterating that we cannot explain such a
contrast merely by reference to literary genres. The sense
of experience rendered by Cooper in *The Spy* was not so
much the result of his chosen form as the reason why he
chose the form in the first place: he became an adventurer
because adventure suited what he had to do. So, too, the
Mohawk valley scene in *Notions of the Americans* lacks
energy and center not because it occurs in a discursive work
but because it is written from an ideological stance—a stance
which constrained Cooper even though, at the time, he
willingly accepted it. It is flaccid, uninteresting, totally
without the drama that gives his other American scenes their
characteristic tension. What else are we to expect of a world
that can be rendered, as the Count suggests, by reference to
a map? We should not be surprised in the pages following
when the Count's guide introduces a real map, for he gives
the traveler thereby an utterly public explanation of the
scene before them. The European misses "the recollections
and monuments of antiquity"—already an ancient saw in
comments on America—and Cadwallader draws his attention
from the landscape to the "open map of the country" the

American has spread out. "The moral feeling with which
a man of sentiment and knowledge," Cadwallader officially
intones, "looks upon the plains of your hemisphere, is
connected with his recollections; here it should be mingled
with his hopes."[42] That he proceeds to gesture toward the
past is not important in this context, for the past he calls
up has the haste of rapid change: "Draw a line from this
spot, north and south"—he obviously is still pointing to
his map—"and all of civilization that you shall see for a
thousand miles west, is what man has done since my infancy."[43] Cooper himself could have made the same claim,
and on the same ground; in a sense, he was doing just that in
giving these orthodox sentiments to a character said to have
his home just west of Otsego.[44] Cadwallader is also said to
be about the same age as Cooper was when he wrote the
book, but the character is orthodox of the orthodox—as
Cooper was not, even at this time. Cadwallader thus suggests
that the landscapes of Europe are "tinged with melancholy
regrets," while those of America point toward hope. Cooper
in *The Pioneers*, as we shall see in the next chapter, found
both emotions properly American; if anything, he gave
far more prominence to melancholy. The Count's guide,
however, is not to be silenced. "I have stood upon this
identical hill," runs his peroration, "and seen nine tenths of
its smiling prospect darkened by the shadows of the forest.
You see what it is to-day. He who comes a century hence,
may hear the din of a city rising from that very plain, or find
his faculties confused by the number and complexity of its
works of art."[45] Even Cadwallader's memory speaks of the
future. Cooper's spoke decidedly of the past, even when the
speaking of it—as in *The Pioneers*—aimed at repossessing what
was no more.

Cadwallader's words nonetheless complete the circle of
dogma in *Notions of the Americans*. The scene abstracted
in his map and his language cannot display of itself the
remarkable changes he says it has undergone; the stated
action of the scene, that is, cannot be presented. Even in
The Pioneers Cooper had difficulty finding the means for

presenting, step-by-step, the process of settlement. But this was a problem in the national mind—or, if one prefers, in the national style. Crèvecoeur was hardly alone in *Letters from an American Farmer* when he portrayed the process as a contrast of vacancy and fulfilment: "barren spots fertilised, grass growing where none grew before; grain gathered from fields which had hitherto produced nothing better than brambles; dwellings raised where no building materials were to be found; wealth acquired by the most uncommon means."[46] Hence Cadwallader's trust in the past and the future supplies what his eye might not find in the landscape.

But his words and gestures are compelling for the Count. The two men leave their vantage point "in silence" and return to the carriage that awaits them. The Count, however, is inwardly alive. He has suffered there on the hill what we can only call a "conversion," a conscious reformation of his opinions and outlook. "I began to look around me with new eyes," he writes to Waller, "and instead of seeking subjects of exulting comparison between what I saw here and what I had left behind me [in Europe], I found new subjects of admiration and of wonder at every turn."[47] Brought to this hill by his American friend, and perceiving from it the stated ideals of American life, he can only assent to the revelation tendered him. Now, like Lafayette, he is a European by birth but an American by conviction. In this change of heart we at last perceive why it was that Cooper, in writing *Notions of the Americans*, had to keep so many complex facts so strictly in control.

Panoramas of the sort Cooper created in the fourteenth letter of *Notions of the Americans* derived, of course, from current literary and painterly fashion. But surely we can trace this hilltop scene, and others in Cooper, back to a personal source as well: to the heights of Judge Cooper's "Vision," the mountain from which he first looked down on Otsego. Throughout his career, the Judge's son looked to this powerful moment of the family past as if to a memory of hope. He used it directly and subtly in *The Pioneers*, and in books

as widely spaced as *The Spy* and *Satanstoe* we can find traces
of the same luminous instant. Indeed, as Susan Fenimore
Cooper recalled, the whole of *The Deerslayer* was conceived
in "the vision" that came to her father as they rode home
one day from Cooper's "Châlet," his farm that was located
on "the Vision" itself. As his eye went out over the lake,
Cooper told Susan that he had to write one more book set
there.[48] Significantly, *The Deerslayer* erased from Otsego
all that Judge Cooper had done, all that he had envisioned
from his mountain in 1785. Having lost the social landscape,
Cooper consistently aimed his own wonder toward nature;
as we shall see in the next chapter, this was one source of
Natty Bumppo's relation to the novelist. Cooper could
possess only in spirit, only intangibly through words, what
his father had possessed in utter fact.

The Pioneers opens, we recall, on the road that leads
across "the Vision" to the village of Templeton. The Judge
in the novel later will recount for his daughter Elizabeth
the first sufferings of the region, which she is too young to
clearly remember; and he will tell then, too, of the "mingled
feeling of pleasure and desolation" which overwhelmed
him as for the first time he looked "on the silent wilderness"
from the hill.[49] But Elizabeth herself has experienced something of the same sensations in her homecoming at the start
of the book. There she looks down on "a scene which was
so rapidly altering under the hands of man"—a scene that
leaves her fixed "in mute wonder" (p. 40). And the novel
gives us on several other occasions this same glimpse of the
village. Its meanings change from occasion to occasion—
witness the doleful "vision" of Chingachgook in chapter
36—but the gesture remains immutably, mythically set.
Cooper returned to his father's moment, but he brought
with him emotions his father did not feel in 1785.

Elizabeth's own survey of the valley at the beginning is
the most naively pleasurable of all of them. Yet even the
young woman, unlike the traveler in *Notions of the Americans*, must come down from the heights. Here again Cooper's
sense of experience, rather than his ideas, was controlling

him. She comes down in the gathering darkness, down into "the cold gloom of the valley," and the home she has come to rediscover presents "nothing...but [its] cold, dreary stone-walls." "Elizabeth felt," Cooper writes, "as if all the loveliness of the mountain-view had vanished like the fancies of a dream" (p. 59). Shifting in appearance and meaning, the landscape offers no obvious threats but it nonetheless eludes control; no one formula is adequate to it.

Notions of the Americans violated this apprehension of reality as much in its handling of landscape as in its slick ideology. By suggesting that the world was passively malleable to eye or idea, something to be shaped by whoever viewed it, the travelogue pushed, though in a bogus fashion, toward a transcendental position. Cooper's own position in his novels, on the contrary, was that of a realist; those who survive in his tales are those who see rather than project, who take in the world rather than patly dismiss it. The remarkable acuity of Harvey Birch or "Hawkeye" is merely one example. In book after book, scene after scene, the crucial need is for attention: close sight, quick thought, ready response. And the alternative is death.

Cooper put his characters in such a world because the world as he himself had known it hardly had nourished his illusions. He had reacted with petulance at first, but once he had signalled the recovery of his spirit with the sermon of *Precaution* he went beyond petulance. He did not, as has been claimed, merely retreat from experience into an invented world of safe boundaries and ever-decreasing age. On the contrary, in the Leatherstocking books as in his other tales he imagined over and over again, as if compelled to return to his personal disaster, the trial of hope in a universe of force, violence, and disillusionment.[50] Adventure gave him the means of specifying his vision of life—specifying, exaggerating, and enacting. And adventure as we find it in Cooper has, as a result, a markedly inward cast: it is a test of spirit and mind as well as body, a carefully orchestrated assault of the world on the self. His American tales spring to life when some character, suffering such an assault,

is forced to react and respond. In calling our attention to
Cooper's "sense of the imponderable nature of reality,"
Marius Bewley has pointed us directly toward this pattern.[51]
I would add to his insight only the further fact that Cooper's
characters themselves—not just the reader, as Bewley implies
—are brought face to face with the mystery, the mere given-
ness, of the universe. Forced to act, but more importantly
to deliberate—to measure mind and world in this moment
of intense life—they discover how little besides themselves
they can rely on; old habits, old ideas, old assumptions
fall away. But if they have something beyond what they
must lose, the mortal struggle can become a kind of rebirth.
There is in the very logic of this pattern a fable of the
author's own life.

These points are important enough to warrant some
extended discussion. For this purpose, I would like to raise,
as an example of Cooper's skill in handling adventure, a single
intense scene from one of his later books. This is the long
and difficult vigil forced on Mabel Dunham in chapter 21
of *The Pathfinder*; here, if we pay attention to Cooper's
own stresses, we will find distilled, with all the maturity of
his final phase, the essential action of his American art.

Left relatively alone on a small island in Lake Ontario
while a scouting party is off looking for the French, Dunham
acquires an intensity of inner life precisely as the outer
threat of an enemy force attacks her outpost. The adventure
thus brings her, as Cooper writes, to "the full consciousness
of her situation,"[52] to an awareness of that threat but also
to an awareness of herself. Cooper's very choice of this
phrase for a moment of peril suggests the degree to which
he sought to shape the scene as an expression of psychological themes.

The Pathfinder has pushed Dunham toward isolation and
awakening from the start. In the end, of course, a super-
vening propriety which Cooper rarely wished to violate—
though here, as elsewhere, he questions it—will demand that
this woman be saved by men more skilled than herself in
the arts of survival. During this one long episode, however,

Dunham is clearly the "eye" of Cooper's own narrative, a person seen intensely from the inside as well as the filter through whom events and perceptions reach the reader. Focusing his prose exactly on the confused struggle of her mind with its surroundings and its own impulses, Cooper creates an interior drama richly verified in the literal one of the attack. Moreover, as a person displaced from her familiar world—and just when, ironically, she has been reunited with her father—Dunham expresses the dominant theme of the novel, which is the relation of person and place, self and world, one's "gifts" to one's "circumstances."[53]

Cooper approaches this destination in *The Pathfinder* with leisurely indirection. The characters in the book reveal themselves at first by how they talk and what they say: character itself, that is, is defined expressively. But by the end of the novel they will reveal themselves by the stance they assume in the concrete physical universe; language gives way to act, word to gesture. As we shall see in several instances below, this is one pattern that runs through Cooper's American tales. It springs in large part from that distrust of the social occasion already mentioned, and it leads—with an American logic of which Cooper was arguably aware—to the world of adventure. If we fail to note the presence of this pattern in *The Pathfinder*, we are likely to find the chatty pointlessness of the early dialogue unartful; in fact, it is absolutely essential to Cooper's meaning. The tiring verbal formulas delivered again and again by Uncle Cap— even Natty's bothersome talk is part of the problem—suggest that identity is largely unchanging, uninteresting, and at last trivial. But we must note what finally happens to Cap when, under the pressure of circumstances, he gives up his captious words and begins to act. He does not develop, to be sure, but he does reveal in the crisis "the hardy and experienced seaman, that he truly was" (p. 237). At the same time, intriguingly, Natty becomes on the lake a curiously impotent lubber whose forest skills have little use. Earlier, it is Natty who scoffs at Cap's use of nautical language in the woods: "I know nothing of ports and anchors," he responds when the sailor typically speaks of the Mingos as an enemy ship, "but there is a direful Mingo trail, within a hundred yards of this very spot, and as fresh as venison without salt" (p. 49). Natty also calls on that occasion for a "plainer ... English" more suitable than Cap's formulas to the real condition of the travelers. Once the travelers become voyagers, however, Natty is verbally and actually out of place. When Mabel Dunham remarks to him that the men on the *Scud* seem oddly silent, Natty thus tells her that "a prudent tongue" is of enormous value, that "a silent army, in the woods, is doubly strong; and a noisy one, doubly weak"—especially when the Mingos are afoot. Perhaps piqued by Natty's next truism ("if tongues made soldiers, the women of a camp would generally carry the day"), Dunham rather sharply notes that she and the others "are neither an army, nor in the woods" (p. 186). This ought to recall that much earlier scene in which Natty is talking on and on in the woods as the Mingos close in; on that occasion, Mabel quiets him with a touch on the shoulder and a silent gesture toward the Indians.[54]

Natty in love is as out of place as Cap in the forest or Natty himself on the lake. But the theme does not belong to him; it belongs to the book, and to the adventure plot which the book embodies. What we see in the incidents already mentioned, as in Dunham's vigil, is that dialectic between world and self which energizes much of Cooper's border art. Self is represented in *The Pathfinder* by the old words, old views, even old skills which the characters bring with them into the wilderness: self, that is, as a defense against experience, as the crusty presence of a personal past. Such things once may have had their fittingness—elsewhere they might be fitting still. Clung to in this universe, however, they prove increasingly dangerous.

And so they do for the Scots soldier McNab, the man left in command on the island while the *Scud* goes off on patrol. McNab speaks for the radical inward authority of the self—he approaches experience from a wholly deductive viewpoint—when he lectures Mabel on the military virtue of unthinking traditionalism. Mabel herself has suggested to the corporal that "forethought" should guide them in the event of an attack, that the "precautions that may be necessary in a situation, as peculiar as ours" should not be lightly ignored. This, on the contrary, is largely an inductive, "attentive" stance; Dunham speaks less for thought in and of itself than thought as the result of watchfulness. She has sensed already that McNab and his Old World cohorts on the island, accustomed to European combat, will "overlook" the demands of their "situation." And everything McNab has to say proves how correct her suspicion is. A right military posture, he already has declared, requires "no journey from Scotland to this place," and so her attempt to distinguish American fighting from the sort this European knows merely entrenches the man in his opinions. Indeed, Mabel thus sends him off, as it were, on a sentimental inward journey to his homeland. Dunham tries to jog the man out of it: "I'm not thinking of Scotland at all," she tells him as he repeats his opinion, "but of this island." He talks on and on of Scotland, nonetheless, until Mabel is "almost in despair"; changing her "mode of operating" on him, she concedes the virtues of his native country—the hope being that this may direct him, by cooling his defensiveness, back to his present situation—but she receives in answer a verbal tour of Bannockburn and Culloden! When at last she gets through to him, and tells him that they should retreat into the blockhouse nearby, the Scotsman will have nothing whatever to do with the idea. Let the Americans like her father (McNab's superior, but in McNab's opinion sorely out of place in a Scots corps) hide behind cover: "it goes against a Scotsman's bluid and opinions, to be beaten out of the field, even before he is attacked. We are broad-sword men, and love to stand foot to foot with the foe. This American mode of fighting, that is getting into so much favor, will destroy the reputation of His Majesty's army, if it no destroy its spirit."

McNab thus shuns a wooden wall but continually repairs, word by word, an intellectual one; he praises the open world and its open fighting—this being the proof of his enclosedness

—and accuses the timid colonials of being so worked up in their "fancies and imaginations" that they have "augmented" the dangers of Indian warfare so much that "they see a savage in every bush." But as the man begins to reaffirm his own fantasy once more, he is cut off by a bullet aimed at him precisely by an Indian hidden somewhere in the nearby forest: "We Scots come from a naked region, and have no need, and less relish for covers, and so, ye'll be seeing, Mistress Dunham—." Mabel, of course, sees something quite different as she looks at the corporal's face while he lies dying on the ground. "There was just enough of life left in McNab," Cooper writes, "to betray his entire consciousness of all that had passed. His countenance had the wild look of one who had been overtaken by death, by surprise."[55]

It is this surprising death, along with her prior sense of the danger, that impels Dunham's own "full consciousness." *Notions of the Americans* had declared with a sentimental offhandedness that the American woman was an insulated creature: "Retired within the sacred precincts of her own abode, she is preserved from the destroying taint of excessive intercourse with the world."[56] But this was not an opinion binding on Cooper's imagination. Mabel Dunham has no abode—nor even a social class to which she unequivocally belongs; as to "intercourse with the world," hers is nothing if not "excessive," and Cooper hardly allows us to consider its effect as a "taint." Indeed, what happens after McNab's murder—followed quickly by four others—shows us Mabel with few outer or even inner protections. Appropriately, she is the only character in the novel other than Natty to whom Cooper attributes "self-reliance" (pp. 48, 90). And that trait as they embody it is the opposite of McNab's neat reliance on his closed assumptions.

Mabel retreats into the blockhouse McNab has scorned, but though she is hiding behind a stout wall she strives unceasingly to extend her eye and mind outward. She is "riveted to the spot" near a loophole on the upper floor, and from there she can see the bodies: "They were left in their gore, unequivocally butchered corpses." The "whole horrible scene" hardly repels her; she looks out on it "as if enchained by some charm," so fascinated that "the idea of self, or of her own danger, [does not] once obtrude itself on her thoughts." Suddenly it occurs to her, however, that the Scotswoman who left the blockhouse to rush to her husband—and death—left the door unbarred. With this thought she recovers the sense of her peril and heads toward the ladder. Just then she hears the door pushed open, however, and she sinks to her knees. One suspects a faint, or at least the prayer Mabel readies herself to speak. But Cooper introduces instead a quite startling proposition: Mabel's "instinct of life" is "too strong for prayer"—her lips move, but her "jealous senses" aim at reality rather than heaven.[57] She listens attentively to every sound that comes up from the lower floor, and then once again jumps to her feet, "all spiritual contemplations vanishing in her actual temporal condition," and "all her faculties . . . absorbed in the sense of hearing." This is the moment, copied again and again in Cooper, when only the given universe is *there*: "This was one of those instants," as he puts it, "into which are compressed the sensations of years of ordinary existence." Herein lies the significance of adventure in his works—that it condenses the ordinary rather than avoids or controverts it, that it sharpens the actual world rather than departs from it. It leads to reality.

The working out of Mabel's anxious suspense offers further insights. At first, Cooper describes her as if she can be seen as an immovable work of art: "Life, death, eternity and extreme bodily pain," he writes, "were all standing out in bold relief, from the plane of every-day occurrences, and she might have been taken, at that moment, for a beautiful, pallid, representation of herself, equally without motion and without vitality." But this is, as Cooper soon reveals, a merely superficial view: "while such was the outward appearance of the form, never had there been a time, in her brief career, when Mabel heard more acutely, saw more clearly, or felt more vividly." She is no mere female victim—surely this is part of Cooper's point—and in the contrast of outer and inner (the reader's expectation, say, and the character's felt reality) we have once again in Cooper that old sense of hidden identity. As the intruder she has heard come into the blockhouse starts up the ladder, Mabel has, however, her own wrong expectations. In this, she shares with the reader a certain formulaic mistake—almost, one may say, a view of adventure itself as a merely mortal event. For she sees the dark-haired head as it comes slowly up the ladder (like the "minute hand of a clock," a nicely concrete symbol of the adventure formula) as not only Indian but (therefore) threatening: "Mabel imagined many additional horrors," Cooper writes, "as she first saw the black, roving eyes, and the expression of wildness, as the savage countenance was revealed, as it might be inch by inch...."[58] In part, this excruciating slow motion is intended to tease the reader: the Indian intruder, we soon discover, is Dew-of-June, and she comes as a friend. But Cooper also intends here that the trick should include Mabel Dunham. However harrowing her recent life, however "jealous" her senses have become, she is still imagining life rather than living it. McNab saw no Indian threat to his assumptions, and died; she sees a threat, and lives to find herself in error. This larger irony includes the reader as well: why is it, after all, that we wanted—secretly, with a desire hidden from ourselves—some more brutal conclusion? On all fronts, the action pushes inward.

Edgar Allan Poe, that master of literary torture and death, felt himself compromised in a quite different way by what he took to be the meretricious murders in Cooper's *Wyandotté*, a settlement tale which he reviewed on its appearance in 1843. Poe saw the hasty deaths at the end of the book as excessive because they were "not strictly appertaining to the right fiction."[59] What he meant by this rather pious statement is not wholly clear: one senses, at any rate, a possible contradiction in the idea that certain events obviously in a plot might not be parts of that plot. But what Poe was more generally responding to in Cooper is lucidly evident: "his predilection for great physical violence." The phrase is Marius Bewley's, and it is Bewley who has called our attention most effectively to this trait in Cooper. He describes, as "an important part of Cooper's greatness," his "remarkable ability to delineate the local details of action and violence."[60] Such it undoubtedly is. But the talent has a source as well as a nature, a meaning as well as a presence in the books. We need to ask ourselves at this point where the talent came from, what renewed its edge in tale after tale, and what gave it the power of shaping—as I am arguing it did—the very center of Cooper's imagined world.

To answer such questions we will have to resolve the apparent conflict between Cooper's sense of "discovery"— what Natty Bumppo sees and states as "all creation"[61] —and his insistence on the infinitely repeatable shocks of actual experience. Natty offers one answer: he is allowed his transcendent affirmations because, skilled and attentive as he is, he can survive beyond disaster. One notes how often, as in the case of Mabel Dunham, threat enlivens and envigorates Cooper's characters; violence initiates them into the world and thus is a kind of discovery in its own right. In this sense the conflict in Cooper's art embodies the pattern of his own life. It was the many troubles of his early adulthood, after all, that led to his creativity. But the conflict went deeper. Cooper used violence, but he also seems to have relished it. Thus he could be clinically exact in presenting it, as in the passage which Bewley quotes from *The Water-Witch*, or in that abrupt opening imagined for *Afloat and Ashore*, where the death of the young hero's father proceeds from the fatal demonstration of a gadget he has designed as an improvement for the family mill. One feels a certain chill in each case, as if an unattributable evil has released itself in the world.

It seems to me that we can explain this extraordinary pattern only as a profound movement of Cooper's imagination. That the hero of *Afloat and Ashore* is left alone in the world by his father's death may suggest one particular source in the author's past. But it must have gone beyond that source—beyond, that is, the merely passive losses Cooper himself had suffered. I would suggest that Cooper possessed some need to destroy things close and dear to himself, or to upset whatever balance he might otherwise seek to achieve. What else, beyond the ideological trappings, can explain his ready plunge into the "Point" controversy, the newspaper battles, and the libel suits? Cooper thought, of course, that he was defending himself in all of this—as he claimed he was defending the nation by attacking its foreign critics—but all his victories were another kind of loss. It seems that he was pursuing something larger, some antagonist only conveniently bodied forth in those whom he literally fought. In the "Effingham" case, he was fighting himself: or that part of himself which, since the 1820s, he had identified with the nation. Hence the significance in his belief that *Notions of the Americans* lay at the heart of the problem; the book itself did not—it was what the book meant, as a gesture of his own spirit, that he blamed. His imagination could not inhabit such a blandly uneventful world. It needed what he took to be the reality of disaster, and it could create that reality when the reality did not materialize on its own.

Still, Cooper clung to the ideal. Each of his four major settlement novels—the same theme figures, of course, in several others—returns faithfully to the ground of specifically national hope. Yet with growing violence they as surely question, assault, and at last reverse that American gesture. The end of the dream comes conclusively with *The Crater*, in which a providential cataclysm wipes from the surface of the Pacific the towering "new world" first discovered (and created) there by Mark Woolston, a young American shipwrecked on a barren reef. The cataclysm is the answer of God to the errors of Mark's nation; the book allegorizes the American past and the acrid present of the author. But the book also lingers with extraordinary patience on Mark's early, placid times on his reef, specifying and celebrating the man's "Columbian" emotions; the shipwreck, that is, is his moral and spiritual rebirth. Only after this prolonged opening does Cooper inject into the story the bitter anger of his own debates with America, destroying the idyll and what it spoke to in *his* emotions. Having invested so much of his own wonder in the beginning, Cooper reacted against himself in the swift finish. If the grand violence of the end was meant as a warning to the United States, it also became by necessity a denial of the man who uttered it.

This rhythm of wonder and doom, hope and destruction, gives Cooper's settlement novels—and many of his other works—their characteristic form as well as their themes. Leatherstocking was inevitably right as Cooper's major character because, as I have suggested already, he linked such opposites; he is a man, *The Pathfinder* tells us, who "had often been known to lead forlorn hopes" (p. 398). Standing outside American society as much as he does, "Sir Leather-stocking" (Elizabeth's term for him in *The Pioneers* [p. 187]) thus has what Cooper's first alter ego, Sir Edward Moseley, lacked: the ability to confront life directly, and to solve its problems by means more daring than the slow accumulation of inherited rents. Harvey Birch was Cooper's first experiment along these lines; old Mr. Wharton, the vacillating and spineless patriarch of *The Spy*, signalled at the same time the death of any wish Cooper may have had to find in some American elaboration of Moseley the answer to his question.

Birch's right to represent American principles, like Bumppo's right to represent American nature, comes from his willing need to risk exposure and forlornness. Without their respective skills, both of these heroes would cut a self-destructive path through the world—for their longing to expose themselves indeed is that great. But even the unsought exposure of other characters in Cooper has the reforming, uplifting power seen in the cases of Harvey and Leatherstocking. Elizabeth Temple's rescue from the panther in *The Pioneers* thus is "like a resurrection from her own grave"

(p. 309); while, to take another example from the same book, Ben Pump's near-drowning, comical as it seems in some regards, delivers him to "a new and unexplored country" (p. 272)—he returns to the world, that is, as if death and discovery are twinned events. And Ben, who has regarded Natty before this point as a kind of white Indian—he even jokes now that Bumppo has scalped him with the spear— appropriately comes to share Natty's mistreatment at the hands of the law. The flatly conceived sailor of the earlier chapters takes on a new weight of meaning after his figurative rebirth. His "new and unexplored country" is the same universe seen with new eyes; it is Natty's "creation."

That Natty can as easily kill a fish with the spear—though with a gleaming beauty of appearance and act—suggests in another way the linked themes. In his settlement novels, following as he did the logical order of frontier events, Cooper often made the wonder prior to the doom; but in essence the two coexisted, neither causing the other nor wholly blotting it out. The border regions were congenial to the themes because there, with a riot of abundance and a steady crop of violence, America itself answered the contrasts of Cooper's imagination. The same regions rested as well beyond the social arena, or at its edge, so they could allow Cooper to justify—by reference to American "facts"—the uneasiness of his art on the matter of society. That the wonder of his own unstoppable creativity invented again and again such violent images of the world may have made him something else, indeed, than "orthodox": but this made him, at the same time, the "American author" he claimed to be.

3   The "New Country"

While in the midst of the "Effingham" debacle in 1842, Cooper looked back across the nearly twenty years which separated him from *The Pioneers*. He claimed then that the book had been motivated, in part, by a desire to demonstrate how false the Old World "notion" about America's lack of polished society really was.[1] Hence he had introduced the Effingham family, with its "great wealth" and "high court interest."[2] Like many acts of memory, this one significantly revised the past; Cooper may have intended such a purpose in 1823, but his mentions of it in the 1840s are the first on record. One may conclude that he was reading his personal history in light of his 1828 attack on European "notions." He also was promoting a view of his services on behalf of the American public which, in the thick of his lawsuits, he wished to state as cogently as he could.

Earlier and later, he had different things to say about the first of his border tales. At its publication, he let it be known that the book departed from his two previous ones: "The third has been written, exclusively, to please myself."[3] This was a jaunty overstatement in an offhand first preface— which has the form of a personal letter to the publisher, Charles Wiley—but Cooper held firm to it then and later. He repeated it in 1823, specifying the exact kind of pleasure he had found in writing the novel: "I have already said, that it was mine own humour that suggested this tale; but it is a humour that is deeply connected with feeling. Happier periods, more interesting events, and, possibly, more beautiful scenes, might have been selected, to exemplify my subject; but none of either that would be so dear to me."[4] The "dearness" of his imaginings was so strong that he reaffirmed it in an introduction prepared in 1832, and retained in the edition he was readying just before he died: "the author has had more pleasure in writing The Pioneers, than the book will probably ever give any of its readers."[5]

We shall return later to the precise nature of Cooper's "pleasure"—for *The Pioneers* itself gives ample evidence on the matter. But first we must review, for this is also part of the larger story, the interesting shifts of Cooper's opinion about what the novel had been intended to express and publish to the wider world. *The Pioneers* came to occupy a special place in Cooper's sense of his career.

Notions of the Americans, as we have seen, cites *The Pioneers* as one product of the author's endeavor to "elucidate the history, manners, usages, and scenery, of his native country."[6] This was a gesture, as I suggested above, aimed at bringing Cooper's earlier works in line with his conscious purpose in the 1828 book. How deeply Cooper himself accepted the alliance we may never know; he had the habit of expressing different opinions on such issues, or others, almost from different layers of his mind. It is interesting to note, nonetheless, that in 1831 he instructed his English publishers, Colburn and Bentley, then preparing new editions of several of his books for their "Standard Novels" series, to print the title of *The Spy* as he himself had originally conceived it: "Remember the title is simply—'The Spy, a tale of the Neutral Ground—' All other &c's are damnable adjuncts of the Messrs Whittakers." Those "adjuncts," used by the English firm of the Whittakers in an 1822 edition, were similar, however, to that general point Cooper himself had made about all his American works in *Notions of the Americans*. For the Whittaker title ran as follows: *The Spy; A Tale of the Neutral ground; Referring to Some Particular Occurrences during the American War: Also Pourtraying American Scenery and Manners.*[7]

Cooper's "damnable" in reference to this title probably reflects his protective attitude toward his literary property rather than any new decision to deny the links between his art and the life of his nation. Barely a month before the letter to Colburn and Bentley was written he told the London editor Samuel Carter Hall, who was planning to write an essay on him for Colburn's *New Monthly Magazine*, that "The Pioneers contains a pretty faithful description of Cooperstown in its infancy, and as I knew it when a child."[8] This may have been an excuse for not extending the comments about his life which Hall had requested ("It is not an easy matter to write of one's self, and I got rid of the affair at as cheap a rate as possible," he wrote Colburn himself a few days later regarding Hall's request); but the assertion that Templeton and Cooperstown were essentially interchangeable cannot in any event be dismissed.[9] The "dearness" of his feelings as he first wrote the novel came in part from this very close relation.

By 1840 Cooper had reversed his view of the matter. *The Pioneers* became entangled in the argument over the "Home" books because he had chosen to revive the Effinghams in them, and to use Templeton as their destination following a long European sojourn. He claimed that he had returned to the world of *The Pioneers* for the sake of convenience: "The necessary machinery" for his new purpose, he explained in one of his *Brother Jonathan* letters in 1842, "*stood ready made to my hands, in the Pioneers.*"[10] His opponents grasped the presumed identification of Cooper himself with young Effingham, however, and in the long run it was all too clear that the author in fact had been reviving his earlier imaginations in order to suggest the shock produced on himself by the changes, as he saw them, that had occurred in America during his own absence. He was so testy about the issue because he recognized, if only after the fact, how indulgent the "Home" books were. He was to win the resulting lawsuits, but he would have been better off never filing them in the first place.

The Effingham argument does not directly concern us here. What is interesting about it in the present context is the effect it had, as already indicated, on Cooper's opinion of his first settlement tale. He went out of his way in the *Brother Jonathan* pieces and elsewhere to demonstrate that Templeton and Cooperstown were not intimately related— to deny, that is, the very source of his "pleasure" in writing *The Pioneers* in 1822. He was thus renouncing, temporarily as it turned out, his initially forthright claims that the "exemplification" of his "subject" in the novel was traceable solely to his own whim. What that more general subject was he suggested in 1840: *The Pioneers*, he wrote then, "was intended to describe the sort of life that belongs to a 'new country,' forming a link in the great social chain of the American community."[11] Certainly it had done so from the start, though one wonders how clearly Cooper saw this purpose in 1822. His pleasure came less from the ethnographic form of the novel than from its precious content. Yet here he was, in 1842, asserting that his own personal knowledge of a "new country" had stemmed not from Otsego but from the Ontario frontier where he had served in the navy early in the century. He had been "tempted by his recollections" of Otsego in writing the work, of course, and he admitted now that certain descriptions—very few of them, it appears from his lists—came directly from his memories. In his characters there were "a few *touches*" of Otsego people, but "No person answering to Betty Flannigan ever lived here; no Leather-stocking, no Indian John, no Dr. Todd, no Hiram Doolittle." His own memory of the place was in fact quite vague: "This village was commenced several years anterior to my birth, and before my memory would have served for such a purpose, had grown into more comparative note in the State, than it possesses to-day. I was sent to school, too, at six, and did not have an opportunity of seeing much of a frontier, until ordered, at nineteen, on Lake Ontario, on service.—It was *there*, I obtained most of my notions of a new country, as well as of several of the characters introduced into the Pioneers."[12] One notes, in any event, that "Betty Flannigan" (actually "Flanagan") had come to him from *The Spy*; in *The Pioneers* itself, she appears under a married name ("Mrs. Hollister"). As to Natty Bumppo, Cooper had written of David Shipman in *The Chronicles of Cooperstown*, published four years earlier, that he was "the 'Leather Stocking' of the region."[13] Though the novelist turned historian was using his own label for Natty as a kind of generic term in that case, he was again suggesting that *The Pioneers* had been imagined from the heart of his own memories. The "new country" theme grew from those memories: it provided the general public framework within which Cooper could return to his private past.

By defending the novel in the 1840s as a conscious treatment of that theme, Cooper was retreating, however, from his own pleasure. Ironically, he wrote in his piece for the Philadelphia *Public Ledger*—drafted in late 1840 but not published—that he had chosen Cooperstown for his model in the book because, given his general intent, "actual description" was quite suitable. In essence, he was basing his argument on the prerogatives of fiction itself. This was astute enough given the dogged inability of his critics to distinguish reportage from invention. But by claiming that the choice of Cooperstown as part of his materials proceeded from his artistic judgment ("an intelligent reader understands that an ingenious blending of fact and fancy contributes to the charm of this species of composition"), Cooper was belying what he in fact believed about *The Pioneers*. He had gone "critically through the book," searching for the facts he might have introduced into it twenty years before, but had found few. He clearly was not reading the novel in the spirit in which it had been written.[14]

We may surmise that Cooper regretted the involvement of this early tale in his recent disputes, and perhaps recognized that his revival of the Effinghams and the village of Templeton was a lapse of judgment—even a kind of profanation. In seeking to revise the public view of *The Pioneers*, to downplay its personal sources and stress in their place his "conscious" aims in writing it, he was laying the foundation for a defense of the "Home" books as social criticism rather than an exercise of personal pique. But he also was attempting to protect from the rampant publicity of his present situation the "humour" which had directed him in *The Pioneers*, and which still lingered in his mind at this later time. He defended the craft of fiction at the apparent cost of his own imagination, yet the defense at last, for all its conscious identification of author and nation, sealed off the inner compartments of his fancy. By denying the book he kept possession of it. This was another of his "No Trespassing" signs.

Written after the response to *Notions of the Americans* had, as he thought, begun his undoing, Cooper's introduction of 1832 already displayed—despite his reaffirmation of the "pleasure" he had felt in writing the novel—this same defensiveness. Here he began by conceding that the "descriptive tale" announced on his title page naturally would make the reader wonder "how much of [the work's] contents is literal fact, and how much is intended to represent a general picture." He was aware that, had he "confined himself" to generalities, he would have made "a far better book"; but "in commencing to describe scenes, and perhaps he may add characters, that were so familiar to his own youth, there was a constant temptation to delineate that which he had known rather than that which he might have imagined." Hence he apologized now, in a way, for his "too fastidious attention to originals," since such an attention "destroys the charm of fiction."[15]

He was being more direct here than he would be later, but he still was missing a crucial point. To think of the personal elements of *The Pioneers* as constituting the work's "literal fact" was to grossly oversimplify the process by which it had been composed in the first place. Cooper had not used his recollections as knowledge; they did not flesh out the book so much as give it its form and feeling. He admitted "facts" here, to be sure, which a few years later he would deny: "New-York having but one county of Otsego, and the Susquehannah but one proper source, there can be no mistake as to the site of the Tale."[16] But his introduction presents, in the main, a thumbnail sketch of the history of the region's literal and public past. Only in asserting that "all his first impressions were...obtained" in Cooperstown, or that he had "indulged his recollections freely, when he had fairly entered the door" of the Mansion House, otherwise altered in the tale, was he pointing to the intensely private history which was his real topic.

When Cooper reprinted this introduction in the final edition of *The Pioneers* to appear in his life, he may simply have been grasping at what was available rather than consciously endorsing what it had to say. But he added to the end of the older piece two new paragraphs concerning a point which had been particularly sore for him in the intervening years. This was the supposed identification of Elizabeth Temple with his own sister Hannah, whose death following a fall from a horse—as a footnote he failed to excise in the final edition suggests—had given to *The Pioneers* at least one glancing caution about forest trails. In denying in 1851 that Hannah was his model for Elizabeth he may have been suppressing some larger debt. But the two added paragraphs have another suggestion: for here, in stating that the widespread belief about the supposed link was wrong, Cooper in effect was again seeking to defend his private purposes and premises. As a symbol of his own memories, Hannah still, in 1851, caused him "pain." The "reverence" he bore toward her, "singularly dear" as she had been, was doubtless real and particular. But the pain and the dearness also attached—as I believe he was saying once more at the end of his life—to all he had been doing in 1822.[17]

As a portrait of the American border, *The Pioneers* did have obvious public meanings. But it will be more useful to accept Cooper's private claims for the work, especially since the "pleasure" he derived from it is evident throughout. The opening chapter gives us a tolerably orthodox view of the "new country" which will be the setting of what follows. We are directed, by a series of narrowing gestures, toward "the centre of the State of New-York," then toward "an extensive district of country" situated there, before we discover Templeton itself. The general district is made up of rolling hills and dales embellished—as Judge Cooper himself in effect said—with "beautiful and thriving villages ...neat and comfortable farms...roads...academies, and minor edifices of learning...and places for the worship of God" (p. 15). Cooper's summary of the landscape is like a trial run for the bright scene looked down upon by the Count and Cadwallader in 1828: "In short, the whole district is hourly exhibiting how much can be done, in even a rugged country, and with a severe climate, under the dominion of mild laws, and where every man feels a direct interest in the prosperity of a commonwealth, of which he knows himself to form a part.... Only forty years have passed since this territory was a wilderness" (pp. 15-16). Following the close of the Revolution, New York has expanded from a "narrow belt" of settlement in the Hudson and Mohawk valleys to include this vast new territory, where "a million and a half of inhabitants... are maintained in abundance." There will come an "evil day," the Malthusian last sentence of this general opening asserts, "when their possessions shall become unequal to their wants" (p. 16). But this first eruption of Cooper's private doubts into the public atmosphere of his tale cannot upset the hopefulness of the book's initial burden. We have been delivered into a world of magical changes, as Elizabeth Temple's vision of the village at a later point will amply prove. Absent for four years from the valley, she bears in her own mind—comparing memories with current perceptions —the ideal legacy of the place.

It is with the sleigh ride which leads toward her sudden vision that the tale proper emerges from its framing generalities. It all is like the rebirth of a lost world, a discovery rendered less by absolute newness than by the reseen clarity of known and obvious details. One notes the sharpness of imagery here: the clouds "whose colour seemed brightened by the light reflected from the mass of snow"; the "sky of the purest blue"; the "glittering in the atmosphere, as if it were filled with innumerable shining particles"; the "hoar frost" coating the horses; the "deep dull black" of their harnesses, with "plates and buckles of brass, that shone like gold"; the "glistening black" of Aggy's skin, "now mottled with the cold," and his "shining eyes filled with tears"; the "fiery red" of the sleigh interior, meant "to convey the idea of heat in that cold climate"; the "red cloth, cut into festoons," trimming the buffalo skins; the "expressive, large blue eyes" of the Judge; or the sparkling, "animated jet-black eyes" of young Elizabeth herself (pp. 16–18).

All these images are rendered with the isolating attention of a dream: the colors, for instance, seem assertively separate from each other ("the dark trunks of the trees," Cooper writes later, "rose from the pure white of the snow" [p. 19]); they also seem less like the properties of objects than like absolutes in their own right. And they have an intensity which appears to come less from the oblique light of the midwinter sun than from some inner vitality; they shine rather than reflect. Though the harness lacks the "glossy varnishing of the present day," it is not merely "dull"—it is "deep dull black" (p. 17).

This kind of high resolution gives everything its special claim upon the eye. The whole scene comes to us, as it were, with the freshness of creation itself; it is overdescribed, as if the words conveying it in fact were constituting it. Herein lies, I think, the extraordinary "dearness" of Cooper's imagination in *The Pioneers*. For this is a world remembered with the child's reconstituted eyesight, its edges sharp and its qualities given the hardness of mere mysterious presence. It is a world simply there. And it is, as well, a world of exaggerated sizes, another mark of the child's dreamy realism: the brass hardware is "enormous," the saddles are "huge," with "high" turrets for the reins; Aggy's eyes are "large," as are the Judge's, as well as his stature, the buffalo robes, the cloak worn by Elizabeth, and the sleigh, "which would admit a whole family within its bosom." Elizabeth's cloak has a "thick" lining, and the hood almost concealing her head is "huge"; the Judge's "great-coat" is "abundantly ornamented by a profusion of furs" (pp. 17–18).

All of this across a mere three pages! The hard particulars come so thick that one feels almost an assault of the world. And yet the final effect is that sense of the "marvellously beautiful" which D. H. Lawrence found in the novel.[18] For Cooper's "descriptive" intent, however much he later would tie it to a national purpose, in fact was the defense he might offer on his title page for the free play of his backward-glancing imagination. The wealth of imagery in *The Pioneers* has such a powerful impact on the reader not because Cooper was primarily concerned with creating such effects, but rather because he gave himself so fully to the impulses of his own mind. And he thereby inadvertently committed what he saw even before the book appeared as a tactical mistake. He wrote his English publisher, John Murray, in late November, 1822, that the wealth of description, even in a work announced as a "descriptive tale," might not meet with approval from his readers. Perhaps he had, as he speculated in the letter, "confined myself too much to describing the scenes of my own youth"; and, since "the present taste" was for "action and strong excitement," the book might suffer neglect—even though its "pictures" were "very faithful" and its ending had action and excitement enough.[19]

Cooper customarily addressed his publishers in a tone quite different from that with which he addressed the agenda of his imagination. In the letter to Murray he was treating the book as a commodity—he had a real knack for doing so[20]—and we cannot trust the document as a record of his working intent. The point in this case is that the descriptive lingering in *The Pioneers* was not so much the result of his personal recollections as the thing which enabled them, the mood which they required if they were to serve their imaginative purpose for Cooper. Insofar as he was striving to repossess his past, he had to shun action: for action was what he was, in the profoundest sense, writing against. He did not need time; he needed space.

And so it is that *The Pioneers* gives us space with a frontal directness. It certainly lacks the "intensity" of event Cooper rightly found in *The Last of the Mohicans* when, in 1826, he sought to characterize for Carey and Lea his latest venture, *The Prairie*: "It will be somewhere between Pioneers and Mohicans—More sprightly than the former and less intense than the latter—."[21] Yet *The Pioneers* has a visual exuberance rare in other works by an author who was versed in what Donald A. Ringe has called "the pictorial mode."[22] The childlike apprehension of qualities as things in themselves, the sense of largeness and brilliance, the slow unfolding of plot—even though it is initiated, symbolically, in the first chapter—all this marks Cooper's desire to grasp and not let go of this world called up by his fancy. The novel has, as James Grossman states, "the haunting quality of something just around the corner from memory."[23] It also has an extraordinary capacity for convincing us that, however unturnable the corner in fact may have been for Cooper as the creature of history—he was just four in 1793, the year the tale opens—he has accomplished the feat anyway.

And yet there is a certain melancholy recognition even in these bright opening pages. The "stillness" of the landscape may be part of the dreamlike air of the whole passage; but it is a trait shared by Elizabeth and her father, too, for they are lost in "reflections" as the sleigh glides almost noiselessy over the packed snow of the narrow mountain road. The woman, to be sure, still is responding to the "novel scenery" passing by with "a pleased astonishment" that suggests how much the book's wondering eye is also her own. But mixed with her wonder, we are indirectly told, is the sad memory of her mother, who died shortly after she had "reluctantly consented" to let Elizabeth be sent away to school four years earlier; and the same topic wholly occupies the "melancholy" thoughts of the Judge (p. 19).

The silence of the two, then, is less the proper sign of their own ravishment by the shining world around them than a mark of their withdrawal from it. The "clear, cold day" (p. 16) gives way to a sense of years past; the outer space, to an inner world of time. And with this shift comes an odd change in the book's own emotional mood. Though the epigraph from Thomson's *Seasons* suggests that winter is "sullen and sad" (p. 15), nothing so far in Cooper's description has verified the sentiment of the tag. Indeed, the chapter up to this point suggests an exactly opposite theme; its own vigor spills over, as it were, into the wintry world evoked by it. The "melancholy" of the Judge is the first sad note injected into the tale, aside from the Malthusian glimpse already referred to. And within the next paragraph, as Cooper again returns to the landscape, that same word occurs twice in quick succession. It is as if the author is coming back with the chastened feelings of an adult to the world created just moments earlier—in the reader's mind at least—by the effervescence of his imagination. How else can we explain the following: "The dark trunks of the trees, rose from the pure white of the snow, in regularly formed shafts, until, at a great height, their branches shot forth horizontal limbs, that were covered with the meager foliage of an evergreen, affording a melancholy contrast to the torpor of nature below. To the travellers there seemed to be no wind; but these pines waved majestically at their topmost boughs, sending forth a dull, plaintive sound, that was quite in consonance with the rest of the melancholy scene" (p. 19). Nothing we have seen of this world so far carries the slightest hint of "torpor." Yet there the word is.[24]

But this is not a false move on Cooper's part, only an indication of the complexity with which his "pleasure" was won in the writing of the book. For it was a satisfaction that derived not only from the direct indulgence of his best memories—or the creation of better ones—but also from the acceptance of other feelings that by 1822 had clustered around the lingering images of Cooperstown. One finds the same contrast in the fifth chapter, where Cooper was describing—as he admitted several times—the "real" hall in the Cooper mansion: "the author indulged his recollections freely," the 1832 introduction states, "when he had fairly entered the door" (p. 9). The attention to detail tells a reader as much, as does the exaggeration: the "high, old-fashioned, brass candlesticks," the "enormous stove" and its "large" pipe, the "enormous" handles of the sideboard—which is "groaning under the piles of silver plate"—the pair of "prodigious tables," and the "enormous settee" (p. 63). Here, to be sure, the shift of feeling is more complex. Cooper already has adopted his satiric voice with the entrance of Richard Jones in the previous chapter; and Jones's depredations on the Temple "hall" are described in the present chapter with a full satiric detachment—as the deft handling of the "dark, lead-coloured English paper, that represented Britannia weeping over the tomb of Wolfe" (p. 64) suggests. The satire belittles, much as the naive descriptions enhance, whatever the eye of the prose lights upon: Richard's application of the wallpaper has been so slapdash that Wolfe's extended arm, running onto the next sheet, appears to suffer "numberless cruel amputations" (p. 64). It is the sort of detail (and mood) which Lawrence, who found the book's pictures lacking in "the cruel iron of reality," ought to have noted.[25] Nor is this bemusement the only sign of Cooper's complex emotional bearing on his topic. When the Judge and Elizabeth enter the hall, in the dim light shed by a mere pair of candles, they fall once more into a "melancholy" silence: for the inner darkness suggests the dead woman, and it is only the "blaze" which ensues as the chandeliers and lustres are lighted that dispels the sadness. We are then back, by the logic of the book's imagery—"glitter" is one of its favorite words—to the brilliant world of the sleigh ride (p. 65).

   This flux of emotion is a true sign, I would argue, of the difficulty with which Cooper recovered his feelings as he wrote the tale. The vacillations precisely define Cooper's "pleasure" as a man giving voice and substance to the "dear" scenes he had accepted, in the depth of his private embarassments in the early 1820s, as the absolute material of his tale. But the conflict does not remain as unfocused as it may seem in the passages already cited; if it did, it would leave the work rich in intermittent images but poor in continuity and design. Cooper found a focus for his emotions not in the departed mother, who is the temporary symbol of grief rather than its abiding sign, but in the "impoverished and forlorn" figure cut in the abundant landscape by Bumppo and Chingachgook. The phrase just quoted comes late in the book, and from Oliver Edwards (p. 345), but from the moment Natty comes forth from the forest in the opening chapter, with his "air of sullen dissatisfaction" (p. 22), we sense that the "dull, plaintive sound" of the pines—apparently so out of keeping with the landscape heretofore described —is but the natural chorus for the hunter's habitually melancholic, musing speech. It is in him that Cooper concentrated his own lamentations over the loss of this shining world recalled in his border novel.[26]

It is the wail of the pines that first breaks, for the reader, the dreamy visual silence of *The Pioneers*, sending the book from space into time. The real jolt for the Judge and Elizabeth comes, however, with the "loud and continued howling" that echoes "under the long arches of the woods"— the "cry" of Natty's hounds. With an appropriateness which the novel will bear out later, the old hunter is heard of and recognized, before he appears, by the signs spreading out from him. The next sound is "the light bounding noise of an animal plunging through the woods," and then—though Temple has shot first, and twice—the "sharp, quick sound" of Natty's rifle, followed by that of Oliver's, and then by the "loud shout" of Bumppo himself (pp. 19-20).

Natty is not really a part of the novelist's conscious scene, as the Temples are (and Edwards finally is), but rather its evocation. He does not live in this world so much as

express it: hence, as Cooper writes, "a couple of men instant-
ly appeared from behind the trunks of two of the pines"
(p. 20). How different the words that give us the other
people: "It was near the setting of the sun, on a clear, cold
day in December, when a sleigh was moving slowly up one
of the mountains in the district we have described" (p. 16).
This has all the earmarks of a given, of something wholly
in the landscape, while the other has for the reader as for
Aggy and the Temples the suddenness of a discovery. It is
as if the forest has been given a human shape. Throughout
the pages which follow, Natty and Oliver and Chingachgook
will be "lost to view" (p. 144) behind the trees, much as the
first two of them have come forth from behind trees here.
And at the very end, Natty himself will be seen by Elizabeth
"on the verge of the wood" just before, as he utters "a
forced cry to his dogs"—fittingly, it is the book's last sound—
he enters the forest and is lost to sight (p. 456). His first
exit in the book, at the finish of chapter 1, is a foretaste
of his last: "already nearly concealed by the trunks of the
trees," he is "hid from view" as the sleigh departs (p. 29).[27]

This iconography is one source of Bumppo's mythic aura
in the book. He is allied throughout with the forest, as when
he tells the woodchopper Kirby, not knowing he has been
hired to help search the cabin, that there is no use for his
services here: "I've no land to clear; and Heaven knows I
would set out six trees afore I would cut down one." Kirby
has his ties with Bumppo, but he responds to this avowal
with a glee that marks his own final allegiances: "Would
you, old boy!...then so much the better for me" (pp.
334-35). For trees once planted must inevitably be cut down.
Natty, as we readily expect, prefers "good hunting grounds"
to "stumpy pastures"—so he tells the Judge when the latter
tries to suggest that an "alliance in sentiment" ties the two
men together (p. 266). And, as to "clearings"—though, as
the book reminds us, Natty lives on a "little piece of cleared
ground" (p. 356)—he has no real use for them: "Woods!
indeed! I doesn't call these woods, Madam Effingham, where

I lose myself, every day of my life, in the clearings" (p. 454). The paradox of this last comment, worthy of Thoreau, is a precise sign of Natty's forceful presence in the book. He has the ability to turn other people's terms back against themselves.

Leatherstocking establishes his presence in the novel by his garrulous insistence: it is right that his sounds are the first to set the world of *The Pioneers* going. Yet the great majority of his words are speeches rather than exchanges. His voice is lyric rather than social, the articulation of a silence brooding in the landscape. It is also, as his many recollections indicate, a sad voice of the past that gives the assertively present scene a certain melancholy depth. And, though Natty can once speak of the "howling wilderness" (p. 26)—he is the only character to use that phrase in the tale—he in fact speaks *for* nature throughout: the "betterments" of the settlers have produced for him not a magically changed but a "dreadfully altered" world. "I hunted one season back of the Kaatskills," he says in one of his moody recollections, "nigh-hand to the settlements, and the dogs often lost the scent, when they com'd to them highways, there was so much travel on them" (pp. 154-55). If Elizabeth is "the lost one" (p. 424) when she is trapped on the flaming mountain, Natty is lost whenever he enters the social space where the young woman is so much at home.

That the hunter has a voice at all in *The Pioneers*, that he must state rather than simply enact his viewpoint, suggests just how fully he is made to enter that space, and thus entangle himself in the book's "plot." Yet the novel makes as amply clear Natty's true taciturnity. His first and last utterances, the "shout" and the "cry," are hints of the man's enclosing silence, much as his long description of his perch in the Catskills above the Hudson valley, where he could look down on "all creation" (p. 292), convinces us that he knows far more deeply than Elizabeth, to whom the phrase is nominally applied, what "mute wonder" really is (p. 40). His tale of that solitary place comes forth, significantly, from the "profound silence" of what Edwards calls the "beautifully tranquil and glassy...lake" (pp. 290-91), while he, Natty, and Chingachgook are fishing on it. And the tale ends when the cries of Natty's dogs, whom Hiram Doolittle has let loose, are heard "ringing...on the mountain." The "confused echoes" play on the rocks until, as the dogs reach the lake, their cries peal "under the forest" lining the shore (pp. 294-95). The dogs always have a wild but sad air, for they express their master's source and destiny: their "long, piteous howls" (p. 288) are like the "long and plaintive howl" (p. 212) of the wolves Elizabeth mistakes for them, even like the "low, mournful sounds" (p. 306), the "moaning" (p. 341), of the panthers. It is, again, their cry that opens the book, and Natty's to them that closes it.

Of course, Natty *is* loquacious at times, and even at the oddest moments: thus, in the midst of the forest fire, after the can of powder brought him by Elizabeth is heard exploding, he laughs and then launches into a disquisition about "Sir William"! Edwards, aghast at the gesture, cuts him short: "For God's sake, tell me nothing now, Natty, until we are entirely safe." But Natty is not really out of place here. Like his other recollections of the old wars, this one is a restatement of his essential identity, a kind of victory song. And it is absolutely appropriate here, for as Natty's "coolness" quickly reveals, the group is now on safe ground (p. 417). He has repossessed the world by his deeds, and he exults in the fact—even though at this point the dying Chingachgook is tied helplessly to his own back.

Aside from such moments, Natty takes to silence as if it were his proper atmosphere. At his cabin all is as "quiet as the grave" (p. 315), much as his laugh is typically "inward" (p. 21), and he himself is said at several points to fall into a deep silence, musing and melancholy. When Edwards goes to the hut before joining Bumppo and John on the lake in chapter 26, he discovers a world where "all was as silent... as if the foot of man had never trod the wilderness." This is the absolute ground of Bumppo, his final and complex function as a symbol in the book. He is the rich expression of that "melancholy Wilderness" which Judge Cooper—and a thousand other pioneers—encountered when they left behind them the comforting noise of the older "betterments."

But that noise now reaches even the borders of Natty's small domain. Once he has entered the cabin in the scene just referred to, Edwards still can hear, drifting across the lake from the village, "the sounds of the hammers" (p. 288). At the end, Bumppo himself will claim that he is "weary of living in the clearings, and where the hammer is sounding in my ears from sunrise to sundown.... I crave to go into the woods ag'in, I do" (p. 453-54)—which is just what, literally and symbolically, he does. Elizabeth, to whom Natty states his craving, is more nearly a creature of the borderground between village and forest. In her walk up "the Vision" with Louisa in chapter 28, she takes in with a kind of balanced delight "occasional glimpses of the placid Otsego" as well as "the rattling of wheels and the sounds of hammers" —these last she pauses to listen to, as if she is trying "to mingle the signs of men with the scenes of nature." But it is a balance soon upset by the "low, mournful sounds" of the panthers, which come from a world more wild than that represented by the "placid" lake (pp. 305-6). When Natty rightly but mysteriously appears on the scene to rescue the women, he is announced by "a rustling of leaves." Then he says softly to Elizabeth, with words that stress the stark contrast of civil and wild ground, "Hist! hist!... stoop lower, gall; your bunnet hides the creater's head." This is a good example of the sort of understatement which offsets the man's loquacity. But next comes his real "voice": "the report of the rifle" and "the whizzing of the bullet," followed by "the enraged cries of the beast" (p. 309). It is by such wordless deeds of skill that Leatherstocking makes his best statements throughout the whole series of tales.

At such times in *The Pioneers*, Natty sheds the moodiness which makes him the focus of the book's drifting melancholy. He can laugh during the fire, or jokingly call his dog just after shooting the panther ("Come in, Hector, come in, old fool; 'tis a hard-lived animal, and may jump ag'in" [p. 309]), because these are fleeting moments of recovery. The man who can't do things as he "used to could" (p. 26)— he is failing, but so is his world—has repossessed here the old realm of action which he can only speak of elsewhere in the novel, and speak of as if trying to call it back one more time. Rare as his exultations are, they give a depth, a sense of what he has been forced to lose, to the subdued emotions he more typically betrays. His melancholy is not the fruit of his long isolation earlier in life; he is asocial, but not unsociable. It is the mark instead that he has lost his proper home to others less worthy of owning it. It is the bitterness of dispossession, relaxed just long enough on a few occasions to reveal exactly how great the lost world was.

Thus Natty tells of Otsego, the "cheerful place" he once had all to himself: except for a few transient intruders, "there was none to meddle with the ground" until "the money of Marmaduke Temple, and the twisty ways of the law" jointly fell upon it. This is his response to Edwards when the young man asks, as they are fishing, if the hunter had ever seen the lake "more calm and even than at this moment" (p. 291). Yet Edwards himself, apparently so close to Natty, understands neither his own question nor the hunter's answer. "'It must have been a sight of melancholy pleasure indeed,' said Edwards, while his eye roved along the shores and over the hills, where the clearings, groaning with the golden corn, were cheering the forests with the signs of life, 'to have roamed over these mountains, and along this sheet of beautiful water, without a living soul to speak to, or to thwart your humour.'" That there was nothing melancholy about the place then, however, I think Natty's immediate response suggests: "Haven't I said it was cheerful!" (p. 291). For it is to Edwards's eye that the "clearings" seem to enliven the woods; he reveals himself here, as by his lack of final skill during the fire, to be a creature of the village. He merely hides behind the trees, as he hides within a woodsman's costume, or the mask of his "Indian" nature. Cooper tells us a good deal about the book's polarities by using the same word ("cheer") to express radically opposite visions in the passage, for at last we discover that the work is structured by a dialectic of image, emotion, and ideas. And the source of that dialectic lay in the conflict of Cooper's own recollections.

It is with the "cheerful sound of sleigh bells . . . as they came jingling up the sides of the mountain" (p. 46) that Natty's chief antagonist, Richard Jones, bursts into the tale. Perhaps it would be easier to like a man such as Jones in life than in the world of *The Pioneers*. He has no visibly repulsive traits, and indeed is humored by the Temples and well-liked by the residents of the village. But he represents a subversive force in the settlement nonetheless. Among other things, he is a perfect embodiment of self: the bells with which he has overdecorated his sleigh—the Judge, we note, is still too much of a Quaker to use them (p. 59)—are assertive rather than merry. Ideally, they ought to offer a social contrast to the natural sounds associated with Natty, but here they suggest nothing less than the sheriff's wagging tongue: "In this manner Richard descended the mountain; the bells ringing and his tongue going" (p. 57). His chatter, we learn shortly afterwards, is "much like an accompaniment on a piano, a thing that is heard without being attended to." Hence, on this occasion, the book "will not undertake the task of recording his diffuse discourse" (p. 65).

Elsewhere, however, the recording is extensive. "I" is Richard's favorite word:

> but no, I will let Marmaduke tell a few bouncers about it before I come out upon him—Come, hurry in, Aggy, I must help to dress the lad's wound; this Yankee Doctor knows nothing of surgery—I had to hold old Milligan's leg for him, while he cut it off. (pp. 56–57)
>
> I never could tell yet, whether it was I or Natty, who killed that bird: he fired first, and the bird stooped, but then it was rising

again as I pulled trigger. I should have claimed it, for a certainty.... (p. 88)

Shall I help you, John? You know I have a knack at these things.... Doctor Todd and I cut out the bullet, and I and Indian John dressed the wound. (p. 88)

Now, I have known a farmer, in Pennsylvania, order a sportsman off his farm, with as little ceremony as I would order Benjamin to put a log in the stove. By-the-by, Benjamin, see how the thermometer stands. (p. 93)

I am not afraid of his rifle. I can shoot too. I have hit a dollar, many a time, at fifty rods. (p. 94)

Here, John; drink, man, drink. I and you and Dr. Todd, have done a good thing with the shoulder of that lad, this very night. (p. 163)

But, 'duke, when I fish, I fish.... (p. 266)

As I told you before, I say nothing egotistical. (p. 318)

... with my own eyes—and my eyes are as good as any body's eyes—I have seen them, I say.... (p. 319)

Every body is asleep but myself! poor I must keep my eyes open, that others may sleep in safety. (p. 347)

But this is more than enough rope, especially for a man who, when just appointed sheriff, sets about thinking who will make a good hangman—other, of course, than himself (p. 182).

Jones, too, has a lyrical presence in *The Pioneers*.[28] He sings the song of self interminably, and his version differs radically from Bumppo's: "But I made a mark on the redskin that I'll warrant he carried to his grave. I took him on his posterum" (p. 26). For Natty, though he also is assertive, amply proves his right to be so; his words refer to deeds, whereas for Jones, often enough, the word itself is the only real deed involved. Nothing Jones touches has about it the kind of grace which falls like a disregarded shadow from the actions of Leatherstocking. He spreads disproportion through the village architecture; wastes precious sugar maple trees with the guffaw of a prodigal; shoots at pigeons with a cannon; catches more fish with his net than he or even the whole village can eat; believes in improvements but makes none worth recall; scoffs at coal mines but digs for silver; and calls out the militia against a weak old hunter, only to see the little local army routed and rebuked. He is completely out of touch with the beauty of the book's scene—for his is the promoter's eye rather than the discoverer's. And, more importantly, he is the only one of the book's major characters who is never said to be "melancholy"; he uses the word once himself, but only when admitting that "one of these melancholy days" he will be dead (p. 285). Perhaps it would be very hard to like him, after all. If silence is Leatherstocking's true ambience, noise is Richard's; and it is Richard's noise which most clearly forces Natty to speak as much as he does.

The effects of Jones penetrate beneath the surface where he seems most happily to live. In addition to his self-importance, his boastfulness, his possessiveness, and his taste for competition, the man reveals a definite though cowardly mean streak. It is from Jones, appropriately, that we first hear of the stocks which finally will confine Natty: shown up by Oliver on the mountain road, he vows that "this shooting gentleman ought to be put in the stocks, if he ever takes a rein in his hand again" (p. 110). Earlier, Dr. Todd arrives at the mansion to treat Edwards, only to find Jones in a "busy strut." Angered that Edwards will not let *him* remove the shot, Richard is "pacing the hall and cracking his whip" (p. 76). It is the same whip with which he already has threatened Aggy on the road; and, once Oliver has safely left the mansion, Jones gives "a loud crack with his whip" and tells his cousin Marmaduke that the young hunter clearly committed "trespass" on the Temple lands—"in your woods," as he puts it. In the very same scene, of course, Reverend Grant intones, "Forgive us our trespasses, as we forgive those who trespass against us" (pp. 92–93). But Richard listens no more to him than he does to anybody else. At the start of the Christmas Eve service, Grant reads "the sublime declaration of the Hebrew prophet—'The Lord is in his holy temple; let all the earth keep silence before him,'" at which Jones rises to his feet as an (unnecessary) example to the congregation; then comes the exordium. "Nothing was heard but the deep, though affectionate, tones of the reader, as he slowly went through his exordium; until, something unfortunately striking the mind of Richard as incomplete, he left his place, and walked on tip-toe from the room." He returns during the confession, taking up the "response" to cover the sounds of his feet, and carrying "a small open box, with the figures of '8 by 10' written, in black paint, on one of its sides." This he places in the pulpit as "a footstool for the divine" (pp. 125-26). Not only has his slapdashery left the "temple" incomplete; his officious concern with the physical arrangements causes him to violate the spirit of the moment and the letter of the biblical command. He is at the very least rude, and perhaps even mean here—not cracking his whip any more, but letting the world know of his presence by his little noises. We note that he customarily times the minister's sermons, presumably to assure himself that they are not becoming "Presbyterian" (p. 351)—leave it to Richard, with his "papal" air during his own preachings (p. 103), to regulate the speech of others. Of course it is Jones who strikes the table in the courtroom and cries "Silence!" when everyone is in "a profound stillness" (p. 371-72).

We are meant to laugh at the man, to be sure: Cooper's satiric description of the mansion and the academy tells us as much. But in the book's complex design he becomes something more than a comic figure. If he had no power beyond that of his own being, which is negligible, he would be just the man to dismember General Wolfe's image, but hardly the living soldier. When the Judge secures Richard's appointment as sheriff of the county, however, the man's bad instincts acquire a kind of dangerous validity. He would in any case be thematically opposite to Bumppo; now, with his official position, he becomes the hunter's opposite in the plot as well. Those critics who have seen Natty as a sullen individualist who must be conquered if society is to prevail ought to have paid more attention to the marpeace peacekeeper who seeks to subdue Natty—who preaches "the dignity of my office" when the militia is drawn up before the cave, but who in fact is "burning with a desire to examine the hidden mysteries of the cave." It is Billy Kirby, rightly enough, who with his "sturdy notions of independence" supports Bumppo at this juncture (pp. 430-31). Jones, on the contrary, represents eavesdropping disguised by an impressive title.[29]

It is appropriate that so chattering a character should both disregard and suspect the sayings of others. As his alliance with Hiram Doolittle and Jotham Riddel suggests, Jones has certain "Yankee" traits against which Cooper inveighed in book after book. He is "literally" from elsewhere, is far more talkative than Cooper's typical Yankee, and is bathed, as I have already noted, in a comic liquor not often associated with the likes of Jason Newcome or Joel Strides. Still, he is prying and selfish, has a "cleverness in small matters" (p. 42), and thinks himself capable of doing anything—or at least directing others to do it. He is meddlesome, in short, and Hiram Doolittle (who does much but does it all ill) is merely the outer skin of Richard's inner nature. That "wandering, eastern mechanic" (p. 42) finally "'pulled up stakes,' and proceeded further west, scattering his professional science and legal learning through the land; vestiges of both of which are to be discovered there even to the present hour" (pp. 446-47). Richard is allowed to stay on in the village after Doolittle emigrates and "poor Jotham" dies pursuing another of the sheriff's "visionary" schemes, but Richard has received "a mortifying lesson . . . which brought many quiet hours, in future, to his cousin Marmaduke" (p. 447). He differs from his expendable associates largely in having such a cousin. Yet whatever the reason, the reader is surely grateful for the small quiet space caused by Richard's absence from the final pages of the tale. It is then that Natty can speak his last words.

We know from the moment Richard Jones is appointed sheriff—"Sheriff! High Sheriff of——!" (p. 182), he exclaims with typical flourish at the news—that little good will come of his elevation. Apparently the Judge has meant the appointment as a titular honor rather than a real job for "that quizzing dog, Dick Jones" (p. 22), as he describes his cousin in the first chapter. Up to this point, with a shrewd estimate of the man's character, he has confined Richard to superintending only certain "minor concerns" (p. 42). But Jones of course takes his appointment with utter seriousness. "It sounds well, Bess," he tells Elizabeth when she gives him the Christmas present of his commission, "but it shall execute better.... It shall be well done, cousin Bess—it shall be well done I say" (p. 182). "Doing" is Jones's correctly vacant activity; he is very much as "I" in search of his proper verb, the means of stating his existence in the world. How right, then, that even his actions should be a kind of noise. "I am, I am, I am...DOING!" Richard in effect exclaims at every turn. "I took him on his posterum," responds Natty. The two are bound to tangle.

"Now, Richard,...now I think you will find something to do," Elizabeth tells him. "I have often heard you complain of old, that there was nothing to do in this new country, while to my eyes, it seemed as if every thing remained to be done." But her eyes are decidely not his. "'Do!' echoed Richard, who blew his nose, raised his little form to its greatest elevation, and looked serious. 'Every thing depends on system, girl. I shall sit down this afternoon, and systematize the county'" (p. 182). The task is an especially absurd one for a man who had to paint the roof of the Temple mansion four different colors in order to make it look like it more or less belonged to the house—or a man who, in his rage over Oliver's "trespass," vows that if he were "in 'duke's place," as he puts it, "I would stick up advertisements, to-morrow morning, forbidding all persons to shoot, or trespass, in any manner, on my woods. I could write such an advertisement myself, in an hour, as would put a stop to the thing at once" (p. 93). An hour for a "No Trespassing" sign, and a mere afternoon for a whole county! And, as we note again, words against "the thing." For Jones lets it be known that he is an expert in words: "I read, sir, all kinds of books; of France, as well as England; of Greece, as well as Rome" (p. 93). To which Natty later answers, "I . . . never so much as looked into a book, or larnt a letter of scholarship, in my born days" (p. 134); "I never read a book in my life . . . and how should a man who has lived in towns and schools know any thing about the wonders of the woods!" (p. 293). This is their symbolic dance.

It takes on an institutional significance once Jones's ridiculous "system" lights on Natty as its necessary villain. Jones declares that Leatherstocking "has set an example of rebellion to the laws, and has become a kind of out-law" (p. 355); but this is simply a justification for the sheriff's injured pride, a public excuse for ravaging the old man's just and closely guarded privacy. Jones cannot distinguish between "the laws" he cites and his own self-importance, much as he cannot view any other matter except as a reflection of and on himself. His is the spirit of regulation not for the sake of public order, but for the sake of the regulator's prestige. Hence the "crime" of Leatherstocking's refusals, which pit intense will against mere order, the individual against the claims of such a civilization as Jones represents: "larning" without wisdom or real feeling, action without grace or true effect, a veneer of manner without a heart of oak beneath. Jones is so dangerous as an agent of justice because he knows nothing whatever of the real system of the law: law, Cooper was to write in *The American Democrat*, is "founded on the immutable principles of natural justice."[30] For Richard the law is another kind of whip, a means of giving his "busy strut" a certain ceremonial air— not a principle or body of principles but a device. "An't Marmaduke a Judge? . . . where is the use of being a Judge or having a Judge, if there is no law? . . . if it were in my power, I'd make 'duke a king. He is a noble-hearted fellow, and would make an excellent king; that is, if he had a good prime minister" (pp. 93; 183).

The humor lingers even here, to be sure: a judge without law is as unthinkable as is Richard's actually having the power to make his cousin king. So it is with some larger appropriateness that the chapter in which Richard learns of his appointment bears a tag from nothing less than *Much Ado about Nothing*: "Some treason, masters—/Yet stand close" (p. 177). This should recall to us the malapropisms of Dogberry, the "sheriff" of the play, especially the one he commits when choosing his assistants: "First, who think you the most desartless man to be constable?"³¹ (According to the Judge, Jones's assistant Riddel is a "dissatisfied, shiftless, lazy, speculating fellow" [p. 317].) All of this is funny as long as the novel can maintain its satiric distance from the "new country," whose face is marred by innumerable literal malapropisms like the mansion and the academy; most of what Jones does is, after all, malapropos. But Cooper's satire is not finally contained within the comforting comic security of Shakespeare's universe. In *Much Ado about Nothing*, villainy is laughable and death itself is a ruse; *The Pioneers*, on the contrary, is a problem play which touches on increasingly vital issues.

The tag from Shakespeare thus is transformed as the chapter itself develops. While declaiming on the monarchical potential of the "'duke," Jones suddenly interrupts himself: "—But who have we here? voices in the bushes;—a combination about mischief, I'll wager my commission. Let us draw near, and examine a little into the matter." Richard, that is, smells "treason." The voices belong to Natty, Oliver, and Chingachgook, who are in a setting suggestive of their anomalous position in the world of Jones: "the open space in the rear of the village, where...streets were planned and future dwellings contemplated; but where, in truth, the only mark of improvement that was to be seen, was a neglected clearing." Jones has been leading Elizabeth around to see his "improvements," and they have come by the logic of his incapacity to this appropriated but unused piece of ground. It lies "along the skirt of a dark forest of mighty pines," but is filled with the mere "mimic trees" of second growth—the precise sign of Jones himself, a little man who is as surely associated with "bushes" as Natty is with the untouched forest.[32] He is the cause of this devastation, and Natty must suffer its (and his) effects. The action of the scene is sustained and enriched by such imagistic contrasts.

Jones is all for eavesdropping on the three woodsmen. Elizabeth, however, rebukes him: she and he are the real "intruders," she asserts, "and can have no right to listen to the secrets of these men." Her cousin echoes her, "No right!" and then pleads his solemn duty in defense of his nosiness: "you forget, cousin, that it is my duty to preserve the peace of the county, and see the laws executed. These wanderers frequently commit depredations." (Actually, the three are discussing the turkey shoot; and, of course, the only "depredations" we can see are those of Jones's own "neglected clearing.") The sheriff pities Chingachgook, who "was quite boozy last night, and hardly seems to be over it yet"; but Jones was "boozy" enough himself at the Bold Dragoon, and in fact got Chingachgook drunk by urging liquor on him. In any event, he ignores Elizabeth's scruples, grabs her arm, and pushes forward: "Let us draw nigher, and hear what they say" (pp. 183-84).

Even here, Jones is itching to use and thus abuse his newfound power. From his "system" and his arrogance will arise that test of competing legal codes in which the larger competition of values in *The Pioneers* will finally be expressed. He is no Dogberry; Natty in the stocks will suggest Lear's fool, and his cave will suggest that of bitter Timon.[33] The problem with the law in Cooper's story is institutional, but it also is symbolic. It is Natty who first refers to Marmaduke as "Judge" (p. 21), and it is Natty who also first raises the larger issue: "I don't love to give up my lawful dues in a free country.—Though, for the matter of that, might often makes right here, as well as in the old country, for what I can see" (pp. 21-22). This mournful barb will be sharpened and relaunched by Bumppo throughout: "But might makes right, and the law is stronger than an old man, whether he is one that has much larning, or only one like me, that is better now at standing at the passes than in following the hounds, as I once used to could.—Heigh-ho!" (p. 135); "Well, well—the time will come when right will be done, and we must have patience" (p. 166); and, at the end, when he expresses his benediction for Elizabeth: "I pray that the Lord will keep you in mind—the Lord that lives in clearings as well as in the wilderness—and bless you, and all that belong to you, from this time, till the great day when the whites shall meet the red-skins in judgment, and justice shall be the law, and not power" (p. 455).[34] The "law" in its higher form is Natty's theme from start to finish; for Richard Jones it is simply another talisman for his vacant self. He arrogates rather than embodies it.

Hence the real villain of the book is not the man who tests the law with his aged weakness but the nominal (and nominalistic) upholder of the peace. Natty in the stocks is a pathetic sight that nothing whatsoever in the novel can justify. The only thing that keeps the hunter from being a victim pure and simple is his remembered skill, as well as his exploits in the tale proper: his rescue of Ben from the lake and Elizabeth from the beast, or his miraculous appearance out of the flames of the burning mountain, his clothing scorched and his hair burnt but his inward talents reclaimed. Like Natty's heroic immanence at the start of *The Prairie*, these moments suggest the man's deep and essential activity, thus giving his passive endurance a greater poignancy and meaning. Were he a mere victim the symbolic drama of *The Pioneers* would be flat and formulaic.

In the stocks, Natty views himself as a "tamed bear" (p. 374), a free and natural creature forced to provide for the vulgar villagers some sort of entertainment. But the wild beast is Natty's totem, much as "taming" is the Judge's solemn prerogative: "The enterprise of Judge Temple is taming the very forests!" exclaims Elizabeth (p. 212). This is a piously orthodox gloss on the village and the valley, however, one which the novel as a whole questions if it cannot quite reject it. When Oliver pleads for Natty with the Judge, who has not yet understood the busy machinations of Jones and Doolittle, Temple proclaims that—whatever Natty's services to Elizabeth have been—he must suffer "whatever the law demands." Edwards ironically affirms that "No one...doubts the sense of justice which Judge Temple entertains!" and then urges that "the years, the habits, nay, the ignorance" of his "old friend" may extenuate the punishment awaiting him. "Ought they? They may extenuate, but can they acquit? Would any society be tolerable, young man, where the ministers of justice are to be opposed by men armed with rifles? Is it for this that I have tamed the wilderness?" Temple has the abstract issue on his side here, to be sure; but as he has been responsible for Jones's elevation, he is inevitably responsible for Jones's arrogations. Indeed, his good-humored quarrel with Natty and Oliver over the deer in the first chapter, when he speaks like a judge even though he is involved in a private dispute, suggests a certain arrogance in his own makeup.[35]

So, Edwards responds to Temple's prideful boast about taming the wilderness: "Had you tamed the beasts that so lately threatened the life of Miss Temple, sir, your arguments would apply better." Temple is not Dick Jones; he has borne the "uniformly repulsive" attitudes of Bumppo without seeking, as Richard would, to counter them with the power of his position. But Temple does not, in fact, understand the issue. If his opposition to Oliver himself is based on a simple misperception, and hence can be easily cleared up, his theoretical opposition to Natty, regardless of his own relenting melancholy over the destruction of nature, eludes his grasp. And thus, with more passion than propriety here, as when he gives way to the excitement of the moment during the pigeon shoot, Temple orders Oliver to leave his house: "After this language, we must separate." Temple is a true judge, but before he can reveal his mettle he must commit this further error; it is not just in appointing Richard sheriff that he has made bad judgments (pp. 344-45).

Because he can never step outside its assumptions, Marmaduke Temple remains the tool of the book's orthodox ideology; hence it takes him so long to stop "Dickon," who represents the final bankruptcy of the orthodox as a mere assault on nature, an arrogation of the continent itself. And it is the symbolic purpose of Natty in *The Pioneers* to speak for nature by speaking out for his own assaulted rights; he is socially heterodox because he conforms to a higher sense of what is fitting. Thus, though Cooper poured his own inchoate feeling of dispossession into the figure of Leatherstocking, he gave Natty's laments a cogent public end. The dialectic of the novel lacks a final synthesis (for none had yet been reached in the nation), but it has a certain sharp definition which mere effusiveness could not have given it. The contrasts of village and forest, waste and abundance, noise and silence, disproportion and "all creation," suggest a mind working out with a clear imagistic logic a drama whose struggle is expressed by the very exuberance of Cooper's "descriptions." The most significant plot of the novel is its verbal and gestural debate over values.

The law was not something on which, in 1822, Cooper would be likely to look with much favor, and perhaps we can trace in the deceitful stewardship of Jones some of the author's own bitterness over the role of the law in his personal dispossession. The more interesting question, however, concerns his choice of an old squatter like Natty—for this is his strictly legal status—as the vehicle of his higher claims on the precious landscape repossessed by the tale. Oliver Edwards would have been a more direct choice, and indeed Edwards does represent a part of Cooper's feeling: he is the disregarded heir, a man who is more than he seems to be, and who at last recovers his due by revealing his hidden

claims, appealing to the inherent sense of right which Marmaduke finally represents, and, of course, marrying the Judge's
daughter. As for the Freudian complexities raised by this
last event (or the supposed identification of Elizabeth with
Cooper's dead sister Hannah), we need not worry over them
as some critics have. In portraying a part of himself in Edwards, Cooper may have been suggesting exactly how alienated he felt himself to be at this moment from the legacy
of his own family; or, on the other hand, he may have been
recasting in Oliver's relations with the Temples his own
strained relations with the De Lanceys, to whom he clearly
felt a need to prove his real, if hidden, identity.[36] Oliver's
symbolic alliance with the Indian past, and with Natty, thus
makes sense as a sign of his emotional distance from a world
to which he is temperamentally attached and finally restored.
And Oliver's anger, once expressed and thus defused, seems
to allow Cooper himself a means of stating and dismissing
what must have been the equal anger of his personal dispossession—all the greater because there was not in his case
the simple confusion and the equally simple clarification
which the formulas of the romance plot allowed for Oliver.
The nominal plot of *The Pioneers*, with its loss and its
recovery, reads like a wish fulfillment of Cooper's spirit;
it has obvious ties to the efforts of Sir Edward Moseley in
Precaution.

This brings us back, however, to Natty himself, who is
Oliver's mentor and guardian as well as the deeper symbol
of the young man's losses. Oliver's rights at last are nothing
but legal: he tests the law as a matter of institutional uncertainty, personal error, and subsequent restitution. Bumppo's
claims, on the contrary, aim at the landscape rather than the
land, and as such are beyond adjudication; they are transcendent if not quite Transcendental, for it would take the genius
of Thoreau to elevate the solitary American's philosophizing
into "Higher Laws," or to speak at such length in favor of
"Silence."[37] Hence it is not in his social role as a squatter
that he owns the forest, but in his thematic role as an emo-

tional symbol, a sign of wonder and its inalienable, inviolable right to the New World. Herein lies, I think, Cooper's deepest emotional investment in the man. For it is as if, having lost on the proximate legal ground (and knowing that he had), Cooper sought in some ultimate mythic statement the truer expression of his claim to the land he no longer had and the feelings with which that land had become associated. Insofar as Cooper himself was a "tame" member of society, he had to admit and accept his losses; but insofar as he was "wild," still in touch with his private feelings—and his chronic illness suggests how long the emotions lingered—he had to state and restate, as so many of the descriptions of American landscape in his works do, the heart of his timeless legacy. This enduring gesture toward space, of which Natty is the proper spirit, became Cooper's antidote to his profound suspicions about the depredations of time. Perhaps because he recognized the merely irrational source of Bumppo in his own awareness, he gave the hunter that unlikely surplus of conscience which is one of his more evident traits. He is wild by convention and costume and outward habit, as by his symbolic alliance with the woods; but he is deeply civil by propensity. It is Richard who is the book's anarchist.

Yet Natty is nowhere simply mythic: if in essence he seems timeless, as timeless as the forest itself, Cooper forces him—and thus his own truest imaginings—into the world of time. Like his own "deliberative" characters, Cooper himself sought over and over again in his art some kind of lasting order aligned with his best inward impulses. But he did not let his own imagination dwell in "a world by itself," as H. Daniel Peck has suggestively argued; this is just half of the design which his books make.[38] The answering half is as difficult as history, and as fraught with uncertainty; it also is as essential to Cooper's full meaning as the stasis it upsets. As I argued earlier, Cooper had a profound need to do violence to his own creativity, to set history going against whatever myth he might invent. Even in *The Deerslayer*, as far back as he could push Natty, he wiped Templeton off the

face of nature but introduced Tom Hutter and Harry March
as debased envoys of the civilization already hovering to the
east of the Glimmerglass. The bite of his realism in this final
Leatherstocking tale upsets what otherwise might become a
pure dream. The two white scalpers give the whole series a
fitting shape by suggesting what finally will encircle and
destroy the old man in the logical order of the five novels.
It is a singularly important fact that the hero of American
solitude nowhere lives an isolated life. He is myth born into
a world of history, and thus confronted from the start with
his ultimate undoing. As the symbol of American nature he
cannot escape the contagion of "progress."

And so it is that out of the very center of orthodox
recollection Cooper called forth his doubts. With stunning
and lasting effect, he discovered in Leatherstocking the
means of giving voice to the wilderness—which for most
Americans, even in the romantic age, had no other sound
than the "howling" attributed to it in Deuteronomy. Through
Natty in *The Pioneers*, despite his own use of that ancient
phrase, we see the clearings as a kind of disorder: hence the
larger significance of Cooper's words about the turkey shoot
in chapter 17.

> The ancient amusement of shooting the Christmas turkey, is one of
> the few sports that the settlers of a new country seldom or never
> neglect to observe. It was connected with the daily practices of a
> people, who often laid aside the axe or the sithe, to seize the rifle,
> as the deer glided through the forests they were felling, or the bear
> entered their rough meadows, to scent the air of a clearing, and to
> scan, with a look of sagacity, the progress of the invader. (p. 189)

Untamed but sagacious (like Natty himself), the bear enters
this passage—or the "rough meadows"—as a nominal threat
against which arms are the proper response; but the innocu-
ously orthodox piece of local color becomes, in mid-sentence,
a question rather than a celebration. We have unaccountably
seen the topic from the far side. Description becomes po-
lemic.

It is Billy Kirby who is Leatherstocking's chief opponent in the turkey shoot, and that man's introduction in the same chapter raises similar doubts. Billy at first seems like the perfect agent of Jones, who will use him later in the assault on Bumppo. But if Billy is "a noisy, boisterous, reckless lad," he is also something more. His "good-natured eye," Cooper writes, "contradicted the bluntness and bullying tenor of his speech." He also has a certain purchase on the world which Jones never displays, for the axe comes as naturally to his grasp as the rifle comes to Natty's. They have that much in common, as well as a respect for independence: the woodchopper prefers idleness "to an abatement of a tittle of his independence" ("or a cent in his wages," Cooper significantly adds). Thus, Kirby can "enter the woods with the tread of a Hercules," heroically powerful and possessed of the knowledge of his power.

As a woodchopper, nonetheless, Kirby must stand opposite to the Leatherstocking. His Herculean labors at first seem like the burst of positive energy into the woods. But Billy's efforts are no merely naive expense. Like Jones, he tests himself against whatever resists him: his entrance into the forest upsets an old economy as much as it advances a new one. There is something overdone in his selection of "one of the most noble" trees for "the first trial of his power," as there is in the "listless air" with which—"whistling a low tune"—he moves toward it, "wielding his axe, with a certain flourish." For though Kirby reveals strength, as Jones decidedly does not, he utterly lacks the grace of Leatherstocking, who understates his power with a habitual modesty to which Billy is unaccustomed. The latter's operations on the forest are like warfare or natural disaster, aimed as they may be at a social good:

> For days, weeks, nay, months, Billy Kirby would toil, with an ardour that evinced his native spirit, and with an effect that seemed magical; until, his chopping being ended, his stentorian lungs could be heard, emitting sounds, as he called to his patient oxen, which rung through

the hills like the cries of an alarm. He had been often heard, on a
mild summer's evening, a long mile across the vale of Templeton;
the echoes from the mountains taking up his cries, until they died
away in feeble sounds, from the distant rocks that overhung the
lake. His piles, or, to use the language of the country, his logging,
ended, with a despatch that could only accompany his dexterity and
Herculean strength, the jobber would collect together his imple-
ments of labour, light the heaps of timber, and march away, under
the blaze of the prostrate forest, like the conqueror of some city,
who, having first prevailed over his adversary, applies the torch as
the finishing blow to his conquest.

All of this starts with orthodoxy enough: the ardor, the
native spirit, the magical change. But even in the second
sentence certain opposite suggestions begin to accumulate,
and by the end what ought to have been an exercise in praise
of "the American axe"[39] has become instead a vision of
needless destruction: whatever social good is being served
by Billy, the imperial redundancy of his means leaves us
uneasy about the whole imperative of his actions. No wonder
that the sounds of his work seem "like a distant cannonad-
ing," or that his felling of the trees breaks the sunlight into
"the depths of the woods, with the suddenness of a morning
in winter": for it is all a chill and violent business, apparently
benign but actually distressing. Only in the mocking echoes
of nature, which disperse and enfeeble the man's noises,
do we sense any sanitive balance. And the "mountains"
and "distant rocks" are, of course, Natty's special
domain; the laughing belittlement is symbolically his (pp.
190-91).

Still, Kirby's invasion of the forest is an assault on Natty
himself, a symbolic belittlement in its own way. And it
thus makes sense that the chopper should assault Natty in
a more direct manner as well. When Kirby and Doolittle and
Riddel go after the buck in chapter 30, we have with all the
brilliance of Cooper's schematic plot the perfect opposition
of types. Kirby, of course, is wholly reconciled to Natty by
the latter's "peace-offering" of the animal's skin (p. 338),
rifle or no. But it is Natty's use of the gun in that instance

which will afterwards lead to his conviction, despite Billy's friendly testimony against him. That the case of the state rests on the woodchopper is salient proof of what Natty calls "the twisty ways of the law" (p. 291), for this gives the symbolic opposition of the two men its final and formal expression. Kirby lacks the rancor of Jones, and is willing to accept Natty's superior skill as a marksman after the turkey shoot. But he nonetheless stands for the end of Natty's way. Their partial closeness accounts for part of the book's tragic drama, for the line between them must at last be drawn.

The two have clashed over the law much earlier, in fact. When Natty's gun merely snaps as he takes aim on Brom's turkey, a discussion of the rules of the game ensues. It is Kirby who asserts that "the law of the game in this part of the country" demands Leatherstocking's withdrawal if he cannot or will not pay another shilling. Natty quickly responds, with bristling sarcasm, that Kirby is more likely to "know the laws of the woods" than he himself: "You come in with the settlers, with an ox goad in your hand, and I come in with moccasins on my feet, and with a good rifle on my shoulders, so long back as afore the old war; which is likely to know the best!" But on the appeal of Brom Freeborn, who is anxious to make as much as he can on the sport, it is Richard Jones who next "comes in"—and with the law rather than the rifle or the goad, such being the progress of authority. "It seems proper that I should decide this question," Richard proclaims, "as I am bound to preserve the peace of the county; and men with deadly weapons in their hands, should not be heedlessly left to contention, and their own malignant passions." This is, true to form, a gross overreading of the situation. But it is nowhere near as comical as Richard's further reasonings. In duels, he opines, a snap is as good as a fire; therefore, by analogy, it must hold that a man may not stand snapping all day at a "defenceless turkey"! The logic that makes Jones a defender of the fowl is all part of Cooper's ironic smile (pp. 195–96). A man of regulation, Jones later asserts that the "uncertainty about the rules of this sport" needs to be removed; hence he offers to chair a "committee" to "draw up, in writing, a set of regulations—." But at that moment Marmaduke surprises him with his Christmas greeting, a comeuppance that Jones finds sufficiently distracting to drop the present topic (p. 199). He prides himself, of course, on being the first to wish anyone the joys of whatever holiday is at hand. Prominence is his game.

But this scene, however comic and truncated, is a foretaste of what must follow. Richard voices here, uncouthly but vigorously, that ideal of regulation and rules to which Natty will at last fall victim. The Judge's new game law is itself a fitting premise for Bumppo's "fall," but the fall itself could not occur—or at least would not occur—without the entrapping wiles of Doolittle, who feloniously invades Natty's ground and sets his dogs loose to run down the buck. One may read the ensuing temptation, to be sure, as an Adamic parable. Yet Cooper is more interested, it seems to me, in the errors of the tempter than in the susceptibility of the victim. The heart of the matter is Natty's mysterious cabin, "the only habitation within fifty miles . . . whose door is not open to every person who may choose to lift its latch" (pp. 304). The obvious secret here is Oliver's grandfather, old Major Effingham: the secret, that is, of the past. The nominal plot requires that the soldier be kept hidden away until the right moment, and hence requires the "rudeness" (p. 264) with which Natty guards the place against intruders. But the mystery goes deeper. In the symbolic action of the book, Leatherstocking's hut represents the hunter's rights: it is his domain, and as such it must be violated. Natty's real defense is against the nosiness of Hiram, who "craves dreadfully to come into the cabin" (p. 290), and the officious curiosity of Jones, who is certain that the "ore" being dug up by Natty and his cohorts is stored in the hut (p. 319).

The real motives of Richard take us beyond the issue of law, however. Natty's humble dwelling represents for him the one piece of profoundly "unregulated" ground in the county: it is nothing less than the symbol of nature, the inner sanctum over which Jones must gain control if his notions are to prevail. The cabin is associated, as we have seen, with silence, and to that silence Jones brings the clamor of the village: "You will form yourselves in a complete circle around his hut," he tells "his troop" as they go out to arrest Natty, "and at the word 'advance,' called aloud by me, you will rush forward, and, without giving the criminal time for deliberation, enter his dwelling by force and make him your prisoner" (p. 355). Jones prudently stations himself behind the bank along the shore as the men advance, then "raise[s] his voice in the silence of the forest, and shout[s] the watchword." "The sounds," Cooper writes, "played among the arched branches of the trees in hollow cadences"— the echo again reveals the man—"but when the last sinking tone was lost on the ear, in place of the expected howls of the dogs, no other noises were returned but the crackling of torn branches and dried sticks, as they yielded before the advancing steps of the officers." When even these sounds die away, Jones at last rushes up the bank, only to find the "smouldering ruins" of the hut, a "dim flame" in the midst of the ashes casting an eerie light into the dark woods (p. 356).

The discovery reduces everyone in the party, even Richard, to utter silence. For Natty has won the spiritual battle even though he will lose the temporal one. With extraordinary art, Cooper has the old man come forth "from the gloom" while the officers are standing there in their shock, come forth and surrender himself. He has earned the right to another lament, and he delivers it as "the dusky figures" encircle him; it is an indictment not just of Jones but of everything Jones represents:

> What would ye have with an old and helpless man? ... You've
> driven God's creaters from the wilderness, where his providence had
> put them for his own pleasure, and you've brought in the troubles
> and divilties of the law, where no man was ever known to disturb
> another. You have driven me, that have lived forty long years of
> my appointed time in this very spot, from my home and the shelter

of my head, lest you should put your wicked feet and wasty ways in my cabin. You've driven me to burn these logs, under which I've eaten and drunk, the first of Heaven's gifts, and the other of the pure springs, for the half of a hundred years, and to mourn the ashes under my feet, as a man would weep and mourn for the children of his body. You've rankled the heart of an old man, that has never harmed you or yourn, with bitter feelings towards his kind, at a time when his thoughts should be on a better world; and you've driven him to wish that the beasts of the forest, who never feast on the blood of their own families, was his kindred and race; and now, when he has come to see the last brand of his hut, before it is melted into ashes, you follow him up, at midnight, like hungry hounds on the track of a worn-out and dying deer! What more would ye have? for I am here—one to many. I come to mourn, not to fight; and, if it is God's pleasure, work your will on me. (pp. 356-57)

Though the officers involuntarily draw back out of the glare as Natty, "with the light glimmering around his thinly-covered head," addresses them, the old hunter has no desire to escape from the circle. He faces them down, one by one, until Jones comes forward apologetically and arrests him. "The party now collected, and, preceded by the Sheriff, with Natty in their centre, they took their way towards the village." It is absolutely right that the men should ask Bumppo repeatedly why he has burned his hut, and equally right that he should move on in "a profound silence." They do not know what they have arrested in seizing the man (p. 357).

Fire first gleams forth in *The Pioneers* as a cheering and comforting thing, another bright sign among many. By the time Natty has torched his cabin, however, and then accused the "dusky" citizens of the county, it has become apocalyptic. The book draws to a close with "the Vision" itself ablaze, set on fire by "the kearless fellows who thought to catch a practys'd hunter in the woods after dark" (pp. 414-15)—the mob of villagers that set out after the escaped prisoners. At last, "wearied and disappointed" (p. 395), the pursuers simply threw away their burning pine-knots, with the sort of careless abandon that typifies, and culminates, the blind disregard of the village for the larger world that sustains it. Committed as they may be to the progress of civilization, they spread only "the progress of the desolation" over this world (p. 407). "We must ... disregard trees, hills, ponds, stumps, or, in fact, any thing but posterity" (p. 183): this is Richard's philosophy, and in the profoundest sense Templeton embodies it. Even posterity is largely ignored by those who in their nervous assaults on abundance point ahead to that "evil day" invoked by Cooper at the start. And if the future represented by young Effingham and Elizabeth is theoretically brighter, this upturn of the surface plot cannot wholly or even adequately assuage the doubts raised in the real heart of the novel. Aside from Chingachgook (and perhaps Ben Pump), these two are closer to Natty than anyone. Yet not even they can hold him at the end; whatever stability they may suggest will have beneath it the lingering disorder of Bumppo's dispossession. "'He is gone!' cried Effingham" (p. 456). Judge Temple leads a party out in search of the old hunter but of course cannot find him; he has disappeared as surely as he first appeared, with magical overtones, in the beginning. The man of extraordinary presence has become a symbol of absence. So, too, a novel that opens with such an assault on the senses comes to an end with mere vacancy. "This was the last that they ever saw of the Leather-stocking..." (p. 456).

His departure is the last indictment issued against what in essence has forced him out. In all this space, no place can be allotted to Bumppo, precisely because the settlers are unspacious of mind as surely as they are greedy in spirit. They overassert their claims on the American scene because its own amplitude criticizes their littleness, their lack of that imagination with which Natty is blessed. It is the same amplitude of the world that calls forth their voracious wastefulness: as if they seek to reduce nature to the narrow compass of their awareness. They shoot off their mouths, as they shoot their guns or swing their axes or take to the law, in order to fill space with some proof of their existence. Though Natty in effect is exorcised, he is well rid of the settlements. That he does not, cannot, belong reflects on those who will not have him, who cannot include either the man or the vision he represents in their fierce but bumbling economy. He is not simply an early phase necessarily supplanted by a later and more complex one, as the rough backwoodsman of Crèvecoeur is.[40] He stands instead for an abiding truth which the "pioneers" of Cooper's title will ignore at their peril. For they, too, have lost something even in the wealth of their gains. Elizabeth is literally right in asserting that "these clearings and farms" cannot be converted "again, into hunting-grounds, as the Leather-stocking would wish to see them." But she is also right in stating her sadness: "I grieve when I see old Mohegan walking about these lands, like the ghost of one of their ancient possessors, and feel how small is my own right to possess them" (p. 280). Unfortunately, her sensitivity is rare in Templeton, rare and largely verbal.

And so it is that the site of Natty's cabin becomes a graveyard, a ruined spot devoted to human ruin. But Cooper ends the book with a certain larger justice. Leatherstocking leaves the valley as a last and firm protest, less a surrender than an act of defiance. And Chingachgook likewise appeals in his death to the inherent lawfulness of experience, the inner justness of a right departure. The Reverend Grant is appalled by the Indian's resurgent paganism, as he interprets it, but Natty defends his friend: "I should think 'twould be as well to let the old man pass in peace" (p. 421). And as the fire rages on, the dark clouds gather; Grant's last appeal to the Indian is cut short by the flash of lightning and the crash of thunder, and the quenching rain that follows. To such a miraculous intercession Grant can only reply with the words of the Book of Job: "I know that my Redeemer liveth, and that he shall stand at the latter day upon the earth" (p. 423), for the pagan's death has taught him something about his own faith.[41] And Job, one notes, is singularly appropriate at this point: appropriate to the action of the book as well as to the emotions of its author.

Cooper was trying, as he said, to please himself. That his pleasure involved pain *The Pioneers* amply reveals; Natty's mournful lament over the ashes of his cabin speaks, I think, of Cooper's own lasting distress. For the novel is above all else a personal testament, a mixture of light and gloom, cheer and sadness—and, at the end, an avowal of something beyond the pain of loss. Natty's integrity, his refusal to submit to the order of things that has replaced his own, at last proclaims the integrity of nature itself: the enduring wonder of creation and the creative strength of individual will. Among other things, Natty is the tale-teller of the book. All his deeds likewise shine with the rightness of art. Here, too, he adumbrates the hidden identity of his human "creator."

We would probably be wrong to reduce *The Pioneers* to a theory of the frontier. It has a musical form rather than an argumentative one; it uses its border materials rather than simply states them. Nor does it proceed as we think novels should. Not a single character develops, for instance, while the dialogue often misses the depth of meaning which Cooper otherwise imagines for the tale. "An Indian burn!" Oliver exclaims; "who ever heard of an Indian dying by fire! an Indian cannot burn; the idea is ridiculous. Hasten, hasten, Miss Temple, or the smoke may incommode you" (p. 406). One wonders if anything more silly than this could be conceived and perpetrated.[42] The only real explanation lies not in an equally silly defense but in recognizing that Cooper's imagination was not primarily social—indeed, that it often was decidely asocial. Even Richard Jones, one of Cooper's most successful social caricatures, does not converse with other characters so much as make statements; his language is itself a symbol of the man rather than the means of his authentic social life. At its happiest moments, Cooper's art is symbolic rather than representational: Natty may well represent a certain class of people, but his real importance lies elsewhere.

When Cooper's art faltered, on the other hand, he tended to rely on formulas and conventions which he could copy but not really possess on his own. Perhaps he needed such things to give a certain innocuous outer face to his more essential concerns; perhaps he simply did not trust his imagination enough, though his later returns to Leatherstocking suggest just the opposite. We cannot at any rate ignore the scattered weaknesses of his many books, the crotchets, the repetitions, the mere ineptitude. To dismiss everything else merely because of those flaws, however, is to fail in the act of reading. As I have tried to suggest in discussing *The Pioneers*, a firm and artful design lies beneath what may appear to be the illogic of the book's surface. Cooper's eye was surer than his hand; he could envision better than he could render. Literature was a "new country" for Cooper himself, as surely as it was for the United States. And if his language did not adequately convey what needed saying, the fault belonged to the larger American community as much as to him. Besides, what language, left cold on the pages of a book, can ever contain the fullest of human imaginings? To read well is to reinvent the original, and Cooper, as I hope I have suggested, is far better than his reputation—he is probably better than he himself ever realized.

4   Indian Troubles

Surely we are meant to feel that Templeton, ill-built, contentious, and mistaken as it may seem, will survive and even flourish. All the external threats to its life, or the lives of its inhabitants, keep clear of the village: it is on the lake or in the woods where disaster is thinkable and possible—where Edwards can be shot, Jones can upset his sleigh, Elizabeth can meet the panther, Ben Pump almost drown, or Chingachgook and Jotham Riddel at last die. Space in *The Pioneers* seems radically and firmly divided: in the midst of the fire, Elizabeth looks down with horror at the "peaceful village," where she can see the Judge "standing in his own grounds" and looking up at the burning mountain with detached and innocent curiosity (p. 411). There is not the slightest suggestion that the blaze may rush down on his premises. Experience seems to respect his position; experience, moreover, is something to be watched as much as felt. The novel is an ironic pastoral, but it is a pastoral nonetheless.

To some extent this quality in the book comes from the descriptive purpose Cooper declared for it. Description and action are, after all, stylistic and literal opposites. But we may find other explanations as well. In the simplest sense, Cooper knew that his actual model for Templeton hardly was a straggling and struggling backwoods settlement always on the verge of extinction. The Upper Susquehanna had a population of 3,000 in 1790, when the infant James first arrived; by the end of the decade, the figure had increased tenfold, and by the time Cooper wrote the novel it had more than doubled again.[1] Cooperstown stood at the center of all

119

this growth: not until later, with the opening of the Erie Canal, would the rush of population to the West bypass it.[2] Such facts placed a limit on Cooper's imagination. As much as he wanted to express his own sense of loss, he hardly could convert a story of frontier success into an American nightmare. He questioned, satirized, exposed the village, and showed how it looked in a spiritual sense to someone decidedly outside its assumptions. But he could not disregard its final comic reality. One wonders what might have come from him if Judge Cooper had been killed not in Albany but in his own little home.

Cooperstown had its hints of disaster and absurdity, to be sure, and *The Pioneers* does respond to them. Judge Cooper's section on "Absurdities" in *A Guide in the Wilderness* speaks with goodhumored condescension about the European gentlemen whose "failures ... in new lands" were traceable to a dogged insistence on Old World ideas and Old World practices.[3] And so the novel tells of an Englishman who "not only adhered to his native customs, in attire and living, but usually drove his plough, among the stumps, in the same manner as he had before done, on the plains of Norfolk, until dear-bought experience taught him the useful lesson, that a sagacious people knew what was suited to their circumstances, better than a casual observer; or a sojourner, who was, perhaps, too much prejudiced to compare, and, peradventure, too conceited to learn" (p. 124). Then, too, the oddities of Richard Jones suggest the absurd basis of many native attitudes—as when he sees house lots in a swamp, or argues the likely presence of "mines" in Otsego from the "analogy" of South American riches (p. 319). The only mine in Otsego proves a grave for Riddel—though this, too, lies beyond the village, and it is powerless to swallow Jones himself. That such a fool as Jones leads a charmed life in *The Pioneers* tells us much about the tone of the book.

The real county gave other hints. Otsego had no literal Effingham family, and no literal Chingachgook or Leatherstocking, but it hardly was the virgin land Judge Cooper later claimed it was in writing of his first entrance into it. George Croghan, a man of grand schemes, chronically short means, and questionable allegiances, no longer resided there—he died elsewhere in 1782, impoverished and disaffected—but the memory of his old claims long outlived him, much as his "rude dwelling" at the foot of the lake (the first "ruin" Cooper ever saw) also did.[4] Croghan had not entrusted his lands to Cooper's father, as the Effinghams are said to have done with Judge Temple; but Judge Cooper's moral title to Otsego was less than immaculate, and Croghan's heirs, the Prevosts, eventually returned to Cooperstown to press their claims. In 1814 they filed suit against all landholders in the county, and it was the Judge's heirs who handled the larger defense. According to *The Chronicles of Coopers-town*, the proceedings dragged on for a considerable time until they were "discontinued in consequence of the statute of limitations."[5]

Though the Prevost case turned out well for the Cooper family, as long as it lasted it comprised part of young James's growing troubles. The intriguing thing is that in writing *The Pioneers* Cooper not only gave the Effinghams an un-arguable right to the land but also let them win: for in doing so he allied his own disaffections with the Prevosts, who were partially to blame for them. His imagination seems to have grasped the larger poetic truth of the Croghan story, and to have taken it up for its expressive power. Cooper invested other lingering shades of the region with other portions of his private emotion. Croghan himself, with his log hut and his alliance with the frontier and "Sir William," may have supplied some hints for Natty, though the two Shipmans, David and Nathaniel, probably had a more impor-tant place in Cooper's mind when he envisioned Leather-stocking.[6] Here again, as in his substitution of the weakened and poor Reverend Grant for the robust Father Nash of Cooperstown, the novelist found it possible to imagine suffering and distress around the edges of his village.[7] Thus he also could touch on Hannah's fate, though he kept Eliza-

beth safe from it; and he could have Judge Temple speak of
the early trials of the settlement, though he chose not to
dramatically recreate them.

Otsego had its Indian sites, including a little orchard
on the ground where the Cooper mansion was built.[8] But
neither Croghan nor Judge Cooper after him literally displaced the natives from the valley, so that Chingachgook
as a further symbol of dispossession in *The Pioneers* derived
from a general fact rather than a local one: "Before the
Europeans, or, to use a more significant term, the Christians,
dispossessed the original owners of the soil, all that section
of country, which contains the New-England States, and
those of the Middle which lie east of the mountains, was
occupied by two great nations of Indians, from whom had
descended numberless tribes" (p. 83). Of the moral blame
thus plainly placed by the novel, *A Guide in the Wilderness*
says nothing; nor does it mention, for that matter, the
Croghan affair—for the pamphlet is a song of possession
throughout. Yet the novelist could not bring himself to
make much more of Chingachgook than a symbol. The
Indian can remind Judge Temple, in his second speech in
the book, that the great landowner did not fight against
Britain for the land he now controls (to which reminder
Grant replies, "'judge not, lest ye be judged.' What motive
could Judge Temple have"—a nice conjunction of terms
[p. 87]). When Chingachgook's passion over his wrongs
rises up in the Bold Dragoon later the same night, however,
Natty soothes his old friend, as if the native must not violate
the code that protects the village from violence. His final
rebirth, like his death, thus must occur not in the settlement
but in the surrounding woods. And it must occur there with
a benign and peaceful spirituality that lessens the radical
difference of Chingachgook's way from that of the "Christians." Natty himself may carry his gun into the church
service on Christmas Eve, as Oliver may take his into the
Temple mansion—one hand touches it, while the other rests
on the piano—but guns may not be actually used within the
precincts of the town, just as the forest fire must keep its

distance from Templeton. Indeed, though Natty is allowed to threaten Hiram and Billy with his rifle on his own ground, the threat remains symbolic; the gun is a gesture rather than a weapon. And it is for his gesture that Leatherstocking will be punished. The hunter's words are the only weapon allowed him by the village ("I come to mourn, not to fight; and, if it is God's pleasure, work your will on me"), for *The Pioneers* remains profoundly civil. Cooper imagined a far different world from that of his father's memoir, and he surrounded the village with a wealth of "melancholy" signs. But he could not finally destroy what he wanted so dearly to remember.

In his later settlement tales Cooper freed himself from the constraints of mere memory. *The Wept of Wish-Ton-Wish* was set on ground Cooper had known while attending Yale, but that ground had few deep ties to his spirit. The most important artistic result of the difference was a severity of action in this new novel: violation is the unrelenting motive of its plot, and boundary after boundary falls victim to the violence of the author's own imagination. Written and published just after *Notions of the Americans*, *The Wept of Wish-Ton-Wish* itself violates every pious affirmation of that book. For here field and forest merge not with the aesthetic peace envisioned by Cooper's "Count" but with a kind of ferocious drama more appropriate to *The Last of the Mohicans* than to a tale nominally concerned with "conversion." One can only conclude that Cooper was seeking to give the romance of American expansion a perversely Gothic accent, one expressing his own radical loss.

The result might have bordered on melodrama. Cooper must have known enough of that genre from Cooperstown, where in his youth an "Indian" alarm tingled the spine at least once, and where—as another early resident later recalled —the floating lore brimmed with disaster:

> Stories of Indian tortures and burnings; of Indian tomahawks, and scalping-knives; stories of encounters with wild beasts, of dark nights spent in the woods, and of hairbreadth escapes from the wild dangers

of wading and swimming rivers, and crossing mountain torrents;
stories of children strayed or lost, or torn to pieces, or starved
to death in the woods....[9]

With a working sense of how such tales, by "relating to the
actual, living world around us," far surpassed in their affec-
tive power for Americans the imported lore of "ghosts and
witches," this pioneer sketched the proper basis for a New
World literature. What kept the native horrors from being
melodramatic was their continuing reference to reality.[10]

Cooper based *The Wept of Wish-Ton-Wish* less on the
content of American Gothicism than on its psychological
sources and significance. In the first of his terrific scenes,
when Content Heathcote rides out into the dark woods,
he thus gestures toward the kind of lore which was endemic
to the frontier: "Notwithstanding the influence of long habit,
the forest was rarely approached after night-fall by the
boldest woodsman, without some secret consciousness
that he encountered a positive danger.... Histories of com-
bats with beasts of prey, and of massacres by roving and
lawless Indians, were the moving legends of the border."[11]
Nor is this gesture merely explanatory. Cooper intends it as
an indication that his present tale will hinge on the inward
capacity of his characters to distinguish legend from current
fact, outer reality from psychic disposition. He gives the
settlers here not the charm of insulation allowed to those
in *The Pioneers*, but only the desire for it. They are the
victims of disaster, but they are also the victims of their own
mentality.

The Wept of Wish-Ton-Wish is an ironic nightmare in
which achievement and failure, security and loss, alternately
seem in control. Its general opening points toward the first
days of New England, when the settlers had "transformed
many a broad waste of wilderness into smiling fields and
cheerful villages," but its specific setting in the Connecticut
valley is a "forlorn-hope" (p. 13), a little clearing lost in

"the seemingly endless maze of wilderness" (p. 30). Mark Heathcote, the head of the family, is an English Puritan who originally sought a haven in America from the civil uproar of his native land; the "very day he landed in the long wished for asylum," however, his wife died in childbirth (p. 15). His strong faith buoys him up in this adversity, but it is the same faith that accounts for the "schisms and doctrinal contentions" among the settlers in Massachusetts, Mark's first home, and that leads him at last to part from the others in an attempt to repurify his devotion to God. Sullen, prideful, and determined, Heathcote listens to arguments urging him to stay, yet cannot heed them: "Much have I endured, as you know, in quitting the earthly mansion of my fathers, and in encountering the dangers of sea and land for the faith; and, rather than let go its hold, will I once more cheerfully devote to the howling wilderness, ease, offspring, and, should it be the will of Providence, life itself!" (pp. 17-18). And so the "sternly-minded adventurer," with his son Content and his daughter-in-law Ruth, sets out to test his Lord (p. 19).

All of this is merely background to Cooper's real story, but as background it directs us to the psychological bias of the book. Mark Heathcote's actions in the world—"the wilderness of the world," the novel urges us to say[12] —depend on his inner obsessions far more than his perceptions. Cooper quarrels less with the specific items of the Puritan's faith than with the tenacity with which it possesses him: it is, for instance, "the peculiarity of doctrine, on which Mark Heathcote laid so much stress" (p. 20), that makes him avoid all established settlements and plunge into the woods after leaving Massachusetts. And it is the isolation which his faith thus requires that at last will expose his family to disaster. If he begins his life in the book as Natty ends his own in *The Pioneers*, by departing from a community which seemingly has no room for him, he lacks Leatherstocking's firm sense that his God dwells in nature; he flees west, leading "the march of civilization through the country" (p. 13)—as Cooper writes, almost quoting the last words of *The Pioneers* on the first page of this book—but he has no alliance whatsoever with the world to which his "pilgrimage" (p. 20) leads him. Like his fellow believers, he is "metaphysical, though simple-minded" (p. 26).

There is an abstract inwardness about his little clearing that mirrors the man's own mind. It seems like an arbitrary gap in the forest as Cooper first describes it, and between the settlement and the environing world we already find ominous hints of conflict: rail fences that run "in zigzag lines, like the approaches which the besieger makes in his cautious advance to the hostile fortress"; a collection of rude buildings closed up on themselves in a "hollow square" and surrounded by a high palisade; a tall blockhouse at the dead center; "a large square vacancy" cut into the woods of a nearby hill, balanced within the valley by another one since abandoned, where "straggling, girdled, and consequently dead trees, piles of logs, and black and charred stumps were seen, deforming the beauty of a field, that would otherwise have been striking from its deep setting in the woods" (pp. 27-29). Though the Heathcotes and their fellow settlers have passed several years of peace in the spot by the time the tale proper opens, the very deployment of their signs across its face suggests that the rough idyll soon will end.

Cooper makes it clear that preparedness is a virtue (see pp. 75-76), and we must view the Heathcote citadel as a necessary response to frontier realities. Yet the shrewdness of the colonists in this regard seems overwrought. For all their palisades, loopholes, locks, bars, secret compartments, hidden doors, and cannon—or their "jealous" (p. 29) care for this machinery of survival—they are not as pragmatic as they appear. Indeed, as the book proceeds it becomes progressively evident that they lack essential inner traits, for which their outer defenses perhaps serve as an ineffectual balance. Cooper's recurrent term for them, "borderers" (it supplied the British title), has a psychological as well as literal meaning; and it is in their literal trials that their minds are tested.

That the Indian attack which destroys the settlement takes so long to materialize proves just this point, for during the first third of the book the settlers live in an uneasy state of alarm that tests their mental bearing on the world. Nothing intervenes between them and the threats of the forest but their own walls and the little clearing that at night becomes an extension of the woods rather than a barrier to it. Most of all, the wilderness is a perceptual problem for the Heathcotes, a place of "darkness" and "obscurity" (p. 152) that surrounds them like a vast riddle they cannot solve. And their own weakness for spectral suppositions, for "invisible agencies" (p. 149), gives to the "signs" that come forth from the forest—and the language of signs is at the very heart of the book—a terrific power that things in themselves do not often possess in Cooper. The Gothicism of the novel, that is, stems from the Gothic predilections of the characters. Their faith gives them a ready allegorical formula for the things they see or hear (or think they do), but little means of directly perceiving the world as it is. They lack the "jealous senses" of Mabel Dunham in *The Pathfinder*.

But Cooper develops the spectral theme with a broader purpose in mind. The errors of his characters lead to the truth of his own obsession here, which is the constant challenge of the world to human sense and sensibility. The first chapters of the novel are a case study in "delusion" (p. 63), "deception" (p. 69), "imagination" (p. 166)—and a multitude of other inner agonies. By their "keen and anxious watchings" (p. 102), their "untiring watchfulness" (p. 96), and their desire for "tidings . . . from without" (p. 158), the settlers as a group reveal the extraordinary anxiety with which they invest their physical defenses. Their border architecture is a symbol of their exposed mentality. The stout wall in which they trust will ultimately fail, even though—with their penchant for the Bible—they can assert that "Here are no Sampsons to pull down the pillars on our heads" (p. 127). And it will fail because those who trust in it and what it represents have no real ability to transcend their boundaries.

The forest offers them from the outset a series of opposite icons. The neat distinctions of their life belie the actual complexity of its setting, where the "dusky and imperfect light" dissolves all certainty:

> The broad, nearly interminable, and seemingly trackless forest
> lay about them, bounding the view to the narrow limits of the
> valley, as though it were some straitened oasis amidst an ocean
> of wilderness. Within the boundaries of the cleared land objects
> were less indistinct, though even those nearest and most known
> were now seen only in the confused and gloomy outlines of night.
> (p. 164)

And the destruction which will come out of that confusion and gloom in effect comes from the victims themselves. They do not see the world, for all their watchings, as the novel itself describes it, and they have no better language for it than they have for the young Indian Conanchet, whom they surprise one night "in the fields" (pp. 59, 62), where by the logic of their defensive assumptions he should not be. Most of their exchanges with Conanchet while he lingers in their power are gestural; his face and eyes speak for him, even though what they say is dubious (later he will come to the settlers' aid), and even though all along he in fact is picking up English from his unsuspecting captors. By his curious silence, as by his fondness for looking out toward the forest (see pp. 77, 115), Conanchet extends into the settlement the larger challenge of the woods. And the Heathcotes cannot read him any better than they can read his world.

Indeed, the scene in which he is discovered gives us the first long example, rather stylized but important nonetheless, of how the Heathcotes regard the encircling forest. That Content's dark journey begins with an act of blood is crucial. The regicide Submission, an associate of Content's father in

Old England, has come to Wish-Ton-Wish in search of sanctuary from the authorities who are pursuing him. Apparently from hunger, though in fact as an emblem of his bloody past, he has slaughtered one of the Heathcote sheep on his way hither. The carcass, he now tells Mark, lies in that abandoned field across the valley; Mark sends his son out into the night to recover it, and Ruth accompanies her husband to the gate as he departs. It is in her mind as she waits for his return that the real challenge being issued here —the challenge, we may say, of history, both European and American—comes forth. This is merely the first of several scenes in which the woman, entranced by the woods which typify that challenge but not really able to enter them, stands in a "strange stare" (see Cooper's epigraph from *The Tempest*, p. 54) before what threatens and opposes her.

Ruth watches as the "distant form" of Content moves away into the forest, much as Submission, first seen as a "distant and obscure object" (p. 33), has emerged from it earlier. And indeed the distance throughout this novel functions as a sign of obscurity and loss: Ruth thus is beset by "intensely painful" emotions as her husband's form seems to blend "with the dark trunks of the trees"—unlike Natty's disappearances in *The Pioneers*, this one is a kind of death, and it points ahead to that moment when Ruth's own daughter will be quite literally lost to the wilderness. The "feverish inquietude" she feels has "no definite object" at this point— the real object is that later loss—but she nonetheless passes outside the palisade and the "limits to her vision" which it represents. Her act is, of course, an emblem of the book's larger plot.

Once outside, Ruth is moved farther beyond her limits. The spot where she pauses is, ironically, the very one from which Mark has earlier surveyed "the growing improvement of his estate"—as Cooper now reminds us. But during these "anxious moments" only more darkness is to be seen; it is as if the settled landscape has vanished, as if the forest has resumed its old dominion. The human form Ruth thinks she sees coming out of the woods is merely a passing shadow. Suddenly, recalling that the gate behind her remains open, she rushes back inside her "limits," but not before one "startling object" in the surrounding field strikes her faltering attention. As she later tells Content once he, too, has returned, "in the hollow left by a fallen tree, lies concealed a heathen!" (pp. 54-57, 62). Come to scout out the race which is responsible for his father's death—for another deed of blood is implicit here—Conanchet has been glimpsed, and soon he will be captured. From this point on, the little clearing lost in the "maze" of the woods will be transformed in a quite different sense from that which its settlers had intended. Content's and Ruth's dark journey pushes the story forward into its gathering gloom.

The transformation requires, however, a certain cold disillusionment. Freed from the proprieties of his own past, Cooper here could envision with exact and bitter skill a border tragedy adequate to the emotions he had been able to express only by indirect and symbolic means in *The Pioneers*. Ruth and Content will lose to the forest not their own lives—it will take *Wyandotté* to give that twist to the settlement theme—but their young daughter, another Ruth whose captivity among the Indians balances that of Conanchet among the settlers, and whose return at the end is itself tragic. This balance of fates is the first sign of Cooper's radical intent in the novel. Gone from *The Wept of Wish-Ton-Wish* is that unspoken "charm" of *The Pioneers*, whereby Chingachgook may suffer but not inflict wrongs, Natty undergo assault but not freely repay it, Elizabeth be threatened but not destroyed. Space is more open here as well as more oppressive; actions unthinkable except at the fringes of the earlier book have a tacit license to occur at the center of this one. And so the forest moves in.

The license stems directly from the author himself. Cooper seems to toy with the expectations of his readers no less than

with the fate of his characters. Thus he stops the novel
midway through with a grim vision of destruction:

> That sternness of the season, which has already been mentioned
> in these pages, is never of long continuance in the month of April.
> A change in the wind had been noted by the hunters even before
> they retired from their range among the hills; and though too
> seriously occupied to pay close attention to the progress of the
> thaw, more than one of the young men had found occasion to
> remark that the final breaking up of the winter had arrived. Long
> ere the scene of the preceding chapter reached its height, the south-
> ern winds had mingled with the heat of the conflagration. Warm
> airs, that had been following the course of the Gulf Stream, were
> driven to the land, and, sweeping over the narrow island that at this
> point forms the advanced work of the continent, but a few short
> hours had passed before they destroyed every chilling remnant
> of the dominion of winter. Warm, bland, and rushing in torrents,
> the subtle currents penetrated the forests, melted the snows from
> the fields, and as all alike felt the genial influence, it appeared to
> bestow a renovated existence on man and beast. With morning,
> therefore, a landscape very different from that last placed before
> the mind of the reader, presented itself in the valley of the Wish-
> Ton-Wish.

> The winter had entirely disappeared, and as the buds had begun to
> swell under the occasional warmth of the spring, one ignorant
> of the past would not have supposed that the advance of the season
> had been subject to so stern an interruption. But the principal
> and most melancholy change was in the more artificial parts of
> the view. Instead of those simple and happy habitations which
> had crowned the little eminence, there remained only a mass of
> blackened and charred ruins. A few abused and half-destroyed
> articles of household furniture lay scattered on the sides of the
> hill, and here and there a dozen palisadoes, favored by some acci-
> dental cause, had partially escaped the flames. Eight or ten massive
> and dreary-looking stacks of chimneys rose out of the smoking
> piles. In the centre of the desolation was the stone basement of the
> block-house, on which still stood a few gloomy masses of the timber
> resembling coal. The naked and unsupported shaft of the well
> reared its circular pillar from the centre, looking like a dark monu-

ment of the past. The wide ruin of the out-buildings blackened
one side of the clearing, and, in different places, the fences, like
radii diverging from a common centre of destruction, had led off
the flames into the fields. . . . In all other respects the view was
calm and lovely as ever. The sun shone from a sky in which no
cloud was visible. The blandness of the winds, and the brightness
of the heavens, lent an air of animation to even the leafless forest;
and the white vapor, that continued to rise from the smouldering
piles, floated high over the hills, as the peaceful smoke of the cottage curl[s] above its roof. (pp. 225-26)[13]

This is one of those passages of sustained imaginative power
that mark Cooper at his best. The first richness here comes
from his surprising contrast of vernal rebirth and human
suffering—an inversion, as it were, of the pathetic fallacy.
But this contrast gives the passage merely its gross form,
and the prose has embellishments and innuendos far more
subtle. It inventories with unflinching detail the ruinous
human scene: the "scattered" furniture, the "favored"
palisades, the upright but useless chimneys, the blockhouse
with its "gloomy" timber and "naked" well-shaft, the leveled
outbuildings and the charred fences—each is seen clearly,
and each repeats with accumulating force the fact of history.
One notes, too, the power of a term like "abused" or "accidental," both of which hint at some malice beyond that
mere fact. Then, too, Cooper measures all these details by
framing his description in the delusive peace of an older
moment: the "happy habitations" at the start, like the
peaceful "cottage" glimpsed at the end, return the reader
momentarily to that instant in the second chapter when
Mark Heathcote, returning from the harvest, pauses to look
with self-satisfaction over the bright pastoral world he has
created from the wilderness. There is the added cruelty,
beyond this contrast, in Cooper's forced comparison of the
drifting smoke of ruin to the "peaceful" smoke of the
imaginary cottage. The disjunction of this last image tells
us a good deal about Cooper's intent in the whole novel.

For he placed here at its middle what appears to be an
unequivocal end. The apprehension of his characters seems

to have met at last a sound confirmation from their world, and the reader who has noted the spectral fancies of the Heathcotes is left off-balance. But the apparent confusion at this point finally becomes part of a larger and well-matured design. The young captive, who has aided the settlers during the attack, lingers about the ruins as if in search of some token of their survival. This is a sentimental sign of his partial conversion, or at least his sympathy for the whites, even though he clearly retains his acquired "hatred" for "a race, who were so fast sweeping his people from the earth," and thus feels "the fierce joy of glutted vengeance" as he picks up a bone from the charred earth (pp. 227-28). He is like a young Chingachgook from the world of *The Pioneers*, more torn between his conflicting loyalties than the literally young Chingachgook of the later novels will prove: for Conanchet is an emotional "borderer," one of the few characters in this novel who can survive on either side of its fierce boundaries. Yet his immediate function in this scene lies elsewhere. From the heart of the ruins he seems to hear the voice of the dead settlers; and, acting on the impulses of his own spectral "imagination," he soon leaves the settlement, to be "quickly swallowed," though with no upsetting implications, "in the gloom of his native woods" (p. 228). The incipient terror of the clearing, ironically but appropriately, sends him back across the enduring thematic line of the book.

The sound he hears is no delusion, however. The settlers indeed have survived, even though Cooper himself lingers for a few lines among the ruins: "The work of the savages now seemed complete. An effectual check appeared to be placed to the further progress of civilization in the ill-fated valley of the Wish-Ton-Wish. Had nature been left to its own work, a few years would have covered the deserted clearing with its ancient vegetation; and half a century would have again buried the whole of its quiet glades in the shadows of the forest. But it was otherwise decreed" (pp. 228-29). The resurrection itself requires time; it is several hours before the "seeming decision of Providence" is countered, or the resurgent "silence of the wilderness" can be broken. And the coming forth of the survivors from the dark shaft of the well has its own psychic and mythic overtones, startling as the literal event may seem: "a human head was reared slowly, and with marked suspicion, above the shaft of the well. The wild and unearthly air of this seeming spectre was in keeping with the rest of the scene. A face begrimed with smoke and stained with blood, a head bound in some fragment of a soiled dress, and eyes that were glaring in a species of dull horror, were objects in unison with all the other frightful accessories of the place" (p. 229). Here, as in the frightful attack which has produced such results, the Gothicism of Cooper's earlier chapters receives its just and overwhelming reality.

Here, too, however, as Donald A. Ringe has suggested, Cooper is carefully playing upon the Phoenix myth.[14] The return of the Heathcotes now seems like a vindication of the vernal landscape, a repetition in the human sphere of the shift from lingering winter to a premature and startling spring. The settlers emerge, to be sure, into "the desolation of the valley," but they come literally and figuratively "from the bowels of the earth," to be "restored to the light of day." The family knows, as it gathers "amid the desolation of the valley"—Cooper repeats the phrase—that much has been suffered. But it also knows that much has been avoided, that its "deliverance" warrants deep thanksgiving. After a "brief but solemn" prayer, the survivors set about repossessing what they almost had lost (pp. 229-31).

But there are losses that cannot be recovered. The half-burned body of a young settler, and the bones of two others, must be buried. The service begins just as a "gloomy margin" of shadow spreads out from the woods; the "dusky image" of one pine tree in particular, though cast by a "dark green pyramid of never-fading foliage," points like "an emblem of... oblivion" towards "the open grave" (p. 233). Here the complex symbolism of the book's setting once more asserts itself: for it is from and of the forest that death has spoken, and this further dark invasion of the clearing is like a sign held up before the settlers. They possess, however, signs of their own, and ways of reading experience that derive from those signs. Mark enters into a long humble discourse on the disasters of the recent past, urging acceptance and even joy upon his hearers: "Open thy mouths in praise, that the gratitude of a penitent be not hid!" (p. 234). At this point he turns his "stern eye" toward the young "borderer" nearest to him, as if to force the song he wishes to hear; but the young man looks down at the "relics" in the grave, then casts "a wandering glance at the desolation" round about, remembers his wounds, and at last averts his eyes from Mark's—"so officious a display of submission" is beyond him. The "patriarch" is very much the orthodox voice in the novel, orthodox in the root sense, and so he picks up again the sermon he has just interrupted:

> Hath no one a voice to praise the Lord? The bands of the heathen
> have fallen upon my herds; the brand hath been kindled within my
> dwellings; my people have died by the violence of the unenlightened,
> and none are here to say that the Lord is just! I would that the
> shouts of thanksgiving should arise in my fields! I would that the
> song of praise should grow louder than the whoop of the savage,
> and that all the land might speak joyfulness!

To his insistence, however, there succeeds "a long, deep, and expecting pause." At last Content dutifully answers him, echoing Isaiah ("He that made the wilderness blossom, hath caused the ignorant and the barbarous to be the instruments of his will"), and—inevitably, for such is his father's own source—the Book of Job: "He hath spoken in the whirlwind, but his mercy granteth that our ears shall know his voice" (pp. 234-35).

Job is not the thematic flourish here that it arguably is in *The Pioneers*. From the dark twistings of that biblical tragedy Cooper derived for *The Wept of Wish-Ton-Wish* certain profound hints about his plot and tone. The abstract neatness of the Phoenix myth cannot contain the rough complexity of emotion called forth in this wrenching after-

math of the settlers' rebirth. Yet Mark himself, who raises
the biblical parallel, would impose a myth scarcely less
neat on the events just finished; the very exuberance of his
words tells us as much. He turns next to Ruth, who at this
moment seems like a conventional "image of womanly
sorrow." But, as we already have learned, the "image" has
an inner life of her own, a life Cooper once more reveals.
"Gazing earnestly, but without a tear, on the melancholy
spectacle before her," she is seeking "some relic" of her lost
daughter "among the dried and shrivelled remnants of
mortality" at her feet. She responds to Mark's words in a
distracted whisper that suggests her inwardness: "The Lord
gave, and the Lord hath taken away; blessed be his holy
name." This, too, comes from Job, of course, and in fact it
echoes Mark's own exclamation earlier: "He that hath given
freely, hath taken away...." But Ruth is content with the
single iron sentence; she does not try, as does her father-
in-law, to bury grief in a long sermon on the text of this
horrible—if divinely just—loss. To Mark the lost girl serves
largely as an occasion for biblical exegesis; his "freely" is
ominous of what will follow. He thus goes on to pursue the
higher meaning of the recent war. He asserts young Ruth's
"blessedness" while the girl's mother is crying. And he then
suggests, surely with a callousness Cooper intends us to catch,
that his own loss of his wife in childbirth years before, while
he was "a lone and solitary wanderer, in a strange and savage
land," had been balanced—as if in some account book of the
soul—by Content's birth; furthermore, that Content himself
now has been called, "like Abraham of old," to lay "the
infant of his love" before the feet of God (pp. 235-38).

This last gesture of the patriarch is more than a misreading
of Abraham's story, or his own. Old Mark lacks the Old
Testament ferocity of Ishmael Bush in *The Prairie*; it is
notable that he does not call down on the Indians in this
chapter the wrath of God, that he aims finally and profoundly at Job's wise acceptance rather than retribution. Yet he

has a grim intent nonetheless; his faith is simply another
defense—much like those of the preacher Meek Wolfe, who
conceives of his calling as a kind of warfare, and thus erects
"a wall blank as indomitable obstinacy could oppose" against
all disputants (p. 316). At last, however, the larger human
point is not lost on Mark. His son soon reacts to his mention
of Abraham with "a heavy groan," then "a deep silence,"
and then a steady gaze which seems to disarm the old Puritan. Now Mark himself shakes "with grief" for the first time,
and falls into solemn prayer, as if all his other sallies have
failed. He cannot rebuild his temple from the ashes of this
loss; he prays, but he does not again return to "exhortation"
(pp. 238-39).

And so the miraculous resurrection is no simple event.
Soon Cooper himself—one senses the lingering uplift of
Notions of the Americans here—will offer his own sermon
on the "improvements" which followed the war, converting
"a wilderness into the abodes of abundance and security,
with a rapidity that wears the appearance of magic" (p. 242).
But this shift of tone comes with a suddenness that is part of
his larger design. Like the argument with superficial European travelers which he carries on in this same following
chapter, the new brightness hides problems of a deeper and
more enduring sort.[15] After "several years" have passed
(p. 241), the Heathcote settlement seems to have recouped
its outward losses—much as, apparently dead, the settlers
themselves have been reborn at an earlier point:

> Over the bottom land, for the distance of several miles, all the signs
> of a settlement in a state of rapid and prosperous improvement were
> visible. The devious course of a deep and swift brook, that in the
> other hemisphere would have been termed a river, was to be traced
> through the meadows by its border of willow and sumach. At a point
> near the centre of the valley the waters had been arrested by a small
> dam; and a mill, whose wheel at that early hour was without motion,
> stood on the artificial mound [where the Heathcote house originally
> was located]. Near it was the site of a New England hamlet.

The number of dwellings in the village might have been forty.
(p. 244).

Yet Cooper's return to the language of hopeful èxpansion
is as false in its way as Mark's forced thanksgiving. Young
Ruth, who gives the tale its rather cryptic title (she is the
one for whom Wish-Ton-Wish weeps),[16] has not been found,
and her absence cannot be countered by even the most
shining "improvement." The hamlet pushes back the forest,
but Content knows that if Ruth still is alive she may well
"be buried far in the ocean of wilderness" stretching beyond
the clearings around his home (p. 271). And his wife, driven
to despair and delusion by the loss, hears the girl in every
sound that catches her attention; she is wrapped in grief,
torn by the uncertainty of her daughter's fate. She thus
bears forward into the reclaimed space of the novel the
enfeebling knowledge of history. How right not only that the
two women should bear the same name but that it should
be "Ruth." The larger public comedy of the novel has a
dire private tragedy at its heart.

Young Ruth was drawn by Cooper from the captivity lore
of the country. Yet the sources of her suffering in the novel
have an intriguing complexity, and her symbolic function
raises her into something more than a mere figure. She
represents both the flaws of her native world and the claims
of its encircling reality. Hence in the working out of her
fate lies one key to the meaning of Cooper's tale.

We must note first the immense irony of her original
loss. The attack itself Cooper renders as a foretaste of the
gloomy scene left in its wake—a destruction of "long-sus-
tained and sylvan security" by the "most frightful exhibition
of human horrors" (p. 196). This contrast suggests again
the intensity of the book's Gothic imagery, but here, too,
Cooper draws us to the inner consequences. In this section
of the book his focus falls consistently on the girl's mother.
It thus is the elder Ruth's "meditations" (p. 195) that
occupy the center of his prose in the crucial fourteenth

chapter, and it is her eye that gazes "in fearful sadness" (p. 196) on the events outside her house. As long as she has the freedom to watch, of course, she is protected from actual violence; and the book thereby stresses reaction more than action. Even when an Indian suddenly enters the house and seizes young Ruth, driving the peril inescapably close, Cooper renders the threat visually. It is an icon taken, clearly enough, from the kind of lore recorded in John Vanderlyn's painting of the luckless Jane McCrea: "A naked savage, dark, powerful of frame, and fierce in the frightful masquerade of his war-paint, stood winding the silken hair of the girl in one hand, while he already held the glittering axe above a head that seemed inevitably devoted to destruction" (p. 197).[17] If we read closely, the very frozen quality of the picture will tell us that the real climax is yet to come; the mother's horrified response, and perhaps the reader's, is Cooper's aim here.

And the response increases in pitch page by page. As the fire moves closer, Ruth stands fixed "in impotent helplessness, an entranced spectator of the progress of the destruction." Her eye now is "contracted and sorrowing"—for at last the anxiety of that first night outside the walls has taken a visible shape (p. 202). With its massive timbers and commanding position, only the blockhouse remains for the settlers, and to it, amid the rising confusion, they rush for asylum. In the scurry across the inner courtyard, young Ruth once more seems threatened (again Cooper gives us an icon), but Conanchet comes to the rescue here as he had in the house, and at last mother and daughter are safe within the citadel.

Or so Cooper at first suggests. Ruth and Content in fact have two daughters; the other one, Martha, is a young orphan taken into the family at an earlier time, and by some means not made entirely clear in the narrative she apparently has been lost during the last retreat. When the parents rejoin in the citadel they are willing to balance that disaster against a gain which clearly means more to them: "If we have lost one that we loved," Content says, "God hath spared our own child." Then comes a shock for which no previous irony in the novel can have prepared the reader, though afterwards it seems utterly right. The child is so enfolded in the mother's dress that her face is obscured; Content first discovers the mistake, and then Ruth too sees that, "in the hurry of the appalling scene," the girls were exchanged. "It is not our babe!" she cries, giving in to the "fearfully powerful" impulses which immediately assault her mind. "If not thine, whose am I?" the child asks (pp. 213-14).

Ruth soon recovers herself, but not before we have had a startling glimpse into the emotional economy of the Heathcotes. The later chapters will raise to a higher level and a greater intensity the question asked by Martha, for young Ruth is, as the Indian Metacom states, "one who is neither white nor red" (p. 368). Had her end been as iconic as the threat raised against her in the house no such ambiguity would have resulted. As it is, however, she comes to represent the tragic irreconcilability of her two worlds. In a universe marked by sharp divisions—spatial, cultural, political, psychic —such a being can have no place and hence no real life. The Gothic violence of Ruth's taking-off, in other words, matters far less for Cooper's theme than does the consequence, and the real cause, of her departure. Her "devotion" to the forest is less an act of God, as the Puritans think, than a revelation of the Puritans themselves. Their hidden willingness to consign Martha to that fate gives us but the most profound sign of the rigidity with which they draw elaborate borders and boundaries about themselves. Their enclosure is also their exposure; their fate is the fruit of their denials.

We may return here to the aftermath of the battle, for Cooper's description of that grim scene offers hints of the same sort. The attack has come from without in a literal sense, and has moved in toward the garrison, but Cooper's language suggests just the opposite. "In the centre of the desolation" stands the blockhouse; and from "the common centre of destruction" the "radii" of the fences have "led

off the flames into the fields." At the center of the center
rises up the shaft of the well, "naked and unsupported,"
and "looking like a dark monument of the past." This is all
part of Cooper's spatial insistence, his desire to fix the setting
of the tale so firmly in the reader's mind that the placement
of various events is immediately clear. Yet there is meaning
here as well. The rather abstract, even geometric, images in
the passage lead us inevitably back to the emotional heart of
the action, not just to its spatial center. And it is from that
heart, as the confusion over Martha and Ruth suggests, that
the ill has burst outward. The sufferers are not mere victims.

Despite all subsequent "improvements," the ruins at the
center of the landscape endure. They are young Ruth's sign;
in the end she will be buried near them. But she also has left
an inner memorial. Her mother stands now in a perpetual
vigil before the forest, alternately imagining the girl's death—
a pleasing "fancy"—and recognizing the "stern reality" of her
alienation (p. 270). She is emotionally fixed in this "wasting
and delusory" attitude (p. 269), much as she had been frozen
before the dark woods during Content's night ride. But in
this case there is no return. As long as young Ruth remains
outside the walls her mother cannot reenter them herself.
It is the pull of events on her mind that gives the later part of
the novel its own psychological intensity. If the mother
represents the convention of maternal grief, she also represents much more in the thematic design of the book. Though
in an orthodox sense *The Wept of Wish-Ton-Wish* portrays
the progressive possession of the landscape by the whites,
it counters this bright meaning with a disturbing and lasting
dispossession.

Young Ruth comes back, of course, but her return, as I
suggested earlier, is itself tragic. She remains a psychological
captive even to the end, and it is significant that her literal
reentry into the settlement comes during the second, and
at last frustrated, Indian attack. She comes as an enemy,
as Narra-mattah rather than Ruth, and she speaks at first the
language of her captors. Cooper thus brings to bear on the

girl's mother—indeed, on her whole native world—the results of her alienation, and herein clearly lies the climax of the novel's inner action. If for the elder Ruth the forested landscape is always symbolic of her inner world—this is the highest meaning of her various vigils—for the daughter that same landscape has a depth and reality the other Heathcotes cannot fathom. They prefer to think of the girl as a girl still, an icon of innocent suffering, and so she must come back upon them as a woman, wife of an Indian, and mother herself of a child. Such an entanglement of the two worlds is determined in the largest sense by the desire of the settlers to keep the two apart; it also signifies, in one more manner, the vast difference between this novel and *The Pioneers*. There, in the hints about Edwards, we have only the faint foretaste of what *The Wept of Wish-Ton-Wish* makes unalterably real.[18]

That the second attack ultimately fails serves only to make the psychic failure more profound. Cooper gives us, to be sure, an echo of the earlier scene:

> But the dwelling, the out-buildings, and all the implements of
> domestic comfort, which had so lately contributed to the ease of
> the Heathcotes, were completely in possession of the Indians. The
> open shutters and doors, the scattered and half-destroyed furniture,
> the air of devastation and waste, and the general abandonment of
> all interest in the protection of property, proclaimed the licentious
> disorder of a successful assault. (p. 347)

Yet all of this passes like a dream, and the native who lingers among these ruins is no native at all—it is Whittal Ring, a half-witted settler captured during the previous battle, an "innocent" (p. 348) who wanders among the white prisoners alternately remembering his real nature and feeling, as if in an ironic mockery of Conanchet's genuine ambivalence, the wrongs committed by the whites against the Indians. The aftermath of this assault gives us, in fact, the only real talk between red and white, a kind of rough diplomacy across the border that prepares us for young Ruth's eventual recovery and loss. Metacom eloquently arraigns the whites for the wrongs of their race, with an acidic tongue not allowed Chingachgook in *The Pioneers*, but wholly without the evil overtones of Magua in *The Last of the Mohicans*. His, instead, is the voice of dispossession aimed directly at those responsible for it: "Tell me, why is the mind of a Yengeese so big, that it must hold all that lies between the rising and the setting sun? Speak, for we would know the reason why arms so long are found on so little bodies?" (p. 351). Cooper denies the Indians a real victory, but by their loss they purchase a moral right; the forest speaks back here with a power that may be traced finally, I believe, to his own investment in the tale. One has the surface advancement, ideologically correct, and one has as well the emotional blame and emotional ruin. Young Ruth, neither red nor white, is the author's emanation in the story. She gives to his own mixed memories the sort of expression which the real village he later served as "chronicler" could not. She is projected rather than remembered.

Metacom and the other natives serve as her prologue. The "Great Chief" asks her own question more abstractly: "Why have the people of the Yengeese lost themselves on a blind path?" (p. 355), and though Content upholds against native anger the just behavior of his people, echoing in the process the famous speech of Logan (see p. 356), it is the words of Metacom which are more resonant here. Indeed, that Cooper never shows the Heathcotes as conscious dispossessors merely gives to young Ruth's fate a more exuberant and personal accent. Here once more he is pausing over the sources of his own ruin, exaggerating in order to express them.

Narra-mattah is a dialectical creature without synthesis, a psychological embodiment of the debate of *The Pioneers*. Her mother at first seems convinced that the girl cannot be reclaimed—"that her dominion over the mind of her child was sadly weakened, if not lost for ever." Cooper's rendering of the issue in political terms, as a matter of "dominion," is a shrewd sign of the book's final coherence, landscape and mind being interchangeable in imagery as in action. The elder Ruth cannot easily let go, however; soon she starts to sing a nursery song, and as she sings it for the third time her daughter seems awakened again by the "melancholy melody." In the brief silence that follows, the elder Ruth seems to return to "moments of happiness so pure and unalloyed," for the real rebirth here is that of the mother, from whom the cloud of all those "long and sorrowing years" seems lifted. But the silence must end. Young Mark, son and brother, breaks it with a "heavy step" as he enters from without, bringing to his sister a "burden" given him by Conanchet, her husband. Like a similar concealed child earlier in the tale, this one also tests those to whom it is revealed. Young Ruth rushes toward it, leaving her mother surprised, and then comes back to show her "the patient features of an Indian babe." Recognition and rejection lie side by side in what ensues, with a twist of irony for which the author is consciously responsible. Narra-mattah holds the child up "to the riveted gaze of Ruth"—a last vigil—and Ruth bends over to kiss the boy. The echoes of the original loss sound too strongly, however, for the happy end to realize itself. The boy is both in and out of the family, kin and alien at once, and Narra-mattah keenly senses the "cold salute" in Ruth's kiss. Wrapping the child in its blanket, she leaves her mother again and withdraws "in sadness to a distant corner of the room"—a reminder, in the space of the house, of the greater distance she has suffered. There she begins to sing to the boy, surely as a counter to the other melody, "a low Indian song." Content speaks the moral (that the girl lost is not the woman found, nor without a miracle could she be), and his wife quickly accepts what her instincts have made her unknowingly reject. Our memory of the scene with Martha is ominous, nonetheless, for what must follow (pp. 406-8).

Cooper opens his next chapter with another tragic epigraph, an extraordinary one from *Macbeth:*

It will have blood; they say, blood
Will have blood![19]

This points us back to what has just taken place, the attack as well as the following probe of blood ties and their limits, but it also points ahead to what we know must inevitably occur. Content can express the wish all Wish-Ton-Wish may be thought to share:

> The misfortune that early befell my family is not unknown to any in this settlement; thou seest in this trembling creature the daughter of our love—her we have so long mourned. The wept of my household is again with us; our hearts have been oppressed, they are now gladdened. God hath returned our child! (p. 417)

But God's agency in human events is once more to be questioned. Despite Ruth's tardy embrace of her grandson, Narra-mattah cannot return as the mother of confusion but only as an infantile and helpless symbol of loss. She must deny rather than acknowledge all that has transpired.

The next chapter of the book thus goes farther into the forest than any preceding it, into the "pleasing gloom" and the "imposing silence" that reign there, as they reign in a part of Narra-mattah's psyche (p. 423). Cooper consciously inserts here a long description of the scene, ostensibly for the aid of those readers "who have never quitted the older members of the Union" (p. 422), but in fact to set for all his audience the symbolically fitting stage for the end. Submission, who has lived for the intervening years near that scene, in a rude cabin embowered in the woods, now is traveling through the forest with Conanchet. Yet not even the regicide, with his Leatherstocking-like cabin and his Old World wildness, can assume in this American wilderness the kind of mixed heritage that Natty, let alone young Ruth, complexly represents. When Submission and Narra-mattah's husband meet with Metacom in the "pathless forest" (p. 425), the old chief gestures unanswerably toward the English soldier's odd American innocence: for to Submission's bold sermon about the universality of God Metacom calmly replies, "My pale friend hath spoken very wisely.... But he doth not see clearly in these woods; he sits too much in the shade; his eye is better in a clearing" (p. 429). Literal clearings and inner clarity are, for the Europeans, inevitably associated. The regicide, passional symbol that he is, later declares that although he is "of white blood and of Christian origin," his "heart" is almost "Indian" (p. 437); but he in fact is helpless in the Indian domain, so helpless that an Indian almost kills him on the spot when he says this, and only Conanchet, protector of the race that murdered his father, can save him.

And even Conanchet himself will not survive the gathering end. His wife comes to him in the forest then, accompanied by the settlers and carrying the child that signifies the dark twistings of her tale. Yet the dying Conanchet proclaims the boy "a blossom of the clearings" who "will not live in the shade." This, too, is a rejection of sorts, and to Conanchet even Narra-mattah herself is now a "flower of the open land." With his dying words he urges her back where she cannot go: "Let thy mind be like a wide clearing. Let all its shadows be next the woods; let it forget the dream it dreamt among the trees. 'Tis the will of the Manitou" (pp. 459-60). We have here, with a fine lyrical power, the essential design of the book's outer and inner space.

The real dream, however, is Conanchet's dying wish for his wife. "Mother!" Narra-mattah cries out after Ruth suggests that the girl's "inscrutable path" has finally brought her back. But the whole family at this point is, as Ruth also states, "houseless in the woods"—they have been brought out beyond their border less by the plot than the pressure of theme—and the girl is not so much recognizing her origins as forgetting what has removed her from them. "Mother," she repeats, "—why are we in the forest? ... Have any robbed us of our home, that we dwell beneath the trees?" Ruth lets the "illusion" of her daughter build, so that the girl can speak with the voice of a childhood fear that poignantly, though unknowingly, tells her own tale: "It is not safe, thou knowest, mother, to wander far in the woods; the heathen may be out of their towns, and one cannot say what evil chance might happen to the indiscreet." To Ruth this is the "blessedness of infant innocence," the words of "nature." But to author and reader, clearly enough, it is merely the extension of a fatal mistake; it is a "mysterious hallucination," a disturbingly literal return to childhood. Young Ruth has neither the spirit nor the language with which to join her divergent selves, no middle ground between forest and clearing, no place between red and white. She clings "convulsively" once more to her mother's robe, but "the agitated victim of so many conflicting emotions" has no better substance to grasp. She prays as her mother has urged her to, seems to recognize those whites who are around here, and then is beset again with an "evil spirit" just as her eyes fall on the lifeless face of Conanchet, whose body is propped against a tree some feet away. She starts to pray again— against that "spirit," and in the same "low childish voice" as before—and then dies with her eyes fixed on the Indian. Separated in space but inwardly aligned, the two express by their placement and attitude the tense diagrammatics of the book (pp. 468-71).

Cooper drew the novel to a quick end after this long finale. A perfunctory gesture toward the great "changes which have been wrought on this continent" (p. 471) since the seventeenth century points us again to the larger public landscape which has been the point of departure, in the profoundest sense, for the tale. No sacrificial link connects the Heathcote losses with such diffuse gains; indeed, the two seem to offer us only the starkest contrast, two definitions of "change" which lead in precisely opposite directions. The little valley has advanced, measurably but modestly; it seems to rest, like Irving's "Sleepy Hollow," beyond the currents of rapid alteration, "secluded, little known, and...sylvan" as it is (p. 471). Yet the last scene of the book actually is laid in the small family graveyard near those surviving ruins which have been the spatial and thematic center for the past chapters. Such "melancholy remains of former scenes" (p. 473) have nothing of Irving's lighter touch in his Gothic spoof.

The slowly disappearing ruins give Cooper's novel its essential clock, for in them the "progress of... destruction" endured in the first attack continues throughout the long future. The same gloomy sense of time is recorded earlier in the progressively decaying horse of Submission: seen first as a "jaded beast" (p. 36), then as a "half-demolished carcass" in the woods (p. 99), then as a pile of bones "polished by fowls and frost" (p. 148). In the final landscape we find other signs of the apprehension. The "young and thrifty" orchard of 1675—the year of the many deaths—is "now old and decaying," another symbol, full of "deep moral interest," of the "fearful scenes" that took place "beneath [the] shades" (p. 471). The ruins themselves are "much dilapidated and crumbling" (p. 471), while the catalog of tombstones with which the narrative closes "a few years" before the author's present (p. 472) brings us finally to two graves lost in the grass, side by side, where Conanchet and "The Wept of Wish-Ton-Wish"—the inscription provides the last words of the book (p. 474)—were buried apart from the others. Like *The Pioneers*, this novel thus ends on sacred ground, amid the traces of mortality. But here there are no essential survivors to match Elizabeth and Effingham, or to possess the landscape conveyed forward from the past. And in the "new country" of Templeton, of course, even the graves themselves are fresh.

The orthodox American romance as Cooper gave his version of it in *Notions of the Americans* found no room for ruins in the New World, where "in order to keep pace with the progress of things" an "extravagance of anticipation," according to the Count, "becomes absolutely necessary."[20] *The Wept of Wish-Ton-Wish* seems bent on exposing that sanguine lie with a violence and disappointment equally extravagant. But Cooper was pursuing in these pages something more than his own public optimism. Loosed from his oldest memories, though never abandoning them, he found it possible—and necessary—to record in this "forlorn hope" of the early Connecticut frontier the sorrows of his recent, and still lingering, past. He wished he could believe in the fantasy he described even here, a world subservient to self, passive, secure, enclosing. But he recognized the equal forlornness of such a hope. And he did more than recognize the abstract proposition. He created the hope and then relentlessly upset, undercut, overturned, and then at last destroyed it with clinically probing skill. The Gothicism of the novel had a philosophical meaning for him, and the very psychological force with which he developed it under-scores the intensity of his investment in the work. The battle between the inner and the outer, the center and the edges, the family and the others, the self and the world, was most profoundly his. That he sided with the world tells us much, however, about the strength with which he had faced already, and would face again in fact and fancy, the many challenges of that obscure terrain which, like a forest itself, came up to meet his own defenses. *The Pioneers* let him lament as much as solve the problem; this second book let him, as it were, possess the threats and turn them unflinchingly against what at bottom was also part of himself.

5   Settled and Unsettled

Cooper first conceived of *The Wept of Wish-Ton-Wish* in Paris early in 1828, worked on it in Switzerland that summer, and then finished it in the following months at Florence. This was one of the best periods of his European sojourn; he generally admired Paris, was overwhelmed by Swiss scenery, and found both pleasure and real peace in Italy. But his art may have suffered in the flood of delights, or the mere shuffling about of the household. Cooper himself wrote Horatio Greenough in November, 1829, that *The Wept of Wish-Ton-Wish* "was written too much on the highway" to achieve what a more stable environment might have allowed it.[1] His daughter Susan later hinted that even when settled at Florence Cooper composed the work in an oddly tense atmosphere:

> while throwing himself, with his usual zest and animation, into the outward movement of the hour, a portion of every morning was given to his pen; and wide, indeed, was the difference between the living groups among which he moved abroad, the gay, impulsive, laughing, singing, brown-skinned Italians, and the demure, ideal, Puritan band which surrounded him when in his study in the Casa Ricasoli. In all Italy, from the Alps to Mount Etna, the like of these [Puritans] could not be found—never had existed—the soil of Italy could yield no such growth—their virtues and vices belonged alike to a very different zone of the moral world. The two currents, however, remained wholly distinct in the writer's mind; the family of the Wish-ton-Wish were as clearly drawn as if the book had been written in the valley of the Connecticut, rather than on the banks of the Arno.[2]

Had Cooper been at work then on one of his European tales, Susan might not have found the disjunction so great; her comments on *The Bravo*, in fact, stress how her father's fascination with "the outward aspect" of Venice led him to investigate the history of the place, and how that investigation led him to begin his Venetian novel.[3] But in another sense it was not just the obvious difference between where he wrote *The Wept of Wish-Ton-Wish* and what he was writing about in it that Susan was emphasizing. Her language points toward that conflict between the public and the private, Cooper's social life and the life of his imagination, which we have found, in other forms, at the center of his career. When one recalls that his spirits throughout this period were generally high, and that the reaction against *Notions of the Americans* had not yet set in, one is left with the spectacle of an outwardly happy and successful writer, full of "zest and animation," spending hour after hour in his Italian study in the midst of a dark American tragedy. The division of his time and energy in Florence thus offers a diagram of matters far more essential than Susan recognized. He was still lingering in the most crucial of his inner landscapes.

And yet the novel in hand had its own European edges. It was, in a larger sense, another of the writer's many symbolic returns to his native land, each of them caused quite directly by his alienation abroad. Like the two previous books published while Cooper was in Europe, *The Prairie* and *Notions of the Americans,* or *The Water-Witch*, the next one, *The Wept of Wish-Ton-Wish* marked Cooper's desire to keep possession not only of his fame as an American writer but also of the literary and emotional ground on which that fame rested. That all were written, as it were, "on the banks of the Arno" suggests a more conscious inwardness than the sort I pointed to above. Cooper remembered, as he wrote in his French travelogue, the ominous "You will never come back" which greeted his ears as he left New York in 1826; this was a "raven-like prediction" that often recurred to him later, as from the heart of Europe his mind made "its mysterious flight westward across seas and oceans" to his homeland.[4] Each of the American tales he wrote while abroad was conditioned profoundly by where he was. And each, too, was another such "flight." The Arno and the Connecticut were not so "distinct" as Susan claimed.

Nor did the American landscape of *The Wept of Wish-Ton-Wish* come solely from Cooper's inward recollections. James Grossman has noted "that the stark, somber *Wept* was planned in Switzerland, a country unequaled, in Cooper's opinion, 'in the sublimity of desolation.'"[5] The ruinous and desolate American scene of the novel indeed owed much to what Cooper was seeing and doing in Europe as he intermittently wrote it. There are the simple comparisons, wholly typical of his habits as an American abroad, between what he viewed and what he recalled. The journal of his trip from Paris to Switzerland in 1828 thus gestures at one point toward the "hills of New England," while at another it likens an "avenue" cut up a forested mountain to "a deserted American clearing."[6] Though these two remembered images in fact were quite relevant to the book in progress—one suspects that it was from the book rather than his memory that Cooper derived them—Cooper's European journals, letters, and published travel accounts are filled with American images and lore, as well as Old World "notions" of the New World. Like the more abstract social and political comparisons already discussed, such things were another part of Cooper's "mysterious flight" back to his home, his attempt to solidify his national viewpoint while abroad. This habit of weighing Europe and America against each other may account, in part at least, for Cooper's decision to balance the Indian theme in his new tale against the violence of the English Civil War—to see the larger American settlement, in other words, between the world of its origin and the world of its future. But *The Wept of Wish-Ton-Wish* also owed more particular debts to Cooper's European experience. His fascination with what he several times called the "spectral" unreality of the Swiss Alps was probably as important for the book's atmosphere—its sense that the landscape might tantalize eye and mind with something beyond mere perceptions—as was the "desolation" he found in the rocky terrain of Switzerland generally:

"Note the spectral and unearthly appearance of the Alps when seen through broken intervals in the clouds, which resemble glimpses into the interior of another world."[7]

And for a tale so concerned with the "blind path" of the American wilderness, Cooper's experience of getting lost in the Swiss mountains may have provided certain hints: "The guide did not know which way to turn. In front we could not go far, for a Mountain of rock lay there. To the right and to the left, there were apparently steep ascents, through the naked pastures, and the mazes of paths led to both."[8] Perhaps more instructive, though, was Cooper's interest in the ruined towers he encountered in his Swiss ramblings. Here he saw another kind of loss, and one that became more appropriate as he continued to work on the novel. It may be that the radical truncation and recommencement of the tale was a part of his original idea; it may be, too, that we can trace in it the discontinuity of his labors on the book as he moved about from place to place. But if we remember the Count's point in *Notions of the Americans,* certainly fresh in the author's mind at this moment, about "the absence of ancient monuments" in America, the grim new beginning of the narrative seems all the more striking; this is Cooper's way of deliberately "ruining" an American landscape, of giving the new nation some image of its (or his) broken past.[9] The ruins in Connecticut may be traced, I think, to those Cooper was seeing, and responding to with some vigor, in the Old World scene:

> The ruin consists of a tower built in massive stone, and a main building. The form of the whole is an irregular quadrangle, in which the tower is half buried.

> The path from little Rugen led through a thicket of young larches and pines, along the side of the mountain, on which are many meadows, until it comes suddenly into the cleared land above a low, beautiful and nearly semicircular natural meadow. On the other side of this meadow stands the ruins of Uns[punnen?]. They consist of nothing but the dilapidated ruin of a single tower—... The tower appears to have been a keep, being as usual perched upon an isolate

rock some forty or fifty feet high, while the other buildings lay
against its least precipitous side. . . . The solitude at the ruin, into
which I mounted by a window that had been enlarged, was delicious.
The interior of the tower was covered with ivy, and two black birds
were driven from their roost at my presence.[10]

For in the end this novel of the New World frontier does
have a broodingly "European" accent; it takes as its subject
not the hopeful future but rather a sense of decay and loss
and mere history which was as rare in American literature at
the time as it was in the national awareness. But this is not to
say that *The Wept of Wish-Ton-Wish* was the product of a
Europeanized sensibility. What Cooper found in such ruinous
Old World scenes was the symbol of a moral discovery he had
made years before as he sought to come to terms with his
own ruined condition. The real ruins had their place within
him; the outward ones he saw in Europe merely focused his
feelings, and did so as few objects in the American scene had
been able to do.[11] And they led him to imagine for the
center of the landscape in his new American tale a ruined
tower—"a dark monument of the past"—that came to dominate the visual and psychological setting of the book, there
in the valley of the Connecticut.

Cooper's next settlement tale, *Wyandotté*, was written in and
about the author's real home. He had returned to Cooperstown soon after his arrival from Europe, buying the old
house and updating it in a Gothic style that spoke of more
than his Episcopal leanings, and settling in with a tenacity
that probably came from the cost of his many prior wander-
ings. Like *The Deerslayer,* however, *Wyandotté* imagined
Otsego stripped of all its later decorations, Cooperstown and
the Cooper house among them. The actual setting of this tale
is another valley west of Cooper's "Glimmerglass"; yet the
settlers bound for that valley as the book opens in the 1760s
pass down Otsego and camp "on the site of the present village of Cooperstown, but just twenty years anterior to the

commencement of the pretty shire town that now exists on the spot" (p. 38).

That sounds innocuous enough until we recollect what those preceding twenty years had meant for the region. Cooper's preface to the book already should have reminded us. It opens with a terse reference to "the sufferings of isolated families, during the troubled scenes of colonial warfare" (p. v), and in what follows it is the muse of Cherry Valley, not Judge Cooper's *Guide*, which shapes Cooper's approach to his material. The turning of violence against the progress of order on the frontier, the main motive of *Wyandotté*, came to Cooper, of course, from *The Wept of Wish-Ton-Wish*. But the violence in this case has an oddly domestic air even to its more obvious motions. The war here is not the Indian struggle of the earlier book—which, though it has its own domestic sources, comes visibly and relentlessly from an "alien" quarter. It is instead the American Revolution that lets chaos loose against the orderly expansion of American life. Plunging back into the beginning years of Otsego, back before even the trials recounted by his father, Cooper here turns against each other the two primary deeds of national definition. And, as we shall see, he does so with a persistently paradoxical energy. At last he has found in some verifiable and public legend the adequate sign of his own hidden tale. He portrays a nation profoundly divided against itself, self-destructive, blinded, losing what it hopes to gain.

Local paradoxes are rife in *The Wept of Wish-Ton-Wish*, but in *Wyandotté* Cooper makes paradox itself his formal device. We sense this difference between the two even in the worlds evoked by each. If the physical space of the earlier book remains doubtful and distressing throughout, ruled as it is by a constant tension between forest and clearing, that of the later novel is both deceptively open and deceitfully closed. Even social space in *Wyandotté* becomes cluttered as we read on, filled with figures who jostle each other, who must displace someone else in order to find a ground of action: which is, of course, the lesson of any revolt. The principle of hierarchy which is apparently embodied in the physical order of the settlement (for the main settler's house stands on a commanding knoll at the center) is countered by a subversive social reality.

This point emerges most dramatically when *Wyandotté* is compared with *The Pioneers,* for whereas each actor in the village of that work possesses a separate place, those in the present one only seem to. The layering of society in Templeton allows for greater available room, and hence for greater freedom of action—much as the radical split between woods and town keeps violence out of Temple's world. There are tensions caused by that split, and even within the village Remarkable Pettibone can feel that her domain is threatened by Elizabeth's return.[12] Yet Judge Temple remains at least the nominal leader of the settlement, and no threat to his moral sagacity really undercuts his social position. Only at the fringes, again, does the possibility of profound change seem high. People in *The Pioneers* generally have a freedom to act which, in his later books, Cooper generally denies. In *Wyandotté*, character itself becomes a function of events and location; the collapse of hierarchy brought on by the Revolution, and the closing up of physical space under the pressure of history, force upon each other those who otherwise would be held apart. Even the Heathcote valley, for all its stark divisions, is subversively close.

Wyandotté does not allow even to Captain Willoughby, owner of the patent, the freedom which Judge Temple enjoys. Though he is a retired royal army officer, and accustomed to the perquisites of command, Willoughby himself becomes progressively impotent. His relationship with the Tuscarora Nick (who becomes Wyandotté after his sudden and violent reconversion to native ways), centers on just this problem. The uneasiness between the two men reveals flaws in the Captain much more severe than those of Judge Temple: Willoughby is a weak but assertive leader, a man who gives up his circle of just authority by not understanding the true basis of his power. Though his relations with Nick date from their having campaigned together in the French wars, neither man is comfortable with the other. Nick's allegiance to the Captain remains uncertain throughout—not because the Tuscarora is an unreliable "savage," but rather because he finds himself deeply torn between obeying and rejecting a man who is no longer his commander but who pretends that he is. The Captain, however, hardly seems more assured. Nick acts as his guide and his servant, his messenger and his petitioner. Nick actually serves well in these varied roles (he is far more flexible than the Chingachgook of *The Pioneers*), but his obedience always has an edge to it. And the Captain's faults sharpen that edge. When Willoughby blindly tells Nick that he still has the whip with which he has beaten him into submission in the past, he is rubbing the salt of verbal abuse into the wounds of physical humiliation. We know from the first such brutal and insecure reminder that nothing good can come from a relationship so grotesquely warped. And we know, too, that Willoughby's authority, along with the frontier community raised on its assumptions, rests on the weakest kind of power. The men are close but distant at the same time, intimate but out of touch.

In Cooper's view, clearly enough, the Captain's mistreatment of Nick by word and deed is not incidental: it aims us, like a relentless arrow, toward the very center of his character. It tells us, too, something about his personal history. Despite his long and violent experience in America, the Captain remains tragically European in his biases, even if—unlike Corporal McNab in *The Pathfinder*—he has adjusted his social and political ideas while in the New World. He cannot subtly distinguish between human groups, and thus senses nothing of that distinction between red gifts and white gifts which is Bumppo's proof of adaptation, as well as his means of survival. If beating British soldiers will make them obey an officer more promptly, then beating any presumed inferior will induce better respect. This is the Captain's assumption, and it reveals to us the peculiar blindness that afflicts an otherwise intelligent man. But it reveals something else as well. The whip which enacts Willoughby's theory becomes a tenuous symbol (actually, we sense it only as a word) of his even more tenuous authority, and yet unlike Richard Jones's whip this one has done more than make noise. That he accepts this sort of power will help make him vulnerable to its counterstroke later in the book—subject to the fake revolutionaries who besiege his "Hut," subject as well to the vengeance of Nick. When the two men try, outside the palisades of the Hut but inside the valley, to free the Captain's son from the besiegers, the ostensible relation between them still is that of master and servant. But only the walls of the Hut itself have been able to keep this relation intact. Once outside them, the two have entered a world where, in the collapse of an old hierarchy, individuals acquire an insidious equality. Reminding Nick one more time of the whip and its lesson—for Willoughby feels uneasy about the man's "fidelity" (p. 434)—the Captain must suffer the result of his "fatal error" (p. 447). Overcome with rage, Nick stabs the English officer who has been both friend and enemy ("Good man, sometimes; bad man, sometime" [pp. 446–47]); his weapon is the blade that has shone beneath their dealings through the book.

Wyandotté's fierce reconversion gives us the balancing weight to Chingachgook's passive, and spiritual, ascent in *The Pioneers*. But the Tuscarora does not become, thereby, a merely flat native unredeemed by virtue or our own sympathies. Indeed, Cooper makes Nick's desire for revenge quite believable: his motives are clear and specific, and no vague gesture toward "savage" nature can obscure them. It is the man's abused and self-repressed dignity which strikes out in the scene. Cooper formally rejects the deed, of course, but he finds it hard not to sympathize with the motives for it.[13]

Nonetheless, something more than Nick's own springs of action moves him in this scene. Standing side by side in the doubtful landscape of war, he and Willoughby have become equal as they have not been earlier—except as the violent tie between them before has been an admission of their final equality. Nick's deed can occur in such a naked situation as

it never could in the controlled space of *The Pioneers.* But
the power to make it occur is only technically in Nick's own
hands. He murders Captain Willoughby, in other words, as
much because he can as because he wants to. Their isolation
and their strange intimacy both promote the murder, and in
this way the circumstances in which they find themselves
really are the cause of what happens: "Nick had often meditated this treacherous deed, during the thirty years which had
elapsed between his first flogging and the present period; but
circumstances had never placed its execution safely in his
power" (p. 447). And this same strong influence of "circumstances" directs a good deal of what occurs elsewhere in the
novel. A leveling and disintegrating process affects most of
the other relationships in *Wyandotté*, for one thing, and the
process owes its origins to nothing less than the Revolution.
Independence begets disaster, uncertainty, and deceit.

Near the end of *The Pioneers,* as we have seen, Natty
twists his benediction for Elizabeth with a reminder of the
larger justice which finally will right the wrongs of the Indians. In *Wyandotté*, as Nick's swift violence suggests, no such
verbal deference to heaven is necessary or possible. One cannot help wondering whether Cooper's intent in the earlier
book isn't rather scandalous, whether he isn't hinting that the
whites can do anything they care to do here on their earth—
since America has become their special and exclusive circle of
action (Templeton being its image here), within which anything performable, however ill-shaped, is somehow "right."
Among other things, the gesture toward heavenly justice
separates history and the last things. In *Wyandotté*, on the
other hand, Captain Willoughby's unfair deeds, more graphic,
meaner, and yet more superficial, receive a startling earthly
judgment. And the judgment rests not on justice but on an
opposing power that is, if only for the suspended moment of
extremity, greater than his own. This is a world of realpolitik,
not of theological niceties.

Mrs. Willoughby, to be sure, reacts to the news of her
husband's murder by urging the rest of her family, with gro-
tesque irony, to lie down near his body and await the Judg-

ment itself. But the sound which penetrates into the Hut at this instant, and which seems like "the last trump" (p. 491), in fact is a yell of history—for the Indians and whites are launching their attack outside. Biblical prophecy and current fact are cruelly juxtaposed here: history verifies the myth only by mocking it, and the mockery once more suggests how severely every character in the novel is reduced to the same flat universe—how even the longings of the spirit themselves must be leveled to the earth. Having sought in their little valley a retirement from the world (the Captain wants "to pass the close of his life in the tranquil pursuits of agriculture, and in the bosom of his family" [p. 14]), the Willoughbys find instead a world increasingly active and antagonistic. The Captain's body is brought in near the end as a palpable sign of their common ruin.

The Willoughby story thus shows itself alive, like that of the Heathcotes, to the Gothic horrors and ambiguities of the border. Here, too, the outer action has profound inner consequences. Waiting and watching engross the characters, and the delusiveness of what they see and hear gives their vigils a marked spiritual significance; the "last trump" of the battle is, indeed, a proper illusion. The Willoughbys desire to leave history behind them, and to find in the American wilderness not the doubt they discover there but its opposite: clarity and peace, abundance and civil obedience. But Cooper so arranges his tale that this family must confront, recognize, and accept the world to which they in fact have committed themselves. Time has seized control of their timeless retreat.

Cooper's masterful control of his physical scene in *Wyandotté* fixes his characters immovably in the concrete universe of time. The valley here is ominously constricted, a space of some thousand acres from which, after the first few chapters, neither Cooper's own narrative focus nor the main settlers themselves depart. The small world oppresses the reader by its unavoidable presence, and does so despite the orthodoxly hopeful meaning assigned to it by the Willoughbys. Ironically, the hidden valley remains remote, but no longer hidden, as the action proceeds; it boils with activity and intrusion. And those who have thought to control it now become silent before its growing noise. The forest impinges on the clearing, and the art which originally sought to order this landscape now sees itself mimicked by the fraud, deception, and malice enacted in the valley by the artful agents of an otherwise noble revolt. It is precisely right that most of the rebellious actions committed near "Beaver Manor" should be fake as well as ignoble.

We first encounter this dubious landscape through the descriptions of it given by Nick to the Captain. The Indian claims ownership of it not as an Indian but by right of "discovery"—a white strategy that suggests his moral devastation—and offers to sell it to Willoughby. The Englishman, a long life of struggle and violence (and failure—see p. 28) behind him, accepts the offer and plans to move there with his family. But the moment when he first visits the valley hardly is auspicious: it is 1765, late in April, exactly the moment when news of the Stamp Act reached the colonies and caused such broad disgust. Willoughby thus sets forth on his retreat from history just as history is becoming inescapably urgent. And his own initial deeds in the little wilderness tract have their own violent suggestions. The center of the valley is occupied by a serene old beaver lake from which Nick previously has trapped off the animals, leaving the scene stripped of its life. But Willoughby's opening acts hardly counter those of Nick. The beaver dam, which remains like a relic, at first seems of positive value to him, since the waters held back by it surround a high island on which an impregnable fortified home might be built. Beneath the lake, however, lie acres and acres of cleared ground on which a first crop might be quickly planted and as quickly reaped. Willoughby must choose, in effect, between security and ease, between the wary isolation of an island life and the more open but more vulnerable exposure of a sudden change. His decision is, as we might expect, a minor test of character, and once he makes it we see in this man of military experience a blind pastoral streak. He breaks the dam, but less as a gesture of openness toward the surrounding world than a mark of how severely he has failed to understand that world. In a sense, he thinks of himself as living in a universe like that of *The Pioneers,* with its charm and its reservations of space.

His assault on the dam is necessarily violent, but he does not hesitate to begin it. The act is like an opening of history in the forest, pinpointed in time by Cooper as if the exact date will provide later generations with a benchmark: "The first blow was struck against the dam about nine o'clock on the 2d day of May, 1765," Cooper writes, "and, by evening, the little sylvan-looking lake, which had lain embedded in the forest, glittering in the morning sun, unruffled by a breath of air, had entirely disappeared!" (p. 21). This is a magical change, but an ominously ugly one as well; the beginning is also an end, and the force of the paradox will echo through the succeeding chapters. Cooper notes that in place of the lake "there remained an open expanse of wet mud, thickly covered with pools and the remains of beaver-houses, with a small river winding its way slowly through the slime"— a "cheering" sight to the farmer, but "melancholy" in itself (p. 21). The next day Willoughby nearly mourns his deed, and for the month following all the people in his little party feel the depressing influence of the great alteration.

The scene is important, as I have suggested, for its hints about what ultimately will occur in the book—Cooper, it might be said, does to the grand Revolution what the Captain does to the lake, revealing its bleak underside; and the image might be taken as a concise summary of many other revelations in the novel. More immediately, however, the muddy field strewn with debris is a false sign. Across the next two pages Cooper presents a series of scenes in June, August, and October, culminating in a vision of abundant harvest. By the time Mrs. Willoughby comes to the valley the next spring, believing as she does that "a beneficent nature" (p. 30) awaits her, the "magic" she senses (p. 44) seems like the proper result of such a rapid change.

This book defines settlement with a directness not seen in the previous two. "There is a pleasure in diving into a virgin forest and commencing the labors of civilization," Cooper writes while telling of Mrs. Willoughby's arrival, "that has no exact parallel in any other human occupation. That of building, or of laying out grounds, has certainly some resemblance to it, but it is a resemblance so faint and distant as scarcely to liken the enjoyment each produces. The former approaches nearer to the feeling of creating, and is far more pregnant with anticipations and hopes, though its first effects are seldom agreeable, and are sometimes nearly hideous" (pp. 42-43). The Willoughbys seem, this early in the tale, to have garnered the pleasure and missed the pain. Like Elizabeth in *The Pioneers,* the Captain's wife Wilhelmina takes in with an expectancy whetted by absence—or rather total ignorance, for she has not visited the valley before—a world almost too unnervingly "beneficent." In a mere year the place has assumed a startling finish. And in the decade which follows the Captain will treat his wilderness surroundings like a nascent English park, arranging the whole into a large work of art; already at the start he has pushed the necessary but rough brush fences back into the woods until they are out of sight, "so that the visible boundaries of the open land [are] the virgin forest itself" (p. 44)—a sharp but neatly artful balance. It is in such acts that his "creating" consists, and the zest of this older man for such innocent occupations is one of the happier notes in the book. It suggests Cooper's delight at the "Châlet" outside Cooperstown, where in his later years he renewed his own wonder.

Yet Willoughby's acts are profoundly innocent in another sense. He has sold his own commission and secured one for his son Bob, and he shows himself so blind to the gathering colonial unrest that he proclaims to his wife, "we have a peace"—the "we" being the larger American and British world—"that promises to be endless" (p. 25). It is as if, desiring a peaceful end to his active life, he seeks to speak it into existence. His hope for a retreat from history runs that deep; and, as we might expect in Cooper, that hope will prove the man's undoing—for he regards the larger world much as he regards Nick, with a shallow underestimate of its complexity, and at last that world must answer him. In "the eventful summer of 1776" (it is "genial and generous" in the valley itself), Willoughby busies himself, "with a desire to drive away obtrusive thoughts," in his agricultural projects. That the war, confined so far to the coast, has not yet "produced …those scenes of ruthless frontier violence that had distinguished all the previous conflicts of America" perhaps gives Willoughby a basis for his bland pastoralism. Yet the Captain himself has commented on "this peculiarity of the present struggle," and as a veteran he surely knows exactly how "ruthless" the violence of the border could be in the past. Knowing that, and recognizing the current oddity, he nonetheless tells his friend the Reverend Woods that "there is no use…in bothering ourselves about these things, after all"; hence he urges that the hanging of the palisade gates, a task left undone for a full year, be put off again. "It's a heavy job, and the crops will suffer if we take off the hands this week. We are as safe here as we should be in Hyde Park; and safer too; for there housebreakers and footpads abound; whereas, your preaching has left nothing but very vulgar and everyday sinners at the Knoll" (pp. 200-201). That one of those sinners, Joel Strides, will soon lead an insidious campaign against Willoughby ought to suggest how short of the real moral situation in his valley the Captain's wishful estimate falls. And of course it was Strides who, when the palisades were first erected in 1775, "managed to throw so many obstacles in the way of hanging the gates that the duty"—a word Cooper never uses lightly—"was not performed." The apparent "impunity" which has kept the valley free of violence since then has induced a "feeling of security"; rather than being a matter of "serious discussion," the gates have become "a subject of amusement" (p. 202).

The gates finally are hung, but in the midst of a tense insecurity after Strides has launched his assault against Willoughby's large vulnerabilities. And this is not the first such hint of the old soldier's inattention, and hence of his complicity in what destroys his life. The house in which he and his family are to spend their days shows us, even a decade before the Revolution, the same unwary openness. Built of stone and timber, the Hut then presents to the south—the direction from which Strides will orchestrate his mean little war—an utterly blank face, broken only by a large doorway from which, prophetically, the Captain has left the doors unhung. The massive panels rest against the walls of the new house like "indolent sentinels on post, who felt too secure from attack to raise their eyes" (p. 54). And indeed it is all a kind of drowsy blindness, the mind controlling the eye rather than vice versa. "We are hutted for life," Willoughby tells his wife on bringing her to the place then. She immediately recalls to him two close escapes they have endured in the past: "Only attend to the security, Hugh . . . . Twice have we ourselves been near being destroyed by surprises, from which accident, or God's providence, protected us, rather than our own vigilance."[14] Hugh, however, downplays the threat she fears, for he clearly has little desire for "vigilance" any more: "You exaggerate the danger, wife." She nonetheless persists, urging him twice to hang the doors, and at last extracting his promise to do so. But Hugh dilutes the promise by claiming that his "pride" as "an old soldier" is concerned in the question, and by then telling her for a second time that she "may sleep in peace" (pp. 56-57). Thus her warnings and her gestures toward old troubles are really ignored. It is no wonder that the place in which they are "hutted for life" has a "sombre and gaol-like air" (p. 46). The Captain's kind of enclosure is, indeed, self-destructive.

The "blind wall of masonry" (p. 45) which forms the front foundation of the Hut, and runs back on either side to the cliff where "the hutted knoll" ends, is matched by other blind surfaces in the novel. There is, most importantly, the impenetrable wall of language within which, as within their house, the palisade, or even the surrounding artfulness of their neat valley, the Willoughbys seek to hide themselves. At many points in the tale, the family simply refuses to discuss in a suitable way what is happening outside their frail boundaries. The Captain's devious response to Wilhelmina at the outset clues us to this theme. And though much of the settlers' time as the Revolution begins is spent discussing and debating the matter, the wordy formality of the talk suggests how language, even in uttering the unpleasant, in fact dismisses it. The outside troubles can enter only on set occasions, for they are ruled by a decorum which the characters, not the author, impose on the book's dialogue. The chatter may seem like Cooper's mistake, but it is a mark of his real artistry. The Willoughbys talk when they ought to be listening, and they fall silent when what needs saying would disrupt the larger illusion of their life.

The relationship of Maud Willoughby and her "brother" Bob hinges on just this incapacity. Maud is an adopted child who ironically (as we think back to Martha in *The Wept of Wish-Ton-Wish*) has been accepted too intimately into the family. She and Bob clearly have fallen in love. But the potential conflict of their feelings with the forms of the family represents an assault as disruptive in its own positive way as the gathering storm of the war outside. The two have, as a result, no direct means of stating to each other or proclaiming more broadly what at last must be said. When Bob sends a letter home he mixes with his account of political events to the east the hints of his emotional turmoil since leaving the valley—and Maud: "If I had met with a single woman I admired half as much as I do her pretty self, I should have been married long since." His parents, to whom the letter is addressed, take those hints as a conventional hyperbole; in an earlier letter to his son, Hugh has mentioned Maud's reluctance to write Bob, so this response from the young soldier is dismissed as "the badinage of a brother to a sister."

But "sister" Maud takes the letter to her room and goes over its suggestive words again and again. Later, in "the privacy of her chamber" or "her now solitary walks in the woods," it becomes "her constant companion" (pp. 200-201). She has in fact stolen the letter, for she is the only member of the family who can read it aright.

In a more truly open world the real relation between the lovers might be clarified. Maud struggles to impress on the others, and thus on herself, that she is not literally a Willoughby; that she is grounded outside the bounds of the family and thus can enter it with a certain special freedom. The Willoughbys take her reminders, understandably but significantly, in a wrong light. The assertions are proof to them not of her greater intimacy with Bob but of her mystifying alienation from the whole group. Maud struggles, against herself as well as the others, to state her delicate meaning in a fuller form, but language will not work. Since words have served the family to this point as a means of reaffirming old truths—as, in his relation with Nick, they serve the Captain— her rough new insight must find another way out.

The new way, appropriately, is through a language of signs. Again Cooper reveals his distrust of anything but perception in its less codified form—as well as his enduring fascination, beyond his own wordiness, with taciturnity, silence, and gesture. On the tour of her little artist's studio in the Hut, Maud shows Bob a miniature portrait of her natural mother (a secreted picture of Bob himself, as Cooper recognized, would be too direct),[15] and this gesture toward her real history calls forth from Bob a long and indirect, but telling, story. Older than Maud, he knew her actual parents before they died, and his story of them gives her, as an answering sign, the freedom of her emotional realities. By now, he too is aware of the emerging love. Yet before he can openly state his feelings a shout breaks upon them from the yard outside. A false alarm, the yell serves as a reminder of how nearly hostile an eruption of sex within the lines of the family can be. It is no mistake that Maud and Bob watch an earlier abortive attack from a vantage point in the forest outside the walls, or that Maud's new identity emerges from a conflict of loyalties strangely like that which the Revolution unleashes on the valley—and that which Nick suffers. Indeed, the association of Nick with both Bob and Maud offers the book's most profound hints about the deracinating appearances of love: the native murders Hugh just outside Bob's "prison," then later leads Maud—whom he has reminded, when he brings back news of the Captain's death, "he no fader.... Why you care, now, for dis?" (p. 451)—precisely to the spot near that prison where her "fader's" blood had marked the ground. The larger public war and the native's private one both find in the hidden passion of the lovers a strange echo.[16]

And it is Nick who brings to Maud the gesture of Bob's conscious feelings for her. While still captive, young Willoughby gives Nick a snuff box which is latched by a hidden mechanism, and which conceals, as Maud discovers once she has managed to open it, a folded piece of paper. The reader suspects what Maud herself first does: that the paper will display some verbal avowal of Bob's love. But in fact the paper itself is blank. It is simply another enclosure for the real message, a curl of Maud's own hair. The literal meaning of the sign is absolutely clear, yet Bob's avoidance of language has a meaning too. Like everyone else in the valley, he has been lost in a soundless universe: "All in that direction lay buried in silence, as if the ravine had swallowed its tenants, in imitation of the grave" (p. 317). And Bob has a special silence about him. The forbidden passion must find its own arcane language.

Yet *Wyandotté* remains, within its own definitions, a highly verbal book. The first response of the Willoughbys to rumors of the Revolution is, in fact, a "war of words" (p. 96). The Captain and his friend Woods, a New Englander, seem to take the rumors as more fuel for the library fire, for they share a customary relish for debate. The minister, true to his origins, comes off at the start as a supporter of colonial rights against English authority. Likewise, Willoughby begins by assuming a straightforwardly English position. But each man is so persuasive, and yet so uncertain, that by the next morning the two have switched camps: the retired royal officer now favors the colonials, while the Yankee has become a king's man through and through. Here again the problem of conflicting loyalties arises. And we also sense that, in the web of words, the realities closing in on America—and the Willoughby patent—have been overlooked. It is as if the two men regard history as something utterly malleable under the force of argument.

Debating carries on in the book even after these superficial conversions. But it gradually becomes a means of ignoring, not just reshaping, events. A grammar of action, dire and yet ambiguous, replaces the grammar of words—as surely as, in the love-plot, gesture replaces affirmation. In a world capable of more subtle statement, Captain Willoughby might become an actual revolutionary. Though his loyalties lie with the king, his experience in America has given a democratic cast to his character. He thus scorns Bob's news about the baronetcy which has fallen to Hugh from his English cousin: "what is an empty baronetcy to a happy husband and father like me, here in the wilds of America?" (p. 74). And he seems ripe for a further "American" development; given more room for maneuvering, he well might accept an American commission, and it is in this direction that Cooper seems ready to push him. Unlike that of the Whartons in *The Spy*, his own neutrality is honestly doubtful.

The peculiar world in which Willoughby lives will not allow his political development, however. The quick pace of change in the valley wrongfully elevates him into a symbol of royal oppression, and his Hut soon expresses for the pseudo-patriots drawn up below it at the mill everything on which, with a chill orthodoxy, they pretend to cast their enlightened scorn. Once this polarization of space has occurred, mere words can have no effective use. The library where the Captain and the Reverend Woods have debated no longer is an acceptable scene for action—as "little Woods" himself recognizes when, on an apparently mad impulse, he sets out for the "great woods" in the hope that he can quell the uprising (p. 313). Willoughby later mourns for "Poor

Woods!" (p. 332), but in fact the minister will survive, perhaps because he has exposed himself; the weird end which defeats Willoughby and much of his family leaves the minister intact. It is Woods's apparent madness, ironically, which makes the Indians respect him. He endures by risking his life.

It is the coming of the news of "independence" in chapter 13 that gives an almost vitrified permanence to the tense spatial design of *Wyandotté*. Those who have taken refuge in either end of the valley now make presumptions about the stance of their opposite numbers—some of the presumptions being right and some wrong, but all of them based finally on the polar divisions of space. Location thus has replaced speech as a means of declaration. We see the subtle consequences of this change most forcefully in those characters who still can move between the opposing ends. Nick can do so, for instance, because he is permanently torn between his allegiances. The scheming Joel Strides, on the other hand, can enter the Hut without raising suspicion because, although he is a moral inhabitant of the mill, he continues to assert his loyalty to the Captain. When Willoughby and his disguised son go out into the neutral ground one night to reconnoiter, they chance upon Strides there; no explanation he can offer really counters the simple fact that he is where he ought not be—his physical stance, that is, speaks more loudly than his words. And it is in this direction that the novel as a whole moves.

We thus note that the "lawn" where the Willoughbys have had their teas before the Revolution no longer can serve as the passive scene of polite action or verbal nuance. Tea in any event, as the oblivious family might have recognized, is a proscribed commodity. But the retreat of English ritual in the face of American fact has other meanings. The lawn is the prime symbol of the Captain's landscape fantasies, and his loss of this free space signifies the worsening constraints of history. With a clear sense of social fictions traceable to his European sojourn—and perhaps beyond it to the vanished fiction of his own gentlemanly youth—Cooper presents the ceremonial indulgence of the family as a kind of drifting reverie broken by the first news of unrest, news brought into the valley by none other than Nick. That the native announces the approach of young Bob brings the news closer to the family; and that Bob's own entrance into the book is introduced by a description of the darkening forest gives us, as a logical portent, the first glimpse of the spatial diagram of the novel. This occurs as early as the fifth chapter.[17]

Once the siege of the Hut begins, the Willoughbys have lost their control of anything beyond their inner walls, and the walls themselves at last prove unnervingly penetrable. The evening after Bob's second arrival, in the thirteenth chapter, can be spent in renewed debates (it is Bob who brings word of the Declaration), but from this point on talking gives way to watching, listening, puzzling over the world that lies outside. And it is a world full of disguise and pretense, false clues, contrivance, and disregarded warnings. Its events, furthermore, seem as crabbed and deceitful as its sights and sounds. The signal event in the plot thus never really occurs, and the painful delay of its nonoccurrence in fact is the heart of the matter. That the Willoughbys wait so long for something to happen, only to see it end so quickly—and yet, with a further twist, so tragically—gives to the sense of history in the book a sharp capriciousness. One is forced to wonder whether prudently hung gates and a guarded tongue really could prevail against the syncopated threats gathered up around the settlement. One notes, too, that the reader confronts a similar challenge. The shabby unreality of the military danger leaves one unprepared for what at last happens; where the first casualty is literally a stick figure—"nothing but a stuffed soldier!" (p. 380)—the mortality of the end seems to come from another world and another literary universe.

Some of the syncopation derived, I think, from Cooper's struggle to break the dreamy hold which space had exercised over his imagination through so much of the tale: for if "space appears annihilated" (p. 378) once a real shot is fired toward the Hut from the forces at the mill, during long stretches of the narrative the two places seem almost to push each other apart. And the two opposing parties thus spend much of their time during the loose siege watching the opposite end of the valley—watching or alternately putting on a sort of dumb show for their opponents. When Captain Willoughby climbs up to the "stage" in chapter 22, he examines the lower end of the valley with his telescope, and sees a mockingly peaceful sight: the householders who have deserted from the garrison now seem to have repossessed their dwellings, and Willoughby is "so absorbed" by their pursuit of ordinary ends—they are milking cows, feeding swine, and preparing for breakfast—that he spends a full hour gazing at them. He suspects some "deep plan" in the pastoral picture, to be sure, and he knows that his son remains a prisoner near the mill, but the teasing normality of the landscape gives him, after all, precisely the vision he would wish to have; that the deserters left the Hut only the night before adds to the teasing deception (pp. 387-88). Though it remains true, as I stated earlier, that location and allegiance are linked facts in the later chapters of the book, the very sorting out of the characters into camps keeps them apart, and thus forestalls the catastrophe. Cooper gives space a political meaning of subtle power, but in doing so he subordinates plot to setting.

We may understand this tense poise of events across the setting, from the first faltering assault in chapter 11 (the one Bob and Maud watch from the woods) up to the sudden violence of the end, as a sign of Cooper's reluctance to ruin this landscape as he had ruined that of *The Wept of Wish-Ton-Wish*. A similar reluctance, as we shall see, also is present in *The Crater*, while even in the Heathcote tale the renewal of the settlement restores much of what has been lost. It seems clear that in all three of these later books Cooper's imagination found in space—as it had in *The Pioneers* at the start—a pleasing antidote to the sickening losses time had given him. Space was what he had been forced to give up; and space was what he could, through his art, seek to recover.

The faltering narrative pace of *Wyandotté* speaks of the extent to which Cooper indeed sought to do just that. When Captain Willoughby's last journey from the Hut gives him a lingering glimpse back at the place, a glimpse from which he feels a "reluctance to tear himself away," we catch something of the author's own hesitations. But it is also the author who has Nick climb up the face of the little cliff where Willoughby is resting at this dreamy moment—climb up and suddenly insert his own disturbing visage between the Captain and what the Captain wants to see. The "eloquent calm" of this other pastoral survey thus is broken by the "swarthy face, and two glowing eyes" that intercede; yet at the same time, as Cooper notes, it is only Willoughby's abstracted inwardness that makes him draw his knife against the native. If other deserters have their "plans," Nick decidedly does not; when he turns to the party of whites and asks them, "Why come here? Like to see enemy between you and wigwam?" he is describing exactly what has just taken place, and yet he is doing so in perfect innocence. It is Cooper himself who has made this future "enemy" suddenly enter the Captain's drifting reverie, placing between the eye and its proper space what we can only describe as a fierce emblem of time (pp. 428–30).

This is another rebuke of Willoughby, as indeed his very murder will be. We cannot lay everything on Willoughby, though, for the real deserters whose peaceful show he views clearly share the blame. With few exceptions, they are a nameless and faceless mass who use history rather than make it or give themselves to it, and they cannot find even in Joel Strides, their angular leader, any real power. For his own part, Joel without the mass behind him would have as little control over events as Willoughby does; he is not so much the victim of circumstances as their manipulator, and without the lucky chance of disorder he would have no means of action.

Which is to say that Cooper also delayed the Revolution in *Wyandotté* because, aside from all that I have said, the world of the book is incapable of high purpose: the "stuffed soldier" is nothing less than a symbol of the emptiness of all events here. The "rebels" wilfully misperceive Willoughby's difficult political position, but they also undervalue their own moral nature; they nowhere sense, as Cooper had urged the nation to sense in *The American Democrat* and elsewhere, that the national hope lay in the profound realization of independence as a trait of character rather than a slogan or a figment of memory. What such a trait might require Cooper himself demonstrated by his own tenacious, even crabbed, voice in the decade following his homecoming: balancing "They Say" against the fearless and tireless declarations of his personality as a man and an author. *Wyandotté* contributed to the larger debate by projecting backwards the exact kind of revolution which Cooper could see in the 1840s as the properly ignoble source of the present country.[18] If Willoughby began history in his lands by breaking the peace of an older pastoral moment—hence the significance of Cooper's dating of his assault against the beaver dam—those who later stole history from him knew no more of what they were about.

Even from the start of his career Cooper had certain doubts about the American war. But to attack such a symbol of national piety too directly in the 1820s would have been difficult. Hence Harvey Birch and "Harper" anchor the action of *The Spy* in the rock of national faith. We trust these two implicitly, and it is from them that the war as a series of gruesome events derives its moral order and justness. Even here, however, the sense of disguise, deceit, and ambiguity enriches an otherwise orthodox conception. Patriotism has large costs; public rhetoric masks selfish ends; and history seen on the close plane of battle has a raging, chaotic force. One can speculate, as a result, that Cooper's conscious thematic intent even in his first American tale was at odds with his felt response to the subject; that the complexity of historical action as he imagined it in *The Spy* came not from his orthodox assumptions but from his hidden apprehension of reality. Indeed, if we read Birch's character with care, we will perceive that his real attraction comes from his ability to survive history rather than from his immovable principles. It is his quick eye and nimble body that give him literary life, much as they preserve his actual existence in the landscape of the book. Birch the patriot and Birch the actor share a common name; but the two are disjunctive more than coherent—a symbol and an actuality.

Cooper's two following tales of the Revolution, *The Pilot* and *Lionel Lincoln,* have the same apparent assurance about the essential issues at stake in the war. Here, too, the orthodox view gives particular events a firm anchor. Yet here, too, and with increasing urgency, the disjunction seen in Birch gives us a public scheme—bright, progressive, and unambiguous— that does not jibe with the imagined details of the plots. When the patriot raiders in *The Pilot,* for example, cannot find the British hostages they have intended to capture, they divert their noble sortie toward questionable ends. If the two young American women they now seek to free from English captivity may be taken as symbols of the nation's fate, the women remain symbols of love as well. Hence the public business is given up in a pursuit of private hope, and the selfless struggle becomes in effect an episode of selfish romantic gain. Selfishness in *The Spy,* we recall, is largely confined to the Whartons, the Cowboys, and the Refugees; the theme is introduced most fully, however, in the first description of Birch. And what is a shrewdly false clue in *The Spy* is a central problem in *The Pilot.* Birch's selfishness is a matter of personal survival in the service of public ideals. As James Grossman writes of *The Pilot,* on the other hand, the Revolution seems to verge in this book on the siege of Troy.[19]

The metamorphosis marks the failures of the characters, however, rather than those of the author. He gives them the rope, and they make the incriminating knot. In *Lionel Lincoln* matters become more complex. Cooper wrote this novel just as the country was preparing for the fiftieth anniversary of Bunker Hill. And it thus offers Cooper's most disaffecting portrayal of British wrongs against America. But it shows the firmest patriot in the tale to be an insane fanatic for whom the cause of liberty is a perverse metaphor for his private past: he once escaped from an English asylum for the mad, and he desperately intends to keep his freedom by freeing the colonies from English power. In this case the synecdoche of *The Pilot*—the women there taken in their "American" guise—has assumed a brutally literal and ironic force. Cooper still clings to the orthodox view, counterpointing the disorder visited on Boston by the British army to the inherent orderliness of the Americans. And he creates as his hero a rough opposite of Captain Willoughby—a young American who has lived in England long enough to become a British officer, but whose actual return to America (here the parallel with Willoughby breaks down) moves him toward the colonial cause. Yet Lionel Lincoln proves to be mad Ralph's son, and at last he bolts from his changing sense of loyalties as from America itself. He sails back to England and resumes his old position there.

Though we do not know exactly what causes Lincoln's flight, he surely is fleeing from the moral and mental disorder of his family as much as from the war. Cooper links the two, nonetheless, so that the retreat casts back upon the Revolution some of the Gothic light which glares forth from the house of Lincoln. It is Lionel's observation of the battles around Boston, in fact, that provides the first sustained Gothic episodes in the tale, aside from the grim beating of the witless Job Pray (Lionel's half-brother) by the British. What Cooper treats in his narrative with a lofty omniscience becomes from Lionel's viewpoint a harrowing confusion of sights, events, and feelings. When he returns from his vigil in Copp's Hill cemetery one night—the place now holds an English battery, gruesomely enough—he thus dreams a deathly nightmare in which history assumes the sort of spectral force it will have, more literally, in *The Last of the Mohicans* and *The Wept of Wish-Ton-Wish*. The nightmare reminds us that the daylight world of the Revolution (and a daylight world it generally was to Americans in the 1820s) may mask, as do the intensely logical arguments of mad Ralph regarding independence, a deeply discordant interior. Mouthing the accustomed pieties of American faith himself, Cooper contrasts them to the felt derangements of his displaced, beleaguered, and confused hero. If we believe, as John P. McWilliams suggests we should, that Cooper seems to have set Lincoln up for a tidy conversion to the patriot side, only to abandon that intention at the last moment,[20] we are surely mistaking the book. Lincoln sees history rather than ideology; his failure to embrace the colonial cause is the only result that could come about from what he is allowed to perceive. Perhaps the most we can say on the matter of the hinted conversion and the executed flight is that Cooper was showing thereby his own complex imagination.

When he returned to the Revolution once more in *Wyandotté*, almost twenty years had intervened, and the period in its later reaches had been full of disillusionment for Cooper himself. Thus he understandably detached from this book the sort of pious framework which gave even to *Lionel Lincoln* the appearance of orthodox celebration. *The American Democrat*, as I already have suggested, had fixed his opinions in their final form, and he was content to speak far more directly in the years following than he had before. His career as an American author now had taken on the ironic shape which his private life had displayed in the decade before *The Pioneers:* there was the same hopeful but blighted expansion, the same sense of arrival and loss, the same eminence later undercut by circumstance. Cooper's first response to the reversal of the 1830s was a promise of silence in *A Letter to His Countrymen* (1834). But he could not abide the promise or abide by it, as *The Monikins*, the "Home" novels, and at last the flurry of the 1840s were to demonstrate. *Wyandotté* was important in his renewed career because it came immediately after *The Pathfinder* and *The Deerslayer*, in which Cooper seemed to have abandoned his harsh critical muse in favor of the older "romantic" one—it came after these books

and the movement they suggested, and yet it marked the first
full integration of Cooper's critical sense with his imagination.
The result was an enstrictured vision of the American past in
which the orthodox apothegms of Cooper's earlier period are
present, if at all, as ironic miscues. The novel is rooted in
paradox, as I noted above: it presents advance as retreat,
retirement as commitment, independence as moral chaos,
patriotism as an officious badge pinned to the garments of
selfishness. Irony is the theme as well as the method of the
book.

It thus is appropriate that our first extensive news of the
war here comes through Nick—aside from *The Last of the
Mohicans,* and with a large difference, this is the only Cooper
novel named for an Indian character—and the tale Nick brings
near the opening is, in its very form and accent, a signal of
what will follow. His vividly curt account of Bunker Hill,
an engagement Cooper rendered magnificently in *Lionel
Lincoln,* reduces to absurdity the supposed glories of national
violence. Nick has demonstrated in his earlier exchange with
Willoughby over the beaver lake, as we saw above, his moral
and stylistic devastation: the Captain then asks Nick how he
can presume to own any given place in the wide wilderness,
and Nick responds, "How a pale face come to own America?
Discover him—ha! Well, Nick discover land down yonder, up
dere, over here" (p. 16). In the case of Bunker Hill, Nick's
language reveals his own ignorance, as we may be tempted to
put it, of the issues supposedly at stake in Boston. Yet his
satire here, as in the previous case, has an intentional bite.
Like a knowing "Persian" observer, the native recounts by
means of his skewed style exactly what did happen at Bunker
Hill—or exactly how that event must reach the world of this
book. He gives a vision of history which accords perfectly
with the tone of Cooper's own narrative. "Nick dere—hot
time—a t'ousand scalp—coat red as blood.... Yankee on hill;
reg'lar in canoe. Hundred, t'ousand, fifty canoe—full of red-
coat. Great chief, dere!—ten—six—two—all go togeder. Come

ashore—parade, pale-face manner—march—booh—booh—dem
cannon; pop, pop—dem gun. Wah! how he run!" (p. 188).

Before we take this little piece of histrionic reportage as an
unintentional self-parody on Nick's part, we must notice how
similar to Cooper's own deflationary practice in *Wyandotté*
Nick's Bunker Hill oration is. The Revolution throughout the
novel is as drained of glorious meanings as the Boston battle
is once Nick has done with it—or as the real events in *Lionel
Lincoln* are once Lionel himself has dreamed of them. By
exaggerating the mere spectacle of the war, Nick's jocular
satire sets the outer limits of Cooper's treatment of events in
the valley; Cooper never pushes so far himself, but his manip-
ulation of the narrative leaves little dignity and no serious
question of allegiance attached to the history here enacted.
The debates of Willoughby and the Reverend Woods serve to
remind us of the eloquent speech which the actual Revolution called into being. But the debates are literally out of
place in the book. They are also out of time. The war in
Wyandotté is really that of Cooper himself with his own
nation. And where was eloquence, as Cooper himself asked,
in the Whig press?

Detached from its real setting, the Revolution becomes in
Wyandotté an occasion for power plays, fraud, and self-
promotion. Weak as Strides is, he manages to turn the rumors
of American unrest into a source of potential advancement.
Were the issues more fiercely framed than this world will
allow them to be, such a theft of the public business would
not be possible. But *Wyandotté* has no Birch or "Harper,"
and the book thus must drift without an ideological anchor.
Those who can define the public vocabulary in such a world,
as the author of *The American Democrat* poignantly realized,
also can define the agenda of events. When Joel discusses
with the miller the rosy prospects of a war in which they
may "serve" as suppliers to the patriot army, it is the miller
who raises the idea that "a committee of safety, or something
of that natur'," certainly will have to take control of the

Willoughby patent. But it is Joel who translates the miller's sentiment into the language of the book:

> "A committee of safety will be the thing!"
>
> "What is a committee of safety, Joel?" demanded the miller, who had made far less progress in the arts of the demagogue than his friend, and who, in fact, had much less native fitness for the vocation; "I have heer'n tell of them regulations, but do not rightly understand 'em, a'ter all."
>
> "You know what a committee is?" asked Joel, glancing inquiringly at his friend.
>
> "I s'pose I do—it means men's takin' on themselves the trouble and care of public business."
>
> "That's it—now a committee of safety means a few of us, for instance, having the charge of the affairs of this settlement, in order to see that no harm shall come to anything, especially to the people." (pp. 150-51)

Here is the very basis of Joel's thin power. The miller's definition of a "committee" actually is a lofty one which Cooper himself might have endorsed. Joel takes it, however, as a gauge of the man's innocence. Since he seeks quite literally to "secure" Willoughby's patent, he realizes—his "inquiring glance" and his swift "That's it" tell us as much—that he can do so best of all by taking "charge" of affairs. A committee of safety will make his own sly thefts safe. The "people" are Strides.

In Emerson's phrase, Joel skates well on the surface of things. Yet for all his obvious deceit and his final weakness he represents for Cooper a kind of threat both strikingly modern and uncomfortably artful. Like the demagogues Cooper saw all around him in the 1830s and 1840s, Strides has a verbal skill akin to the novelist's: a talent for constituting things by naming or renaming them (or talking them into existence), and thus a knack for shaping reality according to his desires. Perhaps as a defense, Cooper's view of language in *The American Democrat* is persistently positivistic. Words derive from and refer to things; and of the opposite idea the book entertains, especially in political connections, only the most skeptical and reserved opinion.[21] Cooper thus links the demagogue to the "American *doctrinaire*," who is sentimentally attached to the Old World, and thus clings to "opinions that are purely the issue of arbitrary facts, ages after the facts themselves have ceased to exist." The demagogue is, of course, a scheming timeserver rather than a sentimentalist; yet in allowing present passions "so far to blind his faculties" that they "exclude the sight of positive things," he becomes the companion of the doctrinaire. They are linked as well by their verbal style. Much as the "extreme theoretical democrat" (a term for the demagogue) deals "in cant," the doctrinaire "deals in poetry." The wordstock of each is a corrupt and corrupting argot sorely out of touch with American facts, yet seductively attuned to national fictions.[22]

One of Cooper's checks on his own fictionalizing imagination was his continuing gesture toward history as a body of facts and an idea. He became a historical romancer rather than the mannerist-moralist he tried to be in *Precaution* because he needed the kind of limits which history, even when embellished, could give him. The decision, probably far from conscious, was a wise one nonetheless. Yet he was no slave of facts. *Wyandotté* shows in the boldness of its redefinitions exactly how far Cooper could go in shaping his material to meet his inner needs. In *Lionel Lincoln* he had demonstrated that he could copy, if he wanted to, the exact details of American history—much as he suggested that his political fantasy of *The American Democrat* ought to be called "Anti-Cant."[23] *The Pioneers* proved the same point, though less massively, while Cooper's novel of Columbus, *Mercedes of Castile*, failed because the author, constrained by his study of the "sources," could not free his imagination. *Wyandotté* labored under no such constraints. Cooper's view of the current nation required a revised rather than an embroidered record. He gave the worst words to Nick, and the worst deeds to Nick and Joel together; but for word and deed—and the characters themselves—Cooper was clearly responsible. In his third tale of settlement his own private apprehension of history was, at last, the unremitting guide. Mocking the settler and debasing the patriot, Cooper turned them loose against each other. He allowed them just enough power to leave behind as a legacy (a legacy conveyed by Cooper's novel to his own age) an abandoned and ruined landscape. For in *Wyandotté* the whole valley, not just a part of it (as in *The Pioneers* and *The Wept of Wish-Ton-Wish*), has become a graveyard. When Bob and Maud return to it after their long exile in England, they discover that "some reckless wanderer" (pp. 515–16) has torched the mill and the buildings near it—without any other motive, Cooper suggests, than the fact that he had it in his power to do so. The Hut has survived a similar fate because, now empty, it has proved ironically impregnable. There is no Phoenix here. Nick, Michael O'Hearn, and the Reverend Woods still can linger about the "melancholy scene" (p. 522), and the last two can renovate the Hut itself in later days. But Bob and Maud have come to mourn (and to forgive Nick, as it turns out), rather than to repossess what has been lost. It is the owner in this novel—not the squatter, as in *The Pioneers*—who must leave in the end. Even the battered landscape in the Heathcote tale at last endures and grows; the one here, however, remains fixed in time, frozen as a reminder of the power of history. In its devastations, its resistance to any real new beginning, and yet its hermetic endurance against change—inside the Hut, everything seems unnaturally the same as it was years before—the border settlement suggests Cooper's own tough legacy: the outward losses, the recognition, and yet the memory.

"One of the misfortunes of a nation," Cooper announced in his preface to *Wyandotté*, "is to hear little besides its own praises" (p. v). The barbed aphorism, paradoxical like the novel itself, marks how far Cooper had removed himself, by 1843, from the eulogies he had perpetrated in 1828. Further foreign slanders of the kind *Notions of the Americans* had fought still were appearing—Dickens's *American Notes* had been published the year before *Wyandotté*, and *Martin Chuzzlewit* was just beginning to appear in 1843—but by now Cooper took less interest in national defense than in internal improvements. As an American, he could speak to the country with a homebred severity which, to him at least, was clearly distinct from that of the foreign observers; and it was his desire to do just that, channeled as most of his conscious purposes were through his imaginative capacity, which led Cooper to envision the tragic incompletion of the Willoughby tale. Here the "misfortunes" of a border experiment, though they touched the author's own spirit, had an announced public intent.

Cooper's preface to the novel went on to praise the American Revolution, to be sure, calling it "probably as just an effort as was ever made by a people to resist the first inroads of oppression." Yet this orthodox comment is fulfilled in the novel only by the series of inversions we have already examined: it provides, that is, the consensus view which the tale undeviatingly parodies. And even the preface calls attention to the "evil aspects" of the great war, as well as the unfortunate American tendency to worship the past rather than understand it. "We have been so much accustomed," it states, "to hear everything extolled, of late years, that could be dragged into the remotest connection with that great event, and the principles which led to it, that there is danger of overlooking truth, in a pseudo-patriotism" (p. v). Disgusted by the dull pieties of current American memory—for what could they make of the past but a dead image?—Cooper sought to revive history by affronting the present. In doing so, he was guided by that sense of reality which made him see anything outside the self—or, more specifically here, the nation's image of itself—as something more than a sign of self-satisfaction. Here again his own tale might instruct the public; and it was the "truth" of his own past, indeed, on which the lesson of *Wyandotté* was grounded.

That Cooper's main source for the novel lay in the memoirs of a loyalist, Anne MacVicar Grant, suggests how severe his alienation had become. Had they known the fact, his American critics would have seen it as further proof of his European leanings. But Cooper did not make *Wyandotté* merely a minority report on the American war, which is what Grant's book amounts to in this regard. Nor did he import from it that tidiness of a safe retreat which Grant accorded her family: Grant's father ran off from his own beaver meadow, and back to Britain, once the skulking "patriots" sniffed out his premises.[1] Captain Willoughby does not possess this means of escape, committed as he is to his American land, and even if he did he probably would not use it. Even Maud and Bob, who do possess and do use it, must come home in the end: and they come home, as we have seen, to a landscape fixed in the uncorrectable difficulties of time. That the two find themselves received in the supposedly new republic with a fawning admiration for Bob's new status as a British general and a baronet—for he, American-born, has inherited and accepted the title scorned by his English father—makes the homecoming a further satire on the homeland's failings.[2] In following Grant here, as he would follow her in *Satanstoe*, Cooper rejected her biases as much as he rejected the sanctimonious truth-telling of the nation. His attack on current

American assumptions in fact was a way of praising American ideals.

His own stance in *Wyandotté* was not so much political as prophetic. He aimed history into the future as much as he sent the present distortingly into the past, and so he reported to the country what he thought it did not want to accept. We hear the echo of his position in the words of Michael O'Hearn, the Irish immigrant in *Wyandotté* who does not want to announce Captain Willoughby's death by merely bringing the corpse into the Hut: surely, he says to his companions, they can find some means to "clear the way a little for the arrival of truth, in the form o' death itsal'" (p. 444). Thus Nick, of all people, is dispatched to take in the news beforehand. Yet O'Hearn recognizes that the body itself will have to enter the bastion, that "the severity of an unlooked-for sairtainty" (p. 444), as he puts it, must upset the inner and inward place. Speaking in his own voice five years earlier, Cooper had declared in *The American Democrat* that falsehood was becoming an American habit, especially in public affairs, but that "the severity of truth" could not and would not be avoided by the Republic: "in nothing," he then added, "is the sublime admonition of God in his commandments, where he tells us that he 'will visit the sins of the fathers unto the third and fourth generations of their children,' more impressively verified, than in the inevitable punishments that await every sacrifice of truth."[3] If, as the *Wyandotté* preface asserted, America was prone to overlooking the truth in its self-congratulations, then Cooper had to bear into the house of national memory, page by relentless page, the unwelcome facts of his historical vision in the novel. What he destroyed in the process was not destroyed with the recklessness of that wandering arsonist who leveled the buildings at Beaver Manor. Cooper's violence against the pieties of the nation aimed instead at a kind of renewal toward which *Wyandotté*, though unable to enact it, still could point. The misfortunes unflinchingly imagined here were not Cooper's final word on the irreversible loss of the new republic's ideals; they were instead his attempt to forestall "the arrival of truth," to awaken the country to its peril. In this sense, the novel affirmed American ideals by attacking those who were abandoning them.

This was the conscious intent of the book. Its material, of course, dated from *The Pioneers* and *The Wept of Wish-Ton-Wish,* and derived ultimately from the inward struggles of Cooper himself. That *Wyandotté* was meant to work on its audience in other than literary terms, however, suggests how Cooper's art as well as his ideas had changed since the first decade of his career. Like the Littlepage trilogy, which sought to bring the preceding hundred years of American life to bear on the issues of the 1840s, *Wyandotté* shaped its action according to Cooper's present political self; it employed his old emotional paradigms and assumptions in the service of his public being. Both of his earlier settlement novels had their internal doubts, and both of them surely aimed a part of their hesitation out toward their audience. Neither of them had, though, the correlative for their melancholy mood which Cooper later found in the sad fate of the nation. Each of them was an indulgence of the author's needs rather than an argument; when Cooper came to view the nation itself as a kind of failed settlement, he was able to tell his own tale— for such it remained, profoundly, to the end—as a confirmation of American experience rather than an exception to the bright progress he had dreamed in 1828. Then, he had pretended to speak with a merely public voice; now, recovering his oldest doubts and the form in which he had expressed them in the 1820s, he came before the public as a decidedly separate figure, speaking to it instead of for it, and telling it what it had to hear.

In his last settlement tale, *The Crater,* Cooper used the theme with even more directness. The Willoughby experiment could be misread, by those seeking to misread it, as simply an episode from the past; its enactment of the patterns of American history is tied to a specific site, a given time, and a set of characters in whom, even with Joel Strides present

as a demagogue sent back from the 1840s,[4] it is possible
to find simply a local, realistic cast. The author tries to make
all of this exemplary, representative, and symbolic. Yet he
still cannot dispense with the habits of invention that he had
developed in the past two decades. Despite the larger and
pointed tale he wants to deliver to his readers, he cannot yet
give up the tale of the book itself. To the extent that the two
exist separately—the first in the preface, and only by implication in the text, and the second merely in the text—the
work falls apart. Cooper the prophet and Cooper the romancer remain unintegrated.

The Littlepage series allowed the two to merge more happily
because Cooper gave the tale-telling to a trio of characters,
and cast himself as their "editor." He had used the first-
person form as early as 1828, had picked it up again for his
travel books a decade later, and then had discovered its
fictional possibilities as he remet his old shipmate Ned Myers,
listened to the man's story, and served as its public stenog-
rapher. In his own pamphlets and letters to the press in the
thirties, too, Cooper had spoken in propria persona: he
became then, and in at least two senses, a "character." About
this important pattern in his art, a book in itself might be
written. At present, we need to note only that Cooper's
turn toward a limited narrator coincided with his own growing sense of limitation within the public at large. In particular,
the change in technique allowed him to delegate the plot of
his works to someone else; this freed his own voice for other
uses at the same time that it underscored, for his readers, the
fact that a tale and its purpose might be different things. The
massive detailing of the American past he accomplished in
the Littlepage books has attractions beyond Cooper's intent;
Satanstoe remains one of his finest books merely in terms of
its art. But Cooper's intent is always apparent, as in *Wyandotté* it is not—hence Poe's mystification by the assault of
mortality at the end. Had Cooper wanted to write a revolutionary instalment for the Littlepage trilogy, *Wyandotté*
would have been his model. Indeed, that he left the war itself

out of the trilogy probably reflects his perception that in the earlier book he had had his say on the matter. If *Wyandotté* had appeared as a Littlepage book, nonetheless, its purpose would have stood forth more plainly.

The Crater was published the year after Cooper gave up his experiment with first-person techniques. Its own directness thus owes less to the form of the tale—though the tale is said to derive from the hero's "journal"—than to what Cooper had learned in his stint as an "editor." Acting in that role had taught him how to shape his fiction toward a conscious aim; in *The Sea-Lions,* a slightly later companion piece to *The Crater,* Cooper thus declared in his preface, "the design has been to portray man on a novel field of action"—this being his concession toward the plot—"and to exhibit his dependence on the hand that does not suffer a sparrow to fall unheeded."[5] There is a modern tendency to disregard and even discredit Cooper's final religious phase, of which *The Crater* as well as *The Sea-Lions* gives evidence. This tendency tells more about the critic, of course, than it does of the author; how absurd it is, at last, one can notice by extending it back, say, to Milton or Dante. And it is more than absurd. In *The Sea-Lions,* for instance, Cooper succeeds quite well in developing the "novel field of action" not only in itself but precisely *as* a metaphor of his religious theme. It is as much his directness in announcing the latter, as its simple presence in the narrative, to which critics have responded adversely.[6] They accuse him of forcing the issue merely because he let it be known from the start, as in *The Sea-Lions,* that the issue indeed had been before him, quite consciously, as he wrote. Like some of his contemporaries, they want Cooper to recede into the archetypes of his romances.

Surely the author's desire is as important as the modern critic's. He is to be judged according to the rules he adduced and the means by which he sought to give them a consistent force. The challenge in reading Cooper's final settlement tale centers exactly here. There is absolutely no doubt in this case that Cooper intended the tale—which, of course, has its

own "novel field," a Pacific island group of volcanic origin—
as a sermon on the text of national ills. And the displacement
of the theme to that novel setting, away from the assumptions clustered about the use of any specific American place,
aids in the development of Cooper's greater purpose. What
we have in *The Crater* is almost an allegory of the whole
American past: the book begins in a moment of discovery,
moves through a period of mere survival, then a time of wider
exploration and growth, then a colonial epoch beset with
"Indian" wars and buccaneering. And it ends in a foreshort-
ened national era when independence from outer threats
gives rise, over the last two chapters, to assertive and misled
"democratic" claims. In a mere four hundred pages, we thus
have run from the wonder of Columbus, one of the book's
touchstones, to the gossipy lies of the American press in
Cooper's own life, one of its crotchets. The hero of the book,
Mark Woolston, is the focus of this sweep of events and range
of moods, and he thereby acquires a representational Ameri-
canness not found, at least so directly, in the settlers of
Cooper's previous tales. This is another part of the book's
incipient allegory; so is the fact that Mark, born "only ten
days before the surrender of Burgoyne," is coeval with the
Republic.[7] But Mark also is Cooper's rough contemporary—
Cooper's birth in 1789 had a similar coeval note—and he
surely represents the author as much as the country; or, to
bring the two ideas together, he represents Cooper's divided
sense of the nation as an ideal legacy and a devastatingly
present fact. As *The Crater* pushes these two views against
each other, destroying the first with the force of the second,
we seem to be viewing some battle in Cooper himself—yet a
battle which takes a definite public form. Following out the
Columbian parallel with which it opens, the novel thus ends
with an act of un-discovery: Mark's "new world" (p. 161)
has literally sunk beneath the sea, taking the "lost community" (p. 457) with it. There is no question about Cooper's
wider intent here; the loss of the islands prefigures the im-
pending misfortune of America itself.

Cooper blames the disaster in the book on political mistakes that harbor a larger moral and even spiritual error, for finally politics and religion merge in *The Crater*. *Vox populi, vox dei*, runs the "venerable axiom" Cooper chose as the tag for his next-to-last chapter (p. 429): this sums up the argument concisely enough, for it is an authentic *vox dei* that speaks in the second, destructive earthquake, thereby answering and silencing the voice of the people as the "Crater Truth-Teller" (p. 433), the scandal sheet of the colony, has claimed to enunciate it. The paper's name belongs more properly to Providence, of course, and Providence reclaims it by plunging beneath the sea those who have arrogated it.

All of this Cooper obviously projected from his set purpose. In a summary, it seems simple and rigid enough, full of that deductive air which modern critics have found objectionable. But within the novel the religious matter raises more questions than it answers, and it has a richness of implication which suggests that Cooper was not so much abandoning his own inductive habits as suiting them to the new aims, and the new public atmosphere, of his career. Reading the novel in isolation promotes the view that political ire is its mood, and that the God who assuages this ire is something like a party boss letting loose on the opposition. True as it is in its own way, such a surface impression hardly draws our attention to the real significance of the book; indeed, it is likely to give us but another pretext for dismissing the work. If we pursue Cooper's givens far enough, on the other hand, we will locate in *The Crater* a climactic imprint of his lasting vision—altered, recast, and yet essentially restated.

Let us look first at the role accorded to God in the book. If he is decidedly not the same thing as the people's voice, and thus can act in history with the devastating power of his last surprise, he nonetheless holds no surprises whatever for the author. Cooper has no doubts about the presence of God in the landscape of his story, or about the direction and meaning of God's actions there. He adopts a doctrinal rather than a mystical, or a transcendental, viewpoint; he knows God is there to be found before Mark himself finds him, and thus does not need to read and puzzle over God's traces. Mark's faith grows and deepens; the narrator's need not and perhaps cannot.

It follows that Cooper in his role as narrator seems almost interchangeable with God. Mark Woolston never can speak like God, even though he has received possession of the islands from God; when the "great revolution" at last threatens Mark's control over the colony, he thinks "of knocking the whole thing in the head, by the strong arm"—"as he might have done," Cooper adds, "and would have been perfectly justified in doing" (p. 442). But this recourse, not taken, is as immeasurably distant from God's final coup as the *vox populi* is from the *vox dei*. It would be, of course, utterly physical and thus would rest solely on force; it would have none of the divine authority of the actual end. Cooper's closeness to God, on the other hand, derives from the fact that, as author, he is ultimately responsible for God's intrusion; and the fact that, as narrator, he insistently erupts into the story with a godlike force for which he offers not the slightest apology. One does not know whether he has nothing to learn about God because of his tone, or whether the tone comes from his having learned everything already. Certain it is, in any case, that Cooper in his role as narrator sees little need to persuade his audience of the rightness of his plentiful obiter dicta. They issue forth as revelations rather than arguments. In the discourse of *The Crater* Cooper plays the part given to God in the plot: he corrects the "lost community" of his American audience much as God corrects the wayward Craterinos.

This quality in Cooper's voice certainly has a nettlesome effect. One notes the unintended irony that, while the novel preaches humility and arranges its events so as to create that feeling in Mark and to show its wider uses, Cooper himself consistently demonstrates the opposite emotion. The irony is really beside the point, however, for Cooper's bold verbal presence in the novel surely is intentional. We can explain it in part as a sign of his alienation; in part, perhaps, as a further hint of his self-destructive capacities, since it hardly would prove ingratiating to his readers. Yet we cannot ignore the fact that in this period Cooper increasingly saw offense as one means of shocking his readers into thought. One motive for his treatise on American democracy had been his perception, as in the passage about "the severity of truth" already quoted, that others who shared his own doubts were keeping quiet or joining, though cynically, in the chorus of demagoguery. This cowardly retreat from principle and from its vocal articulation seemed like a grave mistake to him, and a disservice to the country.[8] In *The Crater* itself, we may recall, the misled democrats can seize control only because a majority of the citizens will not vote on matters they regard as illegal—this being, in essence, a similar kind of cowardice.[9] Cooper's preface to *Wyandotté* emerged from the author's concern over an allied conspiracy of silence; the novel itself clearly aimed at the blind vulnerabilities of Cooper's American audience, even the shock of those final "unnecessary" deaths (as Poe thought them) suggesting, by its violation of sentimental formulas, that "the truth" is blunter than art. So, too, Cooper's larger goal in *The Crater* was to wake his neighbors up—his neighbors in Cooperstown,[10] as well as the nation—and for this purpose his "intrusions," as they usually are called, were right. He consciously trespassed against the proprieties of fiction because he no longer was seeking to be merely a fiction-maker. One thing he had learned from his experiments with first-person narrative was that any tale has its "I"; one thing the radicalization of his own viewpoint had taught him in the past decade was that the political drama in which he acted as a man had to find its outlet in his art. And might not his fearless declarations also demonstrate to the public that democracy required, above everything else, just this sort of crabbed individualism? If we regard his voice in *The Crater* as presumptuously godlike, we may be missing the exemplary force it carries: for the self, in its

benign rather than selfish moods, ought to have been godlike—
so American ideals claimed—and Cooper, by dramatizing his
viewpoint within the novel, was thus far orthodox. It was the
others who had abandoned decorum, who had sold out the
most intimate part of their heritage. To set them right, arro-
gant as the effort would seem, was necessary for the salvation
of the Republic.

The Crater begins in the year 1793, the point of departure
for *The Pioneers* as well, and though it quickly shifts to the
ocean scenes where most of its action will occur, it first
lingers in the provincial world of postrevolutionary America,
the same world to which the postscript of *Wyandotté* returns
Maud and Bob. This was, of course, the decade from which
Cooper's own first memories came. But in the present case
Cooper hardly was describing what he may have remembered.
Philadelphia as we see it in the exposition of the first chapters is a city from the 1840s: the bickering competition of
Drs. Woolston and Yardley, each with his favorite medical
theory, shows us, for instance, the inherent littleness of mind
which justifies Cooper's aloof and icy tone here and elsewhere. We will see that same littleness in the native chief
Waally; the struggle between him and Ooroony copies and
magnifies that of the Philadelphia doctors. And we will see
it, too, in the final tragedy, when the colonists, belittling
themselves, call down God's wrath and the author's scorn.
One notes here how often Cooper's image of society, from
The Pioneers to *The Ways of the Hour,* is an argument almost
for the sake of argument; in *The Crater,* it is this human
irascibility which will cause the cataclysm, and which thus
seems to give rise to the narrative tone that in fact has created it. Cooper appears to be so far above his characters that
he has the right to issue his pronouncements; he is godlike
because they are all too human. They have the collective
force of the mob in *Wyandotté,* and the same faceless lives.
    Cooper protected Mark Woolston from the belittling
energy of his tone because Woolston emanated from himself.

Late in the novel, of course, Mark seems like the prig Cooper
was accused of being, but we are not meant to take this trait
ironically, and the young man generally has an ample human-
ity of the sort which the other little characters in his world
generally lack. For this trait, the narrative offers many explanations: he escapes from provincial Philadelphia early
enough to see and feel the wider world, including Europe;
he leaves with a sense of wrong traceable to the family quarrels; he shares with his sister and his fiancée a sort of childlike
innocence and openness from which the parents seem to have
fallen at some immemorial epoch. But these reasons cannot
explain Mark's substantial difference. For that, we must look
instead to his lonely months on the reef.

He lands there because those in control of his ship, like
those in control of his homeland, abuse their small authority.
Captain Crutchely is a genial drunk, while the second mate
Hillson is just a drunk, and a resentful coward to boot. Mark
himself, the first mate, has virtual command of the ship on
the fatal night, but no one else on board can or will confirm
his alert sense of danger. Even Mark's good friend Bob Betts,
with whom he will later live on the reef, succumbs to the
unwary heartiness of the vessel's crew—he has seen the white
breakers, but denies the fact and his friend. Once the ship
strikes, the captain is washed overboard: this is moral punishment of the sort that bolsters the author's control, but it has
a nicely circumstantial air to it as well. A likable but "semi-
prudent" man (p. 39), Crutchely does not follow the course
which, as Cooper's narrative makes clear, a good sailor should
in such straits. When the crisis comes, furthermore, the captain
is so stricken by his "serious blunders" that, less "discreet"
than he ought to be, he jumps into action, intent on securing
the anchor cable that Hillson has bent improperly. Just as he
seems to have succeeded, however, the ship makes a heavy
roll, and Crutchely is "seen no more." Not even the narrator
knows what has happened to him; he appears simply to have
been "carried away to leeward, in the midst of the darkness
of that midnight hour" (pp. 43-44). In its moral causes and

its suddenness, this loss points ahead to the whelming disaster of the book's end, and Cooper reinforces the image twice over the next two pages. Hillson, the first crewman to jump into the ship's launch, is soon carried off in it with the other sailors who join him; Mark can catch only "a dim view of the launch, driving off to leeward, on the top of a wave"—then it also is "lost... in the gloom of night" (p. 45). Already, too, the jolly boat and its crew, sent after Crutchely, have been "lost to view in the gloomy darkness of the terrible scene" (p. 44).

This series of visual and moral desertions leaves young Mark and his friend Betts alone on the *Rancocus,* which at first seems hopelessly trapped in a ring of barely submerged rock. Yet within hours a new influence begins to exert itself. As if to balance the heavy gloom of the previous night, day comes upon the two men with a special, spiritual force; it allows them to see the dangers around them, but the eternal dawn also shows them, as "objects first grow distinct," a higher sign—for at this hour, Cooper writes a bit sententiously, "everything appears as if coming to us fresh and renovated from the hands of the Creator" (p. 49). When we remember the dire situation the sailors are in, abandoned by man and left by God with only the most spare of worlds, the moral sentiment seems piously wrongheaded. But as the book unfolds, God the Creator, rather than God the Judge, indeed reveals himself to Mark and Bob precisely in the lonely terrain of their loss. Delivered from death, they have been delivered into a universe which even now calls forth their "wonder" at the ways of Providence (p. 50). Here *The Crater* bases its own best emotions, and here, too, the full power of its otherwise theocratic God finds a richly substantial expression.

The two mariners first must endure the consequences of their dereliction. Betts jokes that they will have to "Robinson Crusoe it" (p. 50), yet before they can try to live that bookish fantasy they will have to accept, as Cooper himself writes, "the realities of their present situation" (p. 52). The need to do so is a classic one in all of Cooper's works, as we have seen already, and in this case it comes forth with a special intensity. The world to which Bob and Mark awake assaults their wits with a series of difficult propositions. The ship, which has survived almost intact, gives them a familiar home—its cabin remains an almost sacred place throughout the book— and a plenty of provision which not even Crusoe's wrecked vessel in Defoe's book can supply. But the *Rancocus,* named for a creek near Mark's hometown, in effect has ceased to be a ship in this alien world; it is vulnerable to the force of the sea but impotent upon the water. Hence the men, anxious lest the vessel may break up, feel relieved when they first see the faint island nearby; the "forlorn and desolate mariners" (p. 52), though not in fact shipwrecked (as Cooper stresses at several points), are in a state of suspended "captivity" (p. 99) on the faraway ocean, and their emotions understandably return to whatever land may be near them. The larger uselessness of the *Rancocus* is hinted when they fire her cannon as a signal for the men washed away the previous night: the "roar" sounds "strangely enough in the midst of that vast solitude" (p. 55). Mark and Bob, alive as they are, teeter between what they have left behind or what remains of it, and what they have been unaccountably delivered into. Their losses must be numbered before the larger gain suggested by the dawn can reveal itself.

But indeed that gain will prove itself surprisingly large, for loss in this instance, as elsewhere in Cooper, becomes a kind of birth; the violence of the storm enables the lyrical patience of what ensues. Mark's "new world" is no mere gift from the hand of God, to be sure, for he must work to assume the prerogatives of discovery. The reef seems so starkly barren that they first despair of surviving on it; it is safer than the ship, but if the ship in fact has become no ship, the land hardly seems like land at all. Cooper's vocabulary for the place—"naked rock," "nakedness and dreariness," "utter nakedness" (p. 59)—is appropriate for what appears to be "so desolate a place" (p. 58), and the author's style forces

Mark himself, as it were, to reject Bob's jovial reiteration of the Crusoe myth: "He had an island," Mark says, "while we have little more than a reef; he had soil, while we have naked rock; he had fresh water, and we have none; he had trees, while we have not even a spear of grass" (pp. 63-64). The passage neatly reminds Cooper's audience of the relevant differences between *The Crater* and *Robinson Crusoe;* but it also underlines the elemental terms of Woolston's new life. Unlike Cooper's other settlers, Mark falls upon rather than sets out for his "plantation" (p. 80), and what he first encounters does not soothe his expectations. Reduction precedes recovery.

The inward gloom is countered, as I have suggested, by the hidden capacity of the reef for a series of magical changes far beyond those witnessed in Cooper's earlier books. Mark and Bob find a safe berth for their ship alongside the reef, and they turn toward the new home, grim as it is, with a determination to make it give them life. It responds to their moral intent with a startlingly benign energy; it soon proves to be a place of "extraordinary fertility" (p. 157) where nature, aided by the labors of the men, works out "her own benevolent designs" (pp. 227-28). For "nature" in this instance, and elsewhere in the novel, we should read "God," since on the crater the Creator seems to have repossessed the power of Genesis—so much so that it spills over onto Mark and Bob. The barren island thus responds to their fertilizing acts; they quite literally make the soil where the seeds providentially stowed in the *Rancocus* by its owner, the much named but unseen human god "Friend Abraham White," can be planted and thus allowed to flourish. When Mark first sees his melon plants standing forth "on that hitherto barren mount," the "rapture" he feels comes only in part from knowing that he will survive; deeper and more lasting is the sense "of a new creation" which the "specks of incipient verdure" evoke (pp. 101-2).

Perhaps we should think back here to the landscape exposed by Captain Willoughby's assault on the beaver dam at the start of *Wyandotté*—an ugly mudflat soon transformed into a lush pastoral valley. Like that scene, the one in *The Crater* has a primal quality nothing in *The Pioneers* or *The Wept of Wish-Ton-Wish* can match; each of those books begins, after all, in the midst of a world already shaped and at least partly settled. But by comparison to *The Crater,* so does *Wyandotté.* The latter passes quickly over the initial years, and its definition of settlement as an almost divine act (full as it is with "the feeling of creating") finds a far more satisfactory confirmation in the leisurely career of Mark Woolston than in the life of the Willoughbys.[11] We must note, too, that Mark begins in devastation before he passes on to wonder; he pays for his pastoral world by the distresses he suffers on the naked reef, while the Willoughbys affirm hope as a way of denying history. Beaver Manor seems to become progressively smaller, as a result, while the lands of the other book in fact enlarge; God rewards Mark's patience by forcing the rock itself to bloom upward, plantlike, from beneath the sea. Woolston can indulge his hope without incurring Cooper's belittling scorn because he has come to that emotion through the crucible of loss and doubt. It is in this sense, rather than by his simple political alignment with the author, that he may be said to emanate from Cooper.

Naming is Mark Woolston's prerogative in *The Crater,* as "discovery" is one of Cooper's favorite words in the narrative of the book. Both facts accord well with the sense of rebirth that follows on Mark's abandonment; he progressively reaches out to possess, wonder at, and transform a world that itself expands even as he does, so that the Columbian theme takes on a dynamic force—the space of the novel being not so much found as founded. The hero is an agent of change, as Cooper's other settlers are, and of change in the most rudimentary way. But so is nature, especially after the first earthquake reveals to him those "astonishing changes" (p. 167) which he immediately sets out to explore. Only rarely did Cooper imagine with such careful and consistent detail this sort of interrelation of character and world; reality in this instance holds little threat, has no deceit, and does not challenge but rather repays the hero's feelings. For most of the book, Mark has no need whatever for the "jealous senses" of Mabel Dunham in *The Pathfinder*.

When he arrives at the "Peak," the towering island thrust upward south of the reef, Mark thus can land on it in a mood of innocent but right awe: "Like Columbus, he knelt on the sands, and returned his thanks to God" (p. 180). His new lands are already verdant, appropriately, and as he climbs to the top of the island his senses are ravished by what he sees. This is Columbian, too, as the author of *Mercedes of Castile* would have known. Yet what happens as Mark's eye takes full possession of the scene passively organized by his own presence in it had other sources in Cooper's mind; the end of the twelfth chapter, when Mark makes his "solitary repast" of the food he has gathered on the spot, surely echoes Judge Cooper's first Otsego journey, the Peak and the Vision being spatial and emotional equivalents (p. 182). And as Mark afterwards climbs to "the highest point of his new discovery," he looks down on a landscape that lies "spread before him like a map," a landscape that seems to emerge from his own feelings: "All its beauties, its shades, its fruits, and its verdant glades, were placed beneath his eye, as if purposely to delight him with their glories" (p. 183). And again, "There it lay, stretched far and wide, extending nearly a degree of latitude, north and south, and another of longitude, east and west, most truly resembling a vast dark-looking map, spread upon the face of the waters for his special examination" (p. 184). What keeps this attitude and this image from becoming as static as they might—as they are in *Notions of the Americans,* for instance—is the fact that Mark has come to this point through a series of trials which he and the reader both recall. Much of what he sees, too, is as new as his own feelings; the scene can appear maplike because no literal map of it exists.

The problem of *The Crater* is to square such exuberance of act and style with the stated purpose of the book and the

actual end which that purpose gives to the plot. In the most
cynical sense, all of Mark's lingering wonder seems directed
precisely toward the crisis. At the conclusion, Mark will feel
a special pain, for instance, over the attacks against his right
to own the crater on the reef:

> From the first, he had claimed that spot as his private property;
> though he had conceded its use to the public, under a lease, since
> it was so well adapted, by natural formation, to be a place of refuge
> when invasions were apprehended. But the crater he had found
> barren, and had rendered fertile; the crater had even seemed to him
> to be an especial gift of Providence bestowed on him in his misery;
> and the crater was his by possession, as well as by other rights, when
> he received strangers into his association. (p. 449)

Here Cooper's Three-Mile Point controversy erupts into the
book; that piece of land on the west side of Lake Otsego
hardly had any defensive purposes—except, one notes, for the
man who reclaimed it for his father's estate against the inva-
sions of picnicking strangers—but the stress in this passage on
the rights (or even just the fact) of possession surely stems
from that weary episode in Cooper's life. And in a larger
sense the whole climax of *The Crater,* when Mark loses his
property and the thieves lose their lives, may be traced to
the same episode in Cooperstown: one might characterize
the novel as a dreamlike expansion of the local quarrel, a
pushing of county matters into universal terms. That indeed
it is, though only in conception; the anger may have sent
Cooper eagerly into the project, but it was not anger that
sustained him as he finished it. Mark Woolston's claim to the
parcel of real estate in dispute, and to his other holdings, has
its legal aspects: a deed, a lease, the "other rights" not specified. Yet Cooper does not elaborate this side of the hero's
claim as he does the other. Mark's emotional authority, his
right to the landscape rather than the land, rests instead on
discovery, on the divine gift discovery implicates, and on the
fertilizing potential of his awe.

Even such an impressive list as this may have its cynical
uses, to be sure, but the very disproportions of the novel—

twenty-eight chapters devoted to the premise, and only two to the grim consequence—ought to point us toward Cooper's other purposes here. *The Crater* is one of the most designedly public of Cooper's books, one in which the author's rhetorical aims generate the overall plot, and yet at the same time it is extraordinarily private, expressive as well as didactic. It resembles *The Pioneers* in this regard; for *The Crater* also lingers indulgently among images dear to the author, spending much of its force in descriptive acts that do not promote, directly at least, the action of the plot. And this book does not have the obvious justification for doing so that *The Pioneers* possesses. Set in an ocean Cooper never saw, on an island group neither he nor anyone else ever could see; conceived as an allegory whose end Cooper must have foreseen from the start; and intended as a jeremiad on the ruin of the Republic—*The Crater* in fact is a lyrical poem on the extraordinary power of nature and nature's God. It preaches hate but in essence it demonstrates love. And it is in this sense that it reveals something about the author which the author, for all his conscious revelations of his political being, clearly did not mean to publish.

It is possible, of course, to argue that the whole elongated beginning of the novel, in which beginning itself is the theme, amounts to little more than another of Cooper's infamous "wish-fulfillments." Mark is Cooper, in other words, because Cooper gave Mark precisely the sort of solitary possession of his little New World which Cooper, in the Cooperstown he rediscovered on his return from Europe, longed to find or invent. Part of the truth assuredly lies here; one can pick up the hints of the mood as early as *The Deerslayer*, which as I already have suggested comes back to the scene of *Home as Found* (and *The Pioneers*) but which at the same time finds its own home in the unacquired landscape of nature, the violence of its erasures pointing us ahead to the cataclysm of *The Crater*. But the pattern I am trying to uncover in the latter book had more than petulance as its source; besides, to reduce an author's imaginative acts to wish-fulfillment in almost any case begs a chain of questions, and in Cooper's particular case it becomes a pretext for overlooking, because presumably they are childish, the real motions of his art. Hence we may recognize here that the erasing force of Cooper's imagination in fact predated the troubles of the 1830s, or the "vision" which led him, at the quieter end of that decade, to leave out of *The Deerslayer* the social landscape he had sought to repossess in *The Pioneers*. The first Leatherstocking book itself, by its distinction between what could be verbally recovered and what could not or should not be—and thus its many and differing styles: lyric, satiric, moody, angered, ironic—outlined the same basic pattern at the start of Cooper's career. In this case, to be sure, it was Cooper who was erased; and Natty Bumppo at the end as well. What Natty aimed against the village, like Cooper's own satire, nonetheless belittled a world which Cooper sought elsewhere in the novel, as by the magnifying language of his child's eye, to enlarge. *The Pioneers* proceeds by offering and then withdrawing images, discovering and wondering at and then losing a succession of scenes, objects, people, or acts. So, too, with its rhythm of light and gloom; the only refuge in the book being a poise, momentary and shimmering, between such opposites—as when Natty holds his spear above the lake, the torches slightly pushing back the night, and reveals to Elizabeth the wonders of the hidden world below. There may lurk a wish in all such moments in *The Pioneers*, or Cooper's other books, but the wish has a tenuous hold on the eye, the style, and the reader; it gets its preciousness not from its inner sources, its emotional force, but rather from its imminent loss. The very defect in the plotting of *The Pioneers*—events replace what has come before but do not necessarily grow from what is replaced—is a symptom of this larger truth in the book.[12]

The plotting of *The Crater* reveals a similar design. The events of the long beginning, up to the defeat of the pirates, serve mainly to keep the book going; they separate the pastoral and contemplative moments which form the core of the real action. Only after that defeat, which makes the colonists prideful of their own power rather than thankful for God's, does the catastrophe noticeably begin to intrude, and this moral point is made only at the start of the penultimate chapter: "A great change came over their feelings, after the success of the 'Pirate-War,' inducing them to take a more exalted view of themselves and their condition than had been their wont. The ancient humility seemed suddenly to disappear; and in its place a vainglorious estimate of themselves and of their prowess arose among the people" (p. 429). In the allegory, the war seems to represent the last struggle of the British with the French, much as the assault on Mark's prerogatives which ensues serves as a curt image of the Revolution—as seen through the Anti-Rentism of the 1840s. Perhaps the suddenness of this other "great change" in the book comports with the suddenness seen elsewhere; perhaps, too, it vaguely represents the sudden shifts in American opinion after 1763. Yet one must conclude that its real origin lay instead in Cooper's hesitations; if he knew exactly what he had to do in the denouement of the tale, he nonetheless resisted doing it. For by the time he came to this part of his manuscript he had already created—with a richness his purpose did not of itself require—an image of what the colonists were to destroy, and he was reluctant to sink this image into the gloom of his necessary ending. He had seduced himself into believing that the discarded premise of contemporary America, the Columbian freshness, surprise, amazement, might be recovered, since he had succeeded in recovering them here. Having pointed his imagination into a blankly abstract sea where he could work out his critical intent with no distractions from the real spaces of America, Cooper had left behind the traces of his private gloom; thus he could create for once a world commensurate with the capacity of his emotions. He found it necessary, as a result, to preach the end as much as invent it: "the earth revolves, men are born, live their time, and die; communities are formed and are dissolved; dynasties appear and disappear; good contends with evil, and evil still has its day" (p. 444). This is eminently true of the Craterinos, or so we are told, but for the most part it is Genesis rather than Ecclesiastes that rules the novel— and Genesis before the temptation and the fall.

The allure Mark Woolston has found lingers so long that his last real act is a relenting tour of his island paradise. The voyage offers him a summary of his life, a catalog of changes that may restate his "rights" but that in a higher way restates his vision and that of the author:

> The channels were in nearly every instance lined with trees, and the husbandry had assumed the aspect of an advanced civilization. Hedges, beautiful in their luxuriance and flowers, divided the fields; and the buildings which contribute to the comforts of a population were to be found on every side. The broad plains of soft mud, by the aid of the sun, the rains, the guano, and the plough, had now been some years converted into meadows and arable lands; and those which still lay remote from the peopled parts of the group, still nine-tenths of its surface, were fast getting the character of rich pastures, where cattle, and horses, and hogs were allowed to roam at pleasure. (p. 449)

The passage is utterly and straightforwardly orthodox, just the kind of thing about which Cooper felt uneasy when he painted and praised it in *Notions of the Americans.* He could embrace it naively in *The Crater* because by 1847, as he saw things, the country had rejected or at least unknowingly abandoned it—the old iconography of magical change now was itself a victim, lost, laid aside, and all but forgotten, and it thus became available to Cooper as an expression of his own endurance. He could eulogize this America because he at last could distinguish it from the real one he lived in. It was an America of the mind, as the projective energy of his imagination in the novel firmly suggested. He was describing nothing here; he was creating.

Nor did he limit himself simply to such set pieces. The most surprising aspect of the book, stylistically, is its extraordinarily tactile sense of the world—I would go so far as to predict that a concordance of all his writings would show *The*

Crater to have more concrete nouns than any other. Here is one case in point:

> The only time when our men could work at even their awning, were two hours early in the morning, and as many after the sun had got very low, or had absolutely set. Eight holes had to be drilled into the lava, to a depth of two feet each. Gunpowder, in very small quantities, was used, or these holes could not have been made in a twelvemonth. But by drilling with a crowbar a foot or two into the rock, and charging the cavity with a very small portion of powder, the lava was cracked, when the stones rather easily were raised by means of the picks and crows. Some idea may be formed of the amount of labour that was expended on this, the first step in the new task, by the circumstance that a month was passed in setting those eight awning-posts alone. When up, however, they perfectly answered the purpose, everything having been done in a thorough, seaman-like manner. At the top of each post, itself a portion of solid spar, a watch-tackle was lashed, by means of which the sail was bowsed up to its place. To prevent the bagging unavoidable in an awning of that size, several uprights were set in the centre, on end, answering their purpose sufficiently without boring into the rocks.
> (p. 113)

It seems to me that such a passage—which is wholly representative of the novel before the preachy end—shows us a mind at peace with the world; the very wealth of modifications, each calmly aiming at a greater exactness rather than a change of intent, conveys attention rather than anxiety, wonder rather than the kind of fear that facts so often introduce in Cooper. And herein lies one proof of Cooper's investment of his best emotions in the career of his lost hero. Each minute step in Mark's creation of his world is as carefully chronicled as is the raising of this awning in the shipyard; the digging, moving, and mixing of the matter which Mark converts to soil is recorded as if Cooper indeed had someone's journal before him.[13] The descriptive ease of the book's heart in effect is a catalog of actions, but actions aimed at placid habitation. Nowhere else in Cooper's settlement tales can we find this calm blooming forth of human art, or of the serene energy which unfailingly directs it. Rarely do we find anywhere in his art, for that matter, this rendering of the universe as a home, and in the most profound and enduring sense of that term. Woolston touches his world with such a respect for its tangibility and its present reality—despite his incipient spiritual awe, though this also is rooted in the earth—that we hardly can accept the landscape as merely a pasteboard marker in an allegory.

It comes down, as I have said, to creation—to "all creation," for what Natty can speak of in memory Mark can see in fact, enjoy in solitude, and respect in silence. The "youthful hermit" (p. 137) and "solitary man" (p. 139) lives, rightly, in a book that gives very little of its space to dialogue, most of the prose being strictly narrative; this is, I believe, less the result of the hero's given situation than a further sign of the author's happy discovery of his best mood and manner. Mark has his melancholy moments, and thinks longingly about his bride; but their marriage, offensive to both sets of parents, in fact cannot be consummated until the woman comes out to the islands with Betts, as if the fertile isolation of the place somehow allows what the social world, parched and possessive, has forbidden. And in this solitude, where life seems "prodigious" (pp. 143, 155), the couple's first child can be born. Time is likewise fruitful here in what Bridget names "Eden" (p. 206)—there is an "abundance of time" (p. 235), and time itself acts as an agent of benevolent change: "Mark saw that another year or two would convert the whole of that vast range ... into very respectable pastures, if not into meadows" (p. 255); "four or five years would convert them into so many beautiful, if not very useful trees" (p. 256); "for the progress of vegetation in such a climate ... is almost magical, and might convert a wilderness into a garden in the course of a very few years" (p. 260); and, at the end, "notwithstanding all these errors of man, nature and time had done their work magnificently since the last 'progress' of Woolston among the islands" (pp. 448-49). It comes as no surprise that another favorite word in the novel is "flourish," or that its best mood and color is green.

But if so much of *The Crater* thus seems to avoid and evade the ending, Mark's attention to nature, and the attention of nature to Mark's hope, in fact do have a political purpose. I have suggested earlier that Cooper's losses in the social world led him to aim his emotions toward nature; as early as *The Pioneers*, this deflection allowed him to occupy both sides in the dispute—to begin by praising the energy of the woodchopper, for instance, but then to end by sending Kirby's sounds echoing, and diminishing, across the hills. It also allowed him in that book to invent Natty at first from the outside, as if he is seen from the village, and then to progressively possess Natty's viewpoint, and hence see the village from outside its assumptions. That Edwards hides in Bumppo's costume and Bumppo's domain suggests, I think, exactly what Cooper was doing with his own alienation; though in the author's case there was less costume and more real sympathy, a protest rather than a ploy. Cooper had none of Edwards's hope for a literal repossession; hence he stayed with Natty after Edwards reassumed what Templeton forced him to—stayed with Natty and, of course, would return to him. He let nature speak back at civilization through Leatherstocking because civilization itself set the terms of that very opposition.

In *The Wept of Wish-Ton-Wish* and *Wyandotté*, as we have seen, Cooper made the claims of the world outside the settlers' world—nature, the Indian "other," and history— more insistent and intrusive. Neither of those books has an equivalent for Natty: young Ruth might serve this way, but cannot; Submission thinks he does, but is mistaken; Conanchet may enter the clearing, but is regarded there as a complete outsider who must be converted; Nick/Wyandotté, as his double name suggests, is divided rather than focused, his conversion to white ways and his reconversion to native life both being parodic; Joel Strides is merely a deceitful political borderer whose essential world is actually the self. The lack of a true mediator in either case surely explains, in part at least, the violence with which inner and outer must meet and clash. There is no one to protect young Ruth from what most deeply threatens her, as Natty protects and saves Elizabeth (or the Munros, up to a point, in *The Last of the Mohicans*), and there also is no one to shield Willoughby when he leaves the Hut to save his son, but then himself succumbs. In the largest sense, of course, it is Cooper himself who is responsible for denying these books the sort of mediation Natty can give—or Susquesus can in *Satanstoe*. Yet the inner reason is also clear: by closing out the world, the settlers leave no place for such a figure to exist. Their lack of vision, and even of sight, forces the world upon them. They, too, forge the opposition.

The Pioneers enjoys a greater security because Templeton tolerates Natty, even though the end of that toleration has been spelled out with the new law. Bumppo's authority comes not from the village, however, but from his own vision and his own long "ownership" of the landscape. The settlers in this instance hardly close out nature; the very point of Temple's law, after all, is to protect nature from depredation, and his policies thus may be said to rest in wonder. As policies, on the other hand, they have a preconcerted and formal air, a rationality, against which, simply on the face of it, Natty must react. He is as surely a figure of vision as Temple is of foresight and planning; they share an aim, but use different means—indeed, Natty would not see his habits as a means, only as what is right and fitting. Temple distrusts anything that approaches instinct, which is why, despite his gratefulness for Natty's rescue of Elizabeth, he must cling to the idea of justice. The Judge remains within civilization throughout; when he feels mournful over the senseless killing of the pigeons, we must note, he offers cash to the village children who will put the birds out of their misery. He also has offered cash at the very start for the deer killed by Natty and Edwards, while Jones's pretext for seizing the old hunter is that he has been stealing gold from Marmaduke's lands. That Natty's greatest possession in the whole series is his gun suggests how profoundly removed from institutions he is; for it is use, nature, that attaches him to Killdeer, as the weapon's name itself underscores. And that his initiation into violence in *The Deerslayer* occurs in the woods and in the terms of the woods likewise places Natty exactly in the right world.

Mark Woolston hardly comes off as even a genteel version of Leatherstocking. What he undeniably shares with Natty, however, is a courtship with nature akin to that which Natty endures in *The Deerslayer*; for Mark, by his isolation, can offer to those settlers who later come to his islands just the sort of mediation that Leatherstocking represents. And in this case the spiritual and political implications of such a gift are seen with a clarity that *The Pioneers*—with its essentially lyrical form—cannot muster. Cooper here arranges things so that visionary possession is the very basis of legal form, thereby returning law to nature. Natty's complaint has become the just foundation of this alter-America in the Pacific.

The first colonists feel the wonder Mark has won for himself; their visual discovery of the islands after their long sea passage aligns them with Woolston's primal feelings, and even at the close of the Edenic period the old settlers will linger in the memory of this shared exuberance. The more recent arrivals will seize the balance of power, however, and for them the wonder is unseen and unfelt. They do not know, as Cooper implies they should, that "Nature did quite as much as art, in bringing on the colony; the bounty of God, as the industry of man" (p. 429). This is another kind of inattention, inattention to the given world, its miraculous power, and the God responsible for both. Deprived of the awe they should know, the newcomers fall into idleness and pride. They will lose the benevolent energies of nature because they ascribe to themselves the many achievements of the "country" (p. 377).

The Crater can naively proclaim "the progress of things" (p. 211), or the general "progress of the colony" (p. 346) after the first large expansions; by a similar logic of growth,

rooted in the power of nature, the "hermit" Mark becomes
an "explorer" (p. 176), then an "adventurer" (p. 177),
and finally "the governor" (p. 227). But by the finale Woolston is merely "Mark—we must call him the governor no
longer," while the "progress of events" has led to delusions
(p. 443): "The supreme folly of the hour is to imagine that
perfection will come before its stated time" (p. 444). And
thus the process begun in disaster now has reversed itself
because the new citizens know nothing of the sources of their
happiness. Time becomes a negative force rather than the
vehicle of growth, for the same people have seized control
of the clock, forcing what might have come naturally:
"*Progress* was the great desideratum; and *change* was the
hand-maiden of progress" (p. 437). Their own "abundance
of time," to use the term Cooper applies to Mark and Bridget, comes from a frenzied and infertile social busyness:
"not only did each lustrum, but each year, each month,
each week, each hour, each minute demand its reform"
(pp. 437–38). The basis of their reforms, moreover, is not
"natural rights" (p. 438), as Mark knows it should be; it is
the will of the majority, from which "nothing permanent
or settled in human affairs" (p. 437) can come. The slow
blooming forth of progress has given way to an unstable
and pointless condition; we are back to the narrow human
world Mark left behind years before:

> In that distant day, homœopathy, and allopathy, and hydropathy,
> and all the opathies, were nearly unknown; but men could wrangle
> and abuse each other on medical points, just as well and as bitterly
> then, as they do now. Religion, too, quite as often failed to bear
> its proper fruits, in 1793, as it proves barren in these, our own times.
> (p. 12)

> All this time, religion was running riot, as well as politics. The next-
> door neighbours hated each other most sincerely, because they
> took different views of regeneration, justification, predestination
> and all the other subtleties of doctrine. (p. 438)

Mark's homeland has visited itself upon the wonder of his
solitary life—which is to say that America, founded in the

presence of awe and aimed at the best of ideals, had become a contest in bickering. Nature might have cured the nation, as it cured Mark Woolston and the man who invented him, but the illness was perverse enough that health, present in *The Crater* in a hundred positive forms, had come to seem like a sickness itself. Cooper was warning his readers, but he also was trying to recreate in them the kind of eye that might give them the world in its old freshness. Indeed, he was himself giving such a world to them in the book.

Mark's emotions aim back at the islands even after he has left them: "As for the ex-governor," Cooper writes, "he might be said to be rich; but his heart was still in the colony, over the weaknesses of which his spirit yearned, as the indulgent parent feels for the failings of a backsliding child" (p. 453). He and Bridget, now back in Philadelphia, had left the Pacific pacifically, still regarding the colony as "a boon from Providence," "a paradise in the midst of the waters" (p. 452). But their departure effectually abandoned the colonists to their own abandonments, so that Mark's final voyage back to the islands must end in failure—in a "sickening awe" (p. 456) rather than a new wonder. If the quotation from Bryant on the title page unequivocally refers to God's power to create and destroy—

> Thus arise
> Races of living things, glorious in strength,
> And perish, as the quickening breath of God
> Fills them, or is withdrawn

—it also suggests how the withdrawal of Woolston's right spirit has allowed the catastrophe; without his eye and what it sees and comprehends, the islands do not and cannot exist. What he finds of them, aside from the atoll that survives of the towering mountain, is an appropriate sign of how the flesh and spirit of his life have been consumed: "Next day, when the ship was again got under way, the anchor brought up with it, a portion of the skeleton of a goat" (pp. 456–57). We are placed here, as we have been at the end of the other three novels, in a graveyard—but one so vast that there can be little doubt in this book, where a world itself has been buried, about the scope of Cooper's purpose. Natty's brief glimpse of "all creation" in *The Pioneers* has blossomed in *The Crater* into chapter after chapter of glowing prose; so, too, Cooper's own Malthusian glimpse ahead to the "evil day" that awaits the abundant land, inserted almost as an aside in the first chapter of his first settlement tale, has become in his last one an enormously literal fact. It was his vigor that imagined the one, and his violence that enforced the other.

And in this case, as in the others we have examined, the drama of his art was in essence the drama of his being. Cooper absorbed the American border so deeply into his imagination because the patterns he saw in that raw material were patterns he had felt before, and still continued to feel; the material itself was unsettled and almost unused when it came to him, and he shaped it, as he shaped so much of the experience in his many books, into a version of his own story. Though loss thus became one lasting theme in his art, each new telling repossessed the world for him, and each new movement of his creative energy—which was vast and must have been vastly sustaining to him—suggested how Cooper had found, after his private losses, something more than despair. His truest America was the new world he invented again and again with the force of his vision, the new world he wrote into existence with his pen.

Though much of the previous discussion has devoted itself to merely four of Cooper's many novels— and admittedly not four of the best-known ones—I have assumed that what we might learn of Cooper's imagination in these instances could shed light on other instances necessarily bypassed. One defense of this assumption would begin with the simple fact that these four tales have an important mutual relevance; they belong together because they are a sustained meditation on a single complex theme of crucial importance to Cooper, and as such they constitute a larger creative whole more coherent, in some ways at least, than the better-known Leatherstocking series. If one of the lasting hints about his art which Cooper found in *The Pioneers* even as he was writing it was the possibility for an American heroic saga based on Natty Bumppo's career as an adventurer, another was that the settlement theme held as much promise in cultural and personal terms as the heroic one. The seven later novels thus implicated in *The Pioneers* help give that book its large significance as a touchstone in Cooper's whole body of works.[1] This was fertile ground indeed; none of his other books proved so originating for his imagination as his tale of Templeton.

Part of its power came from the very preciousness of what Cooper was there converting into art. And in the simplest sense the same relation of author and theme, the same convergence of public topic and private motive, sustained Cooper as he produced all the books I have examined. Yet as the Leatherstocking series demonstrates, Cooper also explored and appropriated areas of the American landscape beyond the clearings. If the real center of his larger map of the New World lay in the kind of newly opened terrain which he had known while growing up and then had lost, his tales of the actual wilderness—the forest largely undisturbed by settlement—hardly are marginal to what he was doing in *The Pioneers* and the other novels discussed above. The typical setting in the forest tales had already been sketched in *The Pioneers* itself, for one thing, while the continual counterpointing of nature and nation which was to go on even in *The Crater* would have been unthinkable without the larger tensions of Cooper's whole American scene. And it was the national designs on nature, especially as they took on outright political overtones in the 1830s and 1840s, that partly accounted for Cooper's own political insurgency in *Wyandotté* and *The Crater*. In presuming to dispose of such a vast extent of unsettled land, America was making a mistake of the sort Cooper had seen in the history of his family; his specifically political arguments with America were enriched by this doubling of theme. The New World microcosm of Templeton thus was personal in the first instance, but it also was national without being nationalistic, and Cooper later drew on the same equivalencies as his argument with the public became more trenchant and entrenched. One notes that the overt theme of *The Sea-Lions*—the rightness of trinitarian Christianity—has little to do, except in its rhetorical pitch, with the real concern of the plot, which is the poverty of merely exploitative urges as a means of relation to the natural universe. The Antarctic setting of the book is a displaced America akin to that Cooper already had imagined in *The Crater*, and the terms of Cooper's spatial imagination in both books were derived at last from the whole complex scheme he had evolved in all his American tales heretofore, not just those focused on the settlement theme.

It is worthwhile recalling here the fundamental distinction between American landscapes put forth in *Notions of the Americans*—the contrast, as the Count first has it in the fourteenth letter of that work, between settled field and wild forest. One may locate in this distinction the fundamental elements of Cooper's New World as an imaginative terrain. But while the European traveler of *Notions of the Americans* quickly seeks to make the two parts of this "completely . . . American scene" coalesce visually,[2] reducing their difference to a mere contrast of hue—the very finesse of which gives the tamely artful land dominance over the wild—Cooper's own typical practice as a novelist was to stress and intensify the contrast. *The Crater*, with its setting far removed from America, is a somewhat special case here, since in it the New World landscape is a moral rather than a visual source; the three other settlement tales, however, show the clearing and the forest existing in an equal and continually fruitful tension. The landscapes in these books never are easy because they never can be seen merely from one controlling viewpoint. This is to say that the forest refuses to be subsumed in social categories of the sort that the Count blithely applies to what he sees from the safe distance of his vantage point. And in Cooper's books located in the forest itself the same lesson is driven home with, as we might expect, even more insistent force. When his imagination left the clearing it did not discover a wilderness yearning, as Judge Cooper thought that of Otsego was, for the impress of social and personal form.

Another of the Count's points might be kept in mind as one reads even so constricted a book as *The Pioneers*. Only the "blunder of Europeans," the Count proclaims, so jumbles American realities that things actually to be found in the new land, though widely dispersed across it—"churches, academies, wild beasts, savages, beautiful women, steamboats, and ships"—are imagined as existing side by side in the same American landscape: "wolf, beauty, churches, and *sixty*-gun frigates" being thereby brought into "strange and fantastic collision."[3] The Count's own catalogs, of course, inevitably push such dispersed and discordant things up against one another in word if not in fact; yet his larger argument is that a certain decorum rules American space, distributing opposite signs into separate places. Even in *The Pioneers*, however, Cooper himself already had been less than sure about this decorous principle. That novel has neither frigate nor steamboat among its props. But it hardly suggests that the other details listed by the Count— all of which are in fact prominent in the tale—exist only in hermetic isolation. Indeed, Templeton's "academy" and its much argued about "church," nominally signs of civil intent, actually represent the rough clumsiness of those who seek to replace the forest with some settled community. Far from giving the landscape a sense of "finish," the buildings disrupt the visual peace which formerly ruled there.

One notes as well that the threat of the "wild beast" against the "beauty" of *The Pioneers* hardly is presented as an anomalous violation of proprieties otherwise observed in the story; there may be a "collision" here, but it is neither "strange" nor "fantastic."[4] Indeed, the forcing together of such opposites is part of Cooper's thematic purpose in the novel, as even the opening scene on the road reveals. The homecoming turns to argument as surely as the innocent jest of the hunt, as Judge Temple views the matter, turns to serious and portentous harm. In keeping with the enlarged brightness of the imagery in this first chapter, Oliver's unsuspected wound thus is betrayed by the "large drops of blood" (p. 24) which are seen oozing from his shirt. Judge Temple's commanding gentility ought to keep itself separate from such violence, but in this case, of course, he is himself the cause of it, while throughout the tale—however light its final touch—the line between civil and wild space, talk and act, right and force, will be continually violated, obscured, and forgotten. It is not without significance here that the agents of the law act lawlessly, or that the sheriff is in immediate need of a thrashing, preferably with his own noisy whip. In moral terms, as in its landscape, *The Pioneers* forces together things kept unaggressively apart in the vision of America entertained five years later by Cooper's European tourist.

And *The Pioneers*, as I have argued earlier, is the most unaggressive of Cooper's four settlement tales. In *The Wept of Wish-Ton-Wish*, and only in part because of its earlier setting on the Indian frontier of New England, Cooper opposed to the "advance" of white civilization—his father's passion as a man, and theme as an author—something far more potent than that idea of nature which the old hunter and the old Indian, or the echoing hills of Templeton, could suggest in *The Pioneers*. The wilderness has a more prominent place in the Heathcote story, for it is a sign of what the settlers can neither understand nor control; there is no Billy Kirby in this novel, let alone a Natty Bumppo, while young Ruth's naturalization in the shadowy forest is violent, ironic, and at last hopeless. The very terms of the Count's contrast are thus reversed as the wild ground intrudes on the clearing—and does so, what is more, precisely because the settlers have so little capacity for recognizing what encircles them.

A similar intensification takes place in *Wyandotté,* the idyllic pretense of its opening chapters making the political and spatial confusion of the ending ones all the more disastrous. Here, too, few of the settlers seem to have even a small part of Natty's forest skill; however much Cooper may have projected his own taste for landscape art onto Captain Willoughby, Willoughby's indulgence in it is profoundly misplaced, and the little garden he tries to make in the wilds of revolutionary America is primarily a sign of how little he knows of nature, human or otherwise. Neither the real woods nor the native inhabitants of the forest (aside from Nick) are here the direct threat, as in *The Wept of Wish-Ton-Wish* they had been. But it is the shrouded valley, circled by a fringe of ominous woods, that circumscribes the symbolic landscape of the tale, much as it is the forest that cuts the Willoughby patent off from the outside world. And it is as "Injins" that at least some of the spineless rebels attack the Willoughby encampment.

The Crater differs from the earlier novels on this issue as on others. Yet we may observe in passing that the native chieftain Waally is as much an "Indian" as are Melville's islanders in *Typee* and *Omoo*, two of Cooper's possible sources for *The Crater*; we may observe as well that the latter-day Craterinos fail to recognize and accept the gifts of nature and of God as they legalistically secure the islands for their selfish purposes.[5] The settled ground in this case, as in the others, thus can be understood only by reference to what lies beyond and behind it. Cooper does not promote the idea that order inheres in the settlement, or grows outward from it. If anything, he implies in this final book that nature and what it represents are the last sources of design: whereas the valley of Templeton can "answer" Billy Kirby's violence only with a mocking echo, Mark Woolston's islands can respond with a coldly fatal power. As for "collisions," one could hardly imagine a stranger or more fantastic one than that which plunges a whole society and its very land beneath a wild and distant sea. How tame, compared to this denouement, is Elizabeth Temple's encounter with the beast in *The Pioneers*.

Yet all of the settlement tales in effect cling to the outwardly tame and open spaces where much of their action occurs. The valleys of Templeton, Wish-Ton-Wish, and the Willoughby patent are best understood in terms of the conventions of the stage: they dominate their respective tales so thoroughly that events which take place elsewhere are usually reported rather than literally presented in the narrative. However uncertain the settlements may be in moral terms, they are at least visually prominent. Thus, the many forays out into the forest in *The Pioneers* customarily yield those backward glimpses of the village about which I already have spoken; in *Wyandotté* we have, by the same token, that odd confinement of so much of the plot to a small clearing in the midst of the vast woods, even though we are told about—but not shown—more widely ranging movements of the characters.[6]

Given the many associations of the clearing in Cooper's art and life, we cannot treat this broad pattern merely as an accident of form. It has a meaning as well as a presence in the books, and a meaning that is not necessarily elusive. Perhaps the best way to approach that meaning is to speculate on what would happen to any of the novels if the dominance of the clearing were to be broken. Such is precisely the case in Cooper's tales of the actual forest, as I hope to suggest at a later point. For the present, however, we may pause over a piece of information which Cooper's daughter Susan recorded in *Pages and Pictures*. According to her, Cooper at one point in his later life contemplated revising *The Wept of Wish-Ton-Wish*, and revising it in a manner quite relevant to the issue I have just raised. Though the essential action of the tale was to remain unaltered, the stage on which it occurred was to have been significantly extended:

> the leading idea, the abduction of the daughter of the Puritan
> family and her adoption by the savages, would have remained
> the same, but instead of bringing Narra-mattah to her old home
> again with the Narragansett marauders, he would have carried the
> heart-stricken father into the wilderness on the trail of his lost
> child; he would have followed the parent step by step through the
> forest, as he was led onward—now deceived by some false rumor,
> then again guided by the right clue, wandering far and wide, along
> unexplored streams, over nameless lakes, through pathless valleys,
> until, at length, in some remote wigwam of the red man, he finds
> her....[7]

Since the idiom here seems uncannily like that which Cooper himself employed in his wilderness romances—the books in which, as Douglas Grant has put it, the "vast woods and wastes" of America occupy center stage[8] —we should recall that these are Susan's words rather than her father's. That we seem to recognize them is crucial; but so is the fact that they are decidely not in the style of the settlement tales.

Indeed, the source of the idea described by Susan lay in one of Cooper's "other" books, *The Last of the Mohicans*. There, in the abduction of Cora Munro by the wily Magua, Cooper first had touched upon the captivity theme which was to provide *The Wept of Wish-Ton-Wish* with its central motif, and a motif rendered far more subtle by the difficult meanings of the new book; there, too, in Colonel Munro's weary pursuit of his lost daughter through the forest, Cooper had sketched the weary journey he later wished to introduce into the Heathcote tale as he contemplated revising it. In the latter book as it originally stood, the reader is told of Content's search for his daughter in the forest, but that search is not actually presented; one sees young Ruth's mother agonizingly turn toward the woods, but her father's sorrow is reported rather than shown.

Had Cooper changed the novel, the shift of scene into the forest clearly would have altered the meaning of the plot. The shift which does occur near the end, where the theme both demands and controls the journey of all the Heathcotes out into the encircling woods, gives us a taste of what this other shift might have entailed. Surely young Ruth's recovery in the revised version would have seemed more difficult. The recognition scene in the book as we have it takes place in her family's beleaguered house, and though this has its own wrenching symbolism, the mere fact that it occurs where it does—in a familiar part of the dominant setting— is at last reassuring as well as ironic. We are back on the "stage" of the constricted drama at this point, at least, whereas Content's bewildering journey through the forest to "some remote wigwam" would leave us, as it would leave the father himself, adrift in an unknown landscape, a world without center. Meager as the sense of place in the book may be, the mere description and redescription of the Heathcotes' clearing, from the first chapter to the last, gives it a certain comforting identity; it is familiar to the reader as well as to the main characters. As opposed to such a centered scene, the revised version of the book would give us mere space in this one thematically crucial episode, a landscape without visual design or focus or direction except as the faltering track of Content through a "pathless" and "nameless" forest could give it a hint of such qualities. Finding his daughter at the end of that track would be like realizing her original loss over again—indeed, like realizing the depth of it for the first time. Like young Ruth, Content himself would be on alien ground at that moment.

These points extend into the whole group of novels. Although each of them questions the right of the various pioneers to organize space around their assumptions, each of them after all accepts, in the way in which it orders and renders action, the spatial consequences of such organizing impulses. When Chingachgook looks down upon Templeton and recalls another time when the valley had been in effect another place, he is mocking the present order. But he also is reminding us that the present order is not to be denied except by visionary means. His eye solidifies what his heart rejects; only the Indians of *The Wept of Wish-Ton-Wish* can destroy in fact, and then only temporarily, what has usurped their world.

How different, then, the sense of space which a modern reader finds in Cooper's actual forest tales. The American scene in these books is not so much centered as set in motion: only in the minds of those who move through it—as do the harried "way-farers" we meet in *The Pathfinder* (p. 9)—does it seem at all focused, and usually only for a moment. To pass from *The Pioneers* to *The Last of the Mohicans* is to enter a world where flight rather than possession, however insecure or wrongful or finally ironic possession may be, is the ruling relation of actor and scene. The revisions Cooper thought of making in *The Wept of Wish-Ton-Wish* would have brought together in a single work the two major strains of his border art.

The questions to ask here are how and why Cooper himself moved from the clearing to the wilderness, and what place the latter region came to occupy in his imagination. And one way to answer such questions is to note the changes Cooper introduced into Natty Bumppo's career as he made the old hunter of Templeton into a forest hero. It seems plausible to argue that Cooper first invented Natty as simply another of the colorful local characters appropriate to the cast of *The Pioneers*, and that he began to sense other possi-

bilities in this one figure only at a later point.[9] Certainly
it is true that the portrait of Natty deepens as *The Pioneers*
proceeds. Yet some facts fixed earlier, such as Natty's old
age, simply could not be altered as Cooper went on in the
imagining of the tale. Though the hunter seems to demand
some occasion when he can reassume the old self or the old
world which his deepening recollections tell us he once
owned, the initial image of Natty will not allow the change.
The lyrical memories called forth on the quiet lake must
substitute for a literal lyricism of action. This is the reason,
too, why Bumppo must depart at the end; the glorious
repossession of American space with which *The Prairie*
opens may be in the reader's mind at the close of *The Pioneers*, but it surely was not in Cooper's as he wrote that
ending. Natty had no place to go since his place already had
been taken from him along with his power. Cooper could
not have gone farther without violating the major premises
of the whole tale.

Here we can begin to locate, I think, the reasons for the
great alteration we sense as we pass into the universe of
The Last of the Mohicans. Derived in part from memories
only mentioned in *The Pioneers*, Natty's heroic presence
in the typically dark landscape of the later novel is intended
to verify—that is, to give a visible warrant for—what those
memories had suggested. To this extent, the second tale
adumbrates rather than simply extends the first one; it is
imaginatively prior to *The Pioneers*, and in a profound sense.
Hence Natty has his famous rifle as a signet of his heroic
position here, and a sobriquet that derives from the weapon;
the name may come to seem ludicrously unepic as the
Indians repeat it in stylized surprise or scorn or a mixture
of both, but it does serve to indicate that the world of the
novel is indeed Natty's rightful place—that he is known
in and to it. Such is the epic hero's acquired prerogative,
as even the opening of *The Pioneers* may be said to admit.
In the present book, we know by this detail alone the extent
to which what Natty already has been said to have lost

was once really his. The poignancy of his dispossession helps to explain how Cooper shaped the second novel as he did.

In his demonstrated skills, as in such props as the rifle and the name it gives him, Natty initially seems at home in the wilderness of *The Last of the Mohicans*. The *longue carabine* is both stylistically and "kinetically" a metonym for Bumppo; it suggests his skills as well as the identity they have given him, whereas "Leather-stocking" suggests in the main his difference of costume (and allegiance) from those who dwell in the village of *The Pioneers*. Oddly enough, his feats of violence in the earlier book are rather more memorable, probably because they are charged with the actor's own nostalgia. But Natty's repertory of skills does not stop, in any case, with deeds of violence. In the present book, his possession of the forest comes as much from other traits: he is familiar with hidden places and paths, has a subtle feel for his immediate surroundings, and evinces an accumulated depth of experience that he wears like a costume. He also has little but scorn for the white tenderfoots—represented here by Duncan Heyward and David Gamut—who are in the woods without belonging there. This ethical contrast is especially important at the start, where Heyward and Gamut jointly serve as Natty's foils. The former is stridently oversure of himself in the forest, for example, while the latter is madly innocent of the darkness into which he plunges with a song literally in his mouth. Indeed, the relationship between the two tenderfoots before Natty appears prepares us for the form his entrance will take. Heyward thus presumes to set Gamut straight when Gamut intrudes on the Munro party; he speaks demandingly, with hauteur, and in a "bass" tone which Gamut notes and Alice Munro, knowing its false authority, jokes about.[10] Heyward is presuming that he can guide Gamut; but the "private path" the party follows because Heyward thinks it safe—the phrase just quoted is his—is in fact a "narrow and blind" one, a "dark and tangled pathway," as Cooper's narrative immediately makes clear (pp.

24, 25). In order to survive in this world, the travelers evidently will need some guide more attentive (and less assertive) than the American major who nominally leads them.

Natty will be that guide, but before he enters we meet Magua, whom Heyward entrusts with the charge. It is Magua, of course, who makes the chosen path both false and dangerous. That he can do so with such ease surely reflects on Heyward. But even here at the start Magua is not merely the symbol of another character's faults. He is the numinous spirit of the woods, knowing the forest so well that he can get lost in it on purpose—or rather can make the others lose their way while remaining in perfect control himself. He is, moreover, a libidinous sign, as Cora Munro's erotic first response to him powerfully hints. Later, when Natty, Chingachgook, and Uncas set about trapping him along the path, he simply slips into the woods whose dark energy is both mythic and sexual throughout the book. He is so much the spirit of the place that he can assume its shapes with magical ease.[11]

In these ways, Magua gives the challenge of the forest to the Europeans who enter it a human intensity; he is the setting concentrated and given the power to act on them. But by the same token—and here the influence of *The Pioneers* over this tale begins to weaken—he sets a limit to Natty's own naturalization. If Bumppo approaches Heyward, the Munros, and Gamut from within the woods, meeting them on their lost trail ("You are, then, lost," he greets them [p. 43]) and bringing them for a moment to their original destination, in other ways he hardly seems as inseparable from the forest as *The Pioneers* leads us to think him. Natty's insistence on his "white" nature in *The Last of the Mohicans*, as in *The Pathfinder*, is thus more than a racial crotchet; it is the verbal iteration of something plainly visible in the action of the books, something so crucial that we ought to pause over it.

The first chapter of *The Last of the Mohicans* describes the general scene of the tale, as well as its general "bloody" mood,[12] while the second introduces the Munro party and sets it in motion within that scene. It is in the third, by a shift of focus which "penetrate[s] still deeper into [the] forest," rightly enough, that we first meet Natty. He is "lingering" with Chingachgook, in wait for Uncas, along the banks of the Hudson a few miles west of the Munros; a "vast canopy of woods" appropriately spreads above them, shadowing the already "dark current" of the river; the sun is now "beginning to grow less fierce"; a "breathing silence" permeates the forest, broken only by the "low voices" of the men, a woodpecker's "lazy tap" or a jay's "discordant cry," and the "dull roar" of the distant waterfall toward which Natty and the Mohicans will lead the Munros at a later moment. All these details gain their immediate importance from what they suggest about the relation of actor and world: Natty, in particular, is characterized by what surrounds and frames him. He is seen in terms of the environment where he is at rest.

The "feeble and broken" sounds do not disturb the two "foresters"—a significantly spatial term Cooper will use for Natty and the two Mohicans, and only for them, another dozen times in the book—so that whatever portent a reader may find in the gathering gloom, or the undertone of the falls, is not part of Natty's concern; he seems, in fact, to have no concerns at all. Yet there is an important difference here between Natty and Chingachgook, as Cooper's first physical description of the two men makes clear. Chingachgook's painted body bears "a terrific emblem of death" that is both a fitting native symbol and a stark narrative portent; Natty, though he is concealed by a "mask of . . . rude and nearly savage equipments," is visibly of "European" origin. Seen together within a landscape that sets them apart from the other characters who have recently entered it, the two foresters share habits and sympathies and experiences. But they nonetheless have come to this place from obviously separate worlds (pp. 33–34).

We can understand the purpose of this contrast best by recourse to what already has been narrated in the book. For the point of it is that each actor must be seen in terms of the closeness he or she can rightly assume to the forest where all of them henceforth will exist. And it is this very point which the first two chapters have driven home. The contrasts among the Yankee tunesmith Gamut, the Indian guide Magua, and the southern officer Heyward suggests the farthest poles of a rather neat scheme, along with a certain dubious middle ground: innocence, experience, and a denied but real uneasiness. Though we may be tempted to take the two women together at this early point in the tale, in fact they too betray subtle distinctions. Alice thus argues for Gamut against the scorn of Heyward, while Cora speaks for Magua (and herself) in urging the others not to judge this "darker" man by his darkness alone. They thereby prepare for their final fates: Alice, like Gamut, will survive; Cora's hidden attraction to Magua of course points to, if it does not insidiously justify, her death in the heart of the dark woods. Alice, that is, aligns herself with art, since Gamut's singing is proof—Alice herself says—that he is "a disciple of Apollo" (p. 28); Cora, on the contrary, is drawn, as much by an artful contrast as by the logic of race, toward the Dionysian forest in which noise rather than music rules. Cora thus moves closer to the woods, though in a more psychic and symbolic way, than any other member of her party.

What comes forth even in this second chapter, then, is an array of suggestive positions, each of which gains meaning against the sketched environment where we find all the actors. In a simple sense, Natty and the Mohicans are placed in that environment to indicate, by a further contrast like that already drawn between Alice and Cora, a range of positions immeasurably more native than any we yet have seen. Yet in fact Magua, if we attend to the hints about him and not just to the obvious information, is more native still—as I suggested above. And Natty's placement in this world is in fact quite problematic. He may tell Gamut that the travelers are "lost" and "helpless" (p. 43), or "off the scent" (p. 44), but even though he senses Magua's treacherous intent he can do little about it. Natty tries to stop the Indian's flight (which is allowed by Heyward's awkward intervention—a direct contrast between the two white men), but he reveals himself to be impotently ineffective. "I heard the imp," he says, "brushing over the dry leaves, like a black snake, and blinking a glimpse of him, just over ag'in yon big pine, I pulled as it might be on the scent; but 'twouldn't do! and yet for a reasoning aim, if anybody but myself had touched the trigger, I should call it a quick sight; and I may be accounted to have experience in these matters, and one who ought to know. Look at this sumach; its leaves are red, though everybody knows the fruit is in the yellow blossom, in the month of July!" (p. 53). The "everybody knows," like other false clues in this apologia, aims us away from the frustration Natty really reveals; the point is that he has shot and only nicked Magua (hence the blood on the sumach), a stunning introduction to his career as a forest "hero."

We should have seen the clues already. Natty's earlier talk with Chingachgook has shown the Mohican to be in spirit, as well as appearance, more nearly aboriginal to this forest world. By way of contrast, we should recall that when Chingachgook sings his death song in *The Pioneers* it is Natty who, mediating between the red world and the white, translates it for the Reverend Grant. This dramatic moment is a proof of exactly how far Natty has come to understand, if not partly to share as well, the aboriginal myths. In *The Last of the Mohicans,* on the contrary, Chingachgook must tell Natty the myths of the very ground they jointly occupy. It is the native's "musical" voice (p. 39) that serves as the voice of the landscape here, and that instructs Natty in things which, remembering the hunter's lyricism in *The Pioneers,* we somehow expect him to know already on his own. Natty himself stresses in the new book, however, that he knows only the white version of the American story; and in fact all he articulates of it is the assumption, a rather paltry one compared to what his companion can speak of, that "all the Bumppos could shoot, for I have a natural turn with a rifle, which must

have been handed down from generation to generation"
(pp. 36-37). The Mohican enacts tradition as well as conveying it or speaking it; and his vision, significantly, is sweeping
and contintental.[13] Nowhere in this novel will Natty, on the
contrary, invoke the spirit of "creation." That he interrupts
Chingachgook in the present case with a tiresome bit of popular science about the tides—actually he is wrong—gives the
Indian's words an even greater poetic pitch.

Nor is Natty excluded from the woods simply on this level.
While both Chingachgook and his son instinctively sense the
approach of the Munro party, Natty at first senses nothing at
all: "to my ears the woods are dumb. . . . I see nothing, nor do
I hear the sounds of man or beast." Natty self-deflatingly extends the evidence of his incapacity: "'tis strange that an
Indian should understand white sounds better than a man
who, his very enemies will own, has no cross in his blood, although he may have lived with the red skins long enough to
be suspected! Ha! there goes something like the cracking of a
dry stick, too—now I hear the bushes move—yes, yes, there is
a trampling that I mistook for the falls—and—but here they
come themselves; God keep them from the Iroquois!" (p.
42). This is not competence, let alone skill, and the halting
humor of it all is part of the meaning; throughout the book,
Natty will be bound by the limits revealed here.[14]

And indeed the wilderness is primarily a place of limits,
perceptual and otherwise. Nothing significant in the novel is
unconditioned by the "fatal region"—the "bloody arena,"
as Cooper also calls it at the start (p. 13)—where the action
takes place. The very first sentence of the book thus sets the
mood as well as the scene: "It was a feature peculiar to the
colonial wars of North America," Cooper writes, "that the
toils and dangers of the wilderness were to be encountered
before the adverse hosts could meet" (p. 11). The army that
departs from Fort Edward at the outset may break the silence of the lingering night with a burst of martial activity,
but the real active agent here is the world it is about to "encounter": "the forest at length appeared to swallow up the

living mass which had slowly entered its bosom" (p. 17). Fort Edward was, of course, a "real" place, publicly recorded and publicly recalled. But the woods encircling it in Cooper's book are a terrain which his private imagination created as it moved, like the army, from a cleared space to one less consoling, less controlled, and less ordered.

It is important to remember that *The Last of the Mohicans* was Cooper's first imaginative foray into the forest, and that he thus was inventing his terms rather than copying them from some vocabulary previously set. But the ominous note of the army's first entrance into the wilderness suggests that Cooper's imagination recognized from the outset what it had to accomplish. The image of American space which that brief passage puts forth is not in itself strikingly original. Yet the novel as a whole consistently develops, and with some subtlety, a series of such images. How often, for instance, the characters merely disappear into the landscape—as if the ground can indeed swallow any figure placed against it:

> the shapeless person of the singing master was concealed behind the numberless trunks of trees, that rose, in dark lines, in the intermediate space. (p. 32)

> the whole three disappeared in succession, seeming to vanish against the dark face of a perpendicular rock. (p. 63)

> and every vestige of the unhappy Huron was lost for ever. (p. 94)

> [Chingachgook] paused a moment, . . . dropped into the water, and sank. . . . (p. 99)

> then, loosening his hold, the water closed above his head, and [Natty] also became lost to view. (p. 99)

> [Uncas] again sank, and was seen no more. (p. 100)

> it seemed as if the earth had, in truth, swallowed up their forms. . . . (p. 294)

> [Magua's] hold loosened, and his dark person was seen cutting the air with its head downwards, for a fleeting instant, . . . in its rapid flight to destruction. (p. 428)

What are we to make of such a pattern? In a novel to some extent modeled on the *ubi sunt* formula—as, in another sense, *The Pioneers* also had been—one interpretation seems immediately clear. The landscape in the book is an image of death, and though some people manage to survive their journey along what Natty calls the "trail of blood" (p. 232), the carnage of the tale is indeed high, Cooper's rendering of it is sharp and even shocking, and his thematic stress on what it all means is insistent. The series of actual or visual deaths which the passages just quoted refer to makes us aware in scene after scene that—contrary to the American settler's mythos—the New World landscape can appropriate those who would seek to appropriate it.

It is the scene around Fort William Henry after the massacre that gives us the fullest revelation of this imaginative truth. Here we see the American border as a devastatingly mortal terrain which serves less as a historic setting than a spiritual metaphor; this is the "evidence" (in literary rather than documentary terms) that makes the very first sentence of the novel grimly correct. "Death was everywhere, and in his most terrific and disgusting aspects" (p. 222), Cooper writes, and he goes on to portray the "horrid tumult" (p. 225) with a seeming conviction that doing so is necessary to his artistic purposes. He claims at the start of the next chapter, to be sure, that "the bloody and inhuman scene [was] rather incidentally mentioned than described" in the preceding one (p. 228). Yet the carnage there had no real precedent in Cooper's earlier books—how right, in this sense, D. H. Lawrence's view of the beautiful "pictures" of *The Pioneers* must seem—and Cooper's own attraction to it here, questions of propriety aside, seems perfectly evident. Even the landscape along the lake in that following chapter hardly is rendered, for that matter, through some decorously obscuring haze: if Cooper does use a certain abstractly evasive language at times—the scene which had been marked by "violence and uproar" now is marked by "stillness and death"—he also seems intent on pointing to the "blackened" bodies which dot the ground, "stiffening in their deformity" under a suddenly wintry sky.[15]

And nature does not soften the shock of history. Indeed, though scorched by the fire that has leveled the fort, the surrounding landscape now is resuming its old face again, and with horrific rather than soothing suggestions: "here and there, a dark green tuft rose in the midst of the desolation; the earliest fruits of a soil that had been fattened with human blood" (p. 229). This is more than a stylish contrast, clearly enough, between the green world and human bloodshed. For if the Huron warriors are said to have actually drunk English blood during the battle ("freely, exultingly, hellishly," Cooper writes with an increase of horror that matches the general trend of his plot [p. 223]), the "fattened" earth hardly rebukes the debaucheries of mankind. In this sense, nature itself becomes a complex symbol of how, in the violent logic of this book, one thing subsumes another: here in almost a literal manner the army has entered the "bosom" of the wilderness. And, intense as this one landscape may be, Cooper does not suggest that its "wildness and desolation" are exceptional; this place merely shows us life in its "harshest but truest colors, and without the relief of any shadowing" (p. 230). Propriety of any sort is just what the wilderness lacks—just what, Cooper seems to be saying, the world in its naked condition everywhere lacks.

Thus the bloody ground about the fort gives a glimpse of that horrid reality which the whole book seeks to reveal. It is appropriate that the Munro party's first real introduction to this universe comes with the slaughter of Gamut's colt, that "innocent thing" (p. 66) whose death Natty would avoid only because killing it will take precious time from the flight. The deed is less a pragmatic necessity than a blood sacrifice performed at the entrance of the dark woods; it thus gives the party a "terrific warning" of the peril also awaiting them. Uncas and his father dispatch the creature with the "calm though steady resolution" of a ritual act. Then the father throws the animal into the dark river, "down whose stream it

glided away," Cooper writes, "gasping audibly for breath
with its ebbing life" (p. 57).

As this last image suggests, water is as central a fact in the
landscape of the book as is the forest whose vast surface it
serves to break and focus.[16] Ideally, the streams and lakes
here—like Glimmerglass in *The Deerslayer*—are allied with
purity and holiness: hence the significance of the "Horican,"
the "holy lake," which is "green and angry" following the
massacre, and lashes the land "as if indignantly casting back
its impurities to the polluted strand" (p. 229). But, even so,
water cannot always resist becoming tainted in *The Last of
the Mohicans.* The Hudson river is "sweet in the shade"
where it takes its rise, as Natty proclaims, but it becomes
"bitter in the sun" once it inevitably falls toward the salt
sea (p. 37)—the "polution" in this case, we should note, having nothing to do with human violence. And "bloody pond,"
though its impurity indeed comes from the history enacted
on its shore, hardly seeks to cast back what has violated it.
Cooper's own narrative first describes the pond merely as it
appears, "a little basin of water" that seems to innocently reflect "the stars from its placid bosom." Once Natty gives
voice to the history of the place, however, Duncan Heyward
must redescribe the "basin" as a "sheet of dull and dreary
water, . . . the sepulchre of the brave men who fell in the contest." In his brief tale, Natty goes on to note that "the dead,
and some say the dying" were cast into the water: "These
eyes have seen its waters colored with blood, as natural water
never yet flowed from the bowels of the 'arth" (pp. 170–71).
He thus suggests that nature at its source may be unsullied;
but the novel, in the most profound sense, is not about
sources.

Soon after the Munro party has paused to look at the dark
pond, so peaceful except as memory recalls its meaning,
Chingachgook murders the French sentinel whom they have
chanced upon and chatted with, rather touchingly in
French,[17] along its shore. The rest of the travelers hear "a
long and heavy groan," then another groan "more faint," and
then "a heavy and sullen plunge into the water." History thus

repeats itself in act as well as word. As the party continues to make its way around the pond, the sound of the waves keeps echoing the "deed of blood" just committed, as well as the older ones reenacted in it. But then the "low basin," like everything else met in this night-obscured landscape, melts into the ruling darkness, becoming merely another part of "the mass of black objects, in the rear of the travellers" (pp. 173-75). The landscape itself can appear, glimmer, and disappear, just as the Frenchman, singing a song of women and wine in the American woods, has—just as so many other people have or will. Even when Uncas kills a deer at the start of the tale, the creature's blood spills into the river, "dyeing the waters" (p. 41), and thus marking the wilderness with the indelible stain of what will follow. The young Indian's act is perfectly innocent: it lacks the cold calculation of the colt's slaughter, or the cruelty of the sentinel's, but the image here in fact prepares us for those later ones. It is, again, a matter of one thing being lost in another—a transformation of singularly terrifying dimensions.

How much any single character could heroically possess such a world without also dying into it is hardly even a question. Presented in what ought to be his proper environment, Natty himself is alienated from it. For this is not, in any conceivable sense, the natural universe which seems to surround Natty's words, and to grow from his spirit, in *The Pioneers*. There is no time in *The Last of the Mohicans* for contemplative pauses of the sort the earlier book affords, let alone for the perception of beauty, peace, and solitude which those pauses promote. Nor is it altogether clear that nature on its own in this new book is as orderly and pure as *The Pioneers* suggests it is. There may be springs of innocence in "the bowels of the 'arth," as Natty asserts. But his moody description of the Hudson as it falls through the gorge at "Glenn's"— this is the longest meditation the novel gives him—conveys a quite different impression of natural order:

> there are the falls on two sides of us, and the river above and below.
> If you had daylight, it would be worth the trouble to step up on the
> height of this rock, and look at the perversity of the water. It falls

by no rule at all; sometimes it leaps, sometimes it tumbles; there, it
skips; here, it shoots; in one place, 'tis white as snow, and in another
'tis green as grass; hereabouts, it pitches into deep hollows, that rum-
ble and quake the 'arth; and thereaway, it ripples and sings like a
brook, fashioning whirlpools and gulleys in the old stone, as if 'twas
no harder than trodden clay. The whole design of the river seems dis-
concerted. First it runs smoothly, as if meaning to go down the descent as things were ordered; then it angles about and faces the
shores; nor are there places wanting where it looks backward, as if
unwilling to leave the wilderness, to mingle with the salt! Aye, lady,
the fine cobweb-looking cloth you wear at your throat, is coarse,
and like a fish net, to little spots I can show you, where the river
fabricates all sorts of images, as if, having broke loose from order, it
would try its hand at everything. And yet what does it amount to!
After the water has been suffered to have its will, for a time, like a
headstrong man, it is gathered together by the hand that made it,
and a few rods below you may see it all, flowing on steadily towards
the sea, as was foreordained from the first foundation of the 'arth!
(p. 68)

This is such an extraordinary passage that it will be helpful
to linger over it. As Blake Nevius has suggested, one function
it has is to fix the setting clearly in the mind of the reader.[18]
But although there is truth in Nevius's further claim that *The
Last of the Mohicans* proceeds from one such fixed point to
another—each of them similarly focused and rendered for the
reader—I cannot agree with his sweeping claim that such wilderness settings have only a minor role to play in the development of meaning in this novel or in Cooper's other "romances of the forest."[19] The river as Natty paints it in fact is a
precise image of what we elsewhere discover to be the spirit
of the larger world; in this one physical description, that is,
Cooper is centering his tale thematically as well as spatially.
We need only observe, for instance, that in a universe characterized by so many downward energies the descent of the
river—even without Natty's (and Cooper's) embroidering
meditation—would be an especially appropriate feature of the
setting. With the meditation added, it becomes a symbol as
well.

All of this develops with a certain subtle richness which the mere push of the plot may cause us to overlook. We should note first that Natty's speech comes forth in the gathering night: he is not referring to the violent and noisy scene outside the cave where the Munro party is resting, but is instead recreating from precise memories what his eyes clearly have seen and pondered on many past occasions. That he can copy the world without really seeing it again is an important sign, regardless of what I have said earlier, of how native to it he in some ways actually is. The fumbling novice who cannot hear the travelers approach three chapters earlier here seems to proclaim, and with a nice lack of conscious intent,[20] his habitation in the forest. He knows his ground. And yet for a man who also is said to have a skill in reading "the blind signs" of the woods (p. 156), a skill necessary to his survival, the spectacle of the falls is not likely to remain a mere spectacle. In all the Leatherstocking books, Natty approaches the world as a practical symbolist: he sees things, but he also sees beyond them.[21] That he has pondered the falls of the Hudson, fixing the place in his mind and speculating on what the place may mean, ought to tell us as much. Again, the fact that he actually is describing remembered images rather than objects outwardly visible at the moment is crucial. For if all language is symbolic, the language of memory is doubly so. When Natty shifts our attention to something really visible, that scarf worn by one of the Munros, we should sense exactly how interior his monologue has been up to this point.

That shift of attention would be in any case a very artful touch. For one thing, it yokes together—as does the "beast" scene in *The Pioneers,* or indeed the whole plot in the present novel—a delicate emblem of the civil ground and a wild fact of the forest.[22] By thus sharpening the larger contrasts of the book, Natty's quick gesture acquires a deeper meaning; by making us see one thing in terms of another, it also urges upon us the greater symbolism of the entire passage and the entire tale.

Perhaps one can go further by saying that the power of the wilderness to condition human life in *The Last of the Mohicans* is nowhere more finely suggested than in the lingering aura which the Hudson has left aglow in Natty's mind. Nightfall or no, Cooper could have described the place more directly if he had wanted to, as a hundred passages in his fiction will show. He apparently did not want a naive panorama here; he did not want images at all in the simple sense; he wanted the sort of flashing afterimage which Natty's words, emerging from the actual forest and from the psychic terrain the forest has created in him, themselves in turn create. The stylistic consequences of this difference are quite important: that long sentence which evokes the shifting motions of the river with a series of quick, choppy clauses ("sometimes it leaps," and so on) simply would not have been possible had Cooper employed his own typical narrative voice. Natty's speech is more fluid, more improvisatory, and hence more like what it concerns. Just as Chingachgook almost sings his myths earlier in the book, Natty here acquires an almost lyric talent; soon, of course, David Gamut will literally begin to sing in the rough cavern.

We can measure some of these issues best, I think, by recurring to that scene in *The Pioneers* in which Natty offers Oliver Edwards a glimpse of the Catskill landscape where so many of his values seem to center. This earlier scene would appear, after all, to be the most direct source for the one just discussed; similar settings are central in each passage, as is the use to which Cooper puts the eye of memory rather than direct sight, while in both instances Natty is conveying to someone else, through his own words, that world which appears to belong to him alone. But here the parallel largely ends. In the earlier book, we recall, Natty describes how his "lonesome" feelings when he first came into the woods made him go to the edge of the mountains near the Hudson; from there he could look relentingly down on the civil landscape he had left behind. But more recently his face turned in another direction: "there's a place, a short two miles back of that very hill, that in late times I relished better than the mountains; for it was kivered with the trees, and nateral" (p. 293). What Bumppo "relished" in the wilder terrain is absolutely clear:

> Why, there's a fall in the hills, where the water of two little ponds that lie near each other breaks out of their bounds, and runs over the rocks into the valley. The stream is, maybe, such a one as would turn a mill, if so useless a thing was wanted in the wilderness. But the hand that made that "Leap" never made a mill! There the water comes crooking and winding among the rocks, first so slow that a trout could swim in it, and then starting and running like a creater that wanted to make a far spring, till it gets to where the mountain divides, like the cleft hoof of a deer, leaving a deep hollow for the brook to tumble into. The first pitch is nigh two hundred feet, and the water looks like flakes of driven snow, afore it touches the bottom; and there the stream gathers together again for a new start, and maybe flutters over fifty feet of flat-rock, before it falls for another hundred, when it jumps about from shelf to shelf, first turning this-away and then turning that-away, striving to get out of the hollow, till it finally comes to the plain. (p. 293)

All here evinces a will toward order. In name and in fact, the "Leap" itself seems not only to accept but even to rejoice in its fate—the "far spring," the "new start," the "striving," the "merry time it has till it gets down off the mountain" (p. 294) all tell us as much. And the whole landscape seems just as directed and orderly. The rock in the gorge, as Natty goes on to say, "sweeps like mason-work, in a half-round"; and he makes it clear exactly who the "mason" is—"To my judgment, lad," he tells Edwards, "it's the best piece of work that I've met with in the woods; and none know how often the hand of God is seen in the wilderness, but them that rove it for a man's life." Where so much in the visible world seems to cohere, Natty himself is soothed: "It is a spot to make a man solemnize" (p. 294).

Many of the contrasts to be drawn between this scene and the one from *The Last of the Mohicans* are obvious. Perhaps one slightly less so ought to be stressed here. For the very style of the "Leap" passage, like what it conveys, has the kind of linear order and clarity which the other passage lacks. Natty's words in *The Pioneers* thus reflect and reinforce the vision which is Cooper's real subject. We move from point to point in a progressive fashion, while in *The Last of the Mohicans* various details of the setting come up (to borrow Natty's own phrase) "by no rule at all": "sometimes it leaps, sometimes it tumbles; there, it skips; here, it shoots; in one place, 'tis white as snow, and in another 'tis green as grass...." This is a collection of facts without any other sequence than that of the prose itself: a prose as wild as the setting, the action, or the theme of the novel. Natty's speech in *The Last of the Mohicans* calls into being a world without "rule" in all its reaches, and almost without that ruling God whom *The Pioneers* much more directly introduces into the wilderness. Something more than human blood or human violence alone—however potent these forces are—is to blame here. There exists at the very heart of the book a vision of chaos so profoundly upsetting that hardly anything remains untransformed by it. And yet the whole of this novel was written, in one sense, to give a fuller account of Leatherstocking's forest world—that very world which, in his tale to Edwards on Otsego Lake, he had painted with a radically different, a deeply ordered, art.

In some ways, as the spatial scheme of the opening chapters suggests, the wilderness in *The Last of the Mohicans* does have a moral order. Otherwise, the long education of Duncan Heyward—who begins by rattling his sword and ends by acting the part of an Indian—simply could not take place. But Heyward's initiation is part of the book's overt moralism; it seems less imagined than plotted, and the book probes depths of meaning to which Heyward himself, whose Indian role is after all that of a tribal clown, remains oblivious. What the officer learns has its importance, yet it is part of Cooper's attempt to give public design to what he was more privately intent upon. Here we may locate an essentially social theme, an attempt to civilize the forest ethically, to which Cooper acceded without taking it to heart.[23]

How inadequate that theme became as Cooper pushed farther into the wilderness of his imagination the growing chaos of the action hints. That the second half of the novel is more orderly than the first has been argued, with a persuasive marshalling of schematic evidence, by Peck.[24] Yet it remains true in another sense that the shift of scene from the fort to the Indian village, though it may replace the terrain of history with that of myth, after all pushes the action more deeply into the forest. And this deeper penetration yields, by the end, a series of murders more tragically meaningful than any of those that occur, namelessly even if horrifically, during the massacre at William Henry. Carnage is replaced by a discriminating violence which has more impact precisely because its victims are known individually to the reader. The chaos of the close, that is, assaults the very center of Cooper's cast: the deaths of Cora and Uncas seal this final extremity.[25]

But this is not to say that Cooper's mind was so attached to the clearing that he could imagine the forest only as an increasingly uncivil ground. Indeed, we probably should take the wilderness in this novel not as Cooper's attempt to render one part of the public landscape, but rather as a projection of forces at work in his own psyche. Like the clearing itself, the forest served him as a metaphor of something he had to describe regardless of the particular terms he might choose. And to draw basically political conclusions from any given part of his New World scene is thus to reduce to flat statements what Cooper typically rendered with a power greater than that which his ideological attachments usually could release in him. The vision of chaos in *The Last of the Mohicans* is really a vision of the chaotic energies of his own creativity.

After we have assigned to various sources—the Gothicism of the border, for instance, as Brockden Brown had originated it—their various values, we are left with the fact that the novel seems to have been dreamed as much as composed. How else but as a dream should one take, for instance, this description of the Indian village:

> A dozen blazing piles now shed their lurid brightness on the place, which resembled some unhallowed and supernatural arena, in which malicious demons had assembled to act their bloody and lawless rites. The forms in the back-ground looked like unearthly beings, gliding before the eye, and cleaving the air with frantic and unmeaning gestures; while the savage passions of such as passed the flames, were rendered fearfully distinct by the gleams that shot athwart their inflamed visages. (p. 301)

That this is not a fully controlled scene those "unmeaning gestures" ought clearly to suggest. Cooper can indicate action but not really name it, much as, in Natty's speech about the river, the prose jumps here and there about the remembered scene without giving it a linear and rational order. In the present case, moreover, one finds that vaguely indeterminate but nonetheless real sense of threat which dreams often reveal. The "resemblance" noted in the first sentence thus seems to give a metaphoric clarity to what is being literally seen; yet the "bloody and lawless rites" of the "unhallowed" arena are hardly more specific than the literal deeds they ought to explain. We go from one feverish image to another. And all the time, despite the vagueness, we are absolutely certain of the enormous specificity of what is taking place. The felt meaning of the scene comes across with real intensity.[26]

Cooper himself described the novel as more "intense" than either *The Pioneers* or *The Prairie*.[27] He apparently meant that the plot had a faster pace; but the term he chose surely has another kind of justness to it. We know, for one thing, that Cooper wrote *The Last of the Mohicans* with a speed unusual even for him—Susan Cooper said "some three or four months." We also know that, while writing it, he suffered from "a serious illness" apparently brought on, as the attack in 1823 partly had been, by sunstroke. The "nervous dyspepsia" which was to afflict him in later years followed on this

new illness; but the present disorder was characterized
instead by a high fever bordering on delirium. Since he had
been engaged with the new work before its onset, during the
fever itself "his mind was filled with images connected with
the book." Indeed, Susan's phrase here—"filled with images"
—hardly seems strong enough:

> One afternoon, suddenly rousing himself, he called for pen and
> paper; but, too ill to use them himself, he requested Mrs. Cooper,
> watching anxiously at his side, to write to his dictation. Most reluc-
> tantly, and in fear of delirium, the request was complied with, and
> solely with a view of relieving his mind from temporary excitement.
> A page of notes was rapidly dictated, and written out; to his alarmed
> nurse they appeared the wild incoherent fancies of delirium, with
> which the names of Natty, Chingachgook, and Cora, already familiar
> to her, were blended. But in truth there was no delirium; a clear and
> vivid picture of the struggle between Magua and Chingachgook filled
> his mind at the moment, and only a few weeks later the chapter—the
> twelfth of the book—was actually written from that rude sketch.
> And this proved to be one of the very few instances in which prelim-
> inary notes related to a work in hand were thrown on paper.[28]

Clinical questions aside, one certainly feels that part of the
"crisis" described here by Susan was not so much medical as
imaginative. One cannot attribute the feverishness of the
"work in hand," at any rate, simply to the literal fever
Cooper was suffering; the illness and the book seem more like
the joint symptoms of some larger disorder. Indeed, in view
of the nature of the novel, one may go so far as to wonder
whether—sunstroke or no—it was not a catalyst of the
physical delirium.

So at any rate we may speculate, using *The Last of the
Mohicans* itself as part of the evidence. For confirmation of a
sort we can turn as well to Cooper's previous book, *Lionel
Lincoln,* as "intense" in its own way as anything Cooper
so far had written. Though meticulously researched and
aimed in part toward a national audience about to celebrate,
with Lafayette, the fiftieth anniversary of the Republic, this
tale of the Revolution reveals a fascination with dreams and

darkness and violence that hardly can be read as part of Cooper's consciously public purpose. As I suggested earlier, Lincoln's spectral visions give to the historical events exploited in the novel some of the psychic force which events in general were to have in *The Last of the Mohicans* and *The Wept of Wish-Ton-Wish*. In this revolutionary tale, Cooper was experimenting for the first time with the serious potential of the Gothic. And he was doing so in a way most revealing from the present perspective. Although some of the hero's passivity in the face of events surely stems from his political dilemma—American-born, he is a British officer, and thus a "wavering" hero related to those of Walter Scott— much of it comes from the detachment forced on him by the author, a detachment that gives to his experience an odd dreamlike quality. It is as if Lincoln does not really live in the world around him, as if he looks out upon it but cannot enter or affect it, even though it in turn holds a dire threat of affecting him. He in fact is a ceaseless observer whose exact parallel, for all of Cooper's stress on attention and watchfulness, is not to be found in any other Cooper character. And it is here in particular that his present interest centers. For Lincoln's only real way of acting upon the world he watches in scene after scene is to transform it in his mind. He is a study in the mind's inventive power; a study, that is, in the imagination. Placed in a universe dreamily distant from him, he dreams another universe from it. He thus emerges in the novel as a projection of the novelist himself.

This is a tricky matter in which overstatement may amount to falsehood. But the "wild confusion" of Lincoln's nightmare following his dark journey to Copp's Hill clearly is Cooper's attempt to probe the "strange phantasies" of which the mind is fruitful, fantasies which were, after all, Cooper's own stock in trade. That the first of those "visions of the past and future" which arise in Lincoln's sleeping mind presents "the form of his father . . . as he had known it in his childhood" may hold some special importance here; but it is the whole shape of the dream which should concern us. And for *The Last of the Mohicans,* or Cooper's wilderness books as a group, the second of Lincoln's anxious visions matters far more in any event. Here we may find, I think, the real "preliminary notes"—to borrow Susan's phrase—which Cooper sketched for the chaotic landscape of his next work. For the "fantastic phantoms" that perform a dance of the dead on the dark hill in Lincoln's nightmare, led by the idiot boy Job Pray, suggest with real force the demonic Indians whose "unmeaning gestures" give to that nightmarish scene in *The Last of the Mohicans* such an unearthly air. Dispersed by "sudden and loud thunder," Lincoln's "shadows" thus flee "into their secret places," from which he can see, "ever and anon, some glassy eyes and spectral faces, peering out upon him, as if conscious of the power they possessed to chill the blood of the living." The officer's visions grow "painfully distinct" just before he jolts awake to discover—but not before he repeatedly tries to "shake off the images that had haunted his slumbers"—that the "thunder" in fact was the pealing noise of a British bombardment taking place just outside his chamber window (pp. 209–10).

This may be standard Gothic fare, but we should recall that Cooper had not really indulged in the Gothic before writing *Lionel Lincoln*.[29] And in this novel itself the Gothic note seems oddly struck; though there is a stress throughout on sounds and echoes, and thus a generally apprehensive sense of reality, the public events of the plot come across with a clarity and a sweep which Cooper rarely matched in his other writings. The novel thus reads like two books never wholly merged, and two books whose coalescence one is hard put to imagine. It seems as if, in other words, the author was working on two levels between which he was not able to establish compelling and consistent connections—one of which led him toward the objective, verifiable history of the Revolution, and the other of which urged him to make of that history some arcane, fear-ridden, but never wholly realized metaphor. That mad Ralph puts forth the best case for American independence, arguing it with a scrupulous grasp of the issues involved, perhaps indicates that Cooper had glimpsed how to bring the two levels of his imagination together. We have here, at any rate, an aesthetically pleasing effect, but an effect capable, as a contemporary British reviewer sneeringly demonstrated, of befuddling consequences: "we...are...instructed that the separation of the colonies from the mother country was effected principally through the agency of a mad old gentleman, called Ralph...."[30] To take the private motions of the book as part of its public purposes is almost as silly as looking for "instruction" in any novel. The latter foible had the support of criticism in Cooper's period, however, while for the former Cooper himself was to blame. The British reviewer had his point.

In *The Last of the Mohicans* public history comes forth so consistently as a private metaphor that the material of the tale can in no way be mistaken for its essential subject. So, too, that toying with "images" and "shadows" which one finds in *Lionel Lincoln* serves here as the very rationale of the whole plot, not simply as a part of it. Surely the massacre at William Henry had its documentary sources, on which Cooper drew; yet he was not seeking to render that historical event as he rendered Bunker Hill in *Lionel Lincoln*—he was seeking, at some level of his imagination, to use it for its expressive power, its ability to give some determining vision its suitable realization. Cooper thus narrates the massacre with the sort of nightmarish intensity which his previous book can sustain, aside from certain basically undeveloped hints, only by introducing a literal nightmare. The "shrieks, groans, exhortations, and curses" (p. 223) which arise during this "jubilee of the devils" (p. 224), as Gamut calls the massacre, are "real" sounds in their own way. But in them, as in the persistent yells which ring through the tale as a whole—or that general "cry of blood" which in *Lionel Lincoln* bears the news of revolt to the inland settlements (p. 183)—we may hear, I think, the accent of Cooper's own increasingly disordered voice. For the nightmare of *The Last of the Mohicans* is the author's; it is his sensibility which dreams the dream of its action.

We should regard the spectral atmosphere of *The Wept of Wish-Ton-Wish,* to which mysterious sounds contribute much, as another gift which, along with the captivity myth, it derived from *The Last of the Mohicans.* Yet the Heathcote tale has an orderliness which its predecessor, and source, does not. The spectral apprehensions in this case, as I noted earlier, locate themselves firmly in the minds of the characters—so firmly, in fact, that for the first half of the story a reader thinks those apprehensions totally wrong. Only with the Indian attack which results in young Ruth's capture do we realize, for instance, that the weird sounding of the conch shell which hangs at the Heathcotes' gate has been more than a sign of the Heathcotes' shared fear. *The Last of the Mohicans* largely lacks such objective "centers" for its own fear: its anxious patterns, in other words, exist in the texture of the narrative rather than in any developed and controlled dramatic focus. The events which make up its plot have psychic meaning primarily because the way they are told by the author—not the way they are seen by the characters— gives it to them.[31]

Which is to say, without too much reliance on Susan Cooper's teasing anecdote, that the imagination which projected this novel was in a sense trapped within its own creative energies. Indeed, I would argue that the book takes as its main subject not the horrors of the war which forms its objective background but rather the horrific capacity of the mind that chose such a background, and then chose to treat it in such a manner. Its real obsession, in other words, lies with the madness, the "strange phantasies," which cause its own being. *The Last of the Mohicans* is thus among the most private of Cooper's fictions. By leaving behind those parts of the American landscape which he knew better by far than the wilderness, Cooper ironically enough was not detaching himself from his deepest feelings; he was instead inventing an outer terrain which, less restrained by the limits of memory and conscious knowledge, could more passionately represent himself.

It seems hard to imagine Cooper claiming of this novel, as he did of *The Pioneers,* that he wrote it to please his own fancy. And yet there was a different kind of pleasure in-

volved in writing *The Last of the Mohicans.* That Cooper was
making his living, and indeed his identity, by exercising his
imagination is an obvious point. But his lasting emphasis on
the need for attention, a need to which this book accedes
in Heyward's growing sense of "reality," ought to tell us that
Cooper felt continually uncertain about the very faculty to
which he unquestionably owed so much. How else, then, are
we to read Natty's long speech about the river—leaving aside
what I have said about the passage already—but as a worri-
some meditation on the shape-making mind? The speech
indeed seems to direct us, as even Natty's reliance on his
memory suggests, toward that power which "fabricates all
sorts of images," that power which "would try its hand at
everything." For it is not really nature here that is disordered;
it is rather the mind which, fecund but fearfully unfocused,
would break its bounds and cast the word itself into chaos.
Susan Cooper claimed that, before he left the actual falls of
the Hudson during the trip which inspired the novel, her
father "examined closely" the scene, "with a view to accurate description at a later hour."[32] However that actual
journey may have gone, once Cooper began to write his
"description" of the place it was something other than a
desire for accuracy which guided him. He located in this one
piece of the American landscape—which was, at the same
time, the literal "occasion" of the tale—what we can only
take as a symbol of his own capacities and desires. The river
became a compelling sign for him, we may surmise, because
his response to it accorded with something already at work in
his imagination. Indeed, it accorded with his imagination
itself.

    We need not have recourse to psychological theory in
order to understand such patterns or the energies which fill
and sustain them. In fact, the novel in hand provides all we
need in the way of theory; its own fascination with the
change of one thing into another—seen in the many disappearances, in the allied stress on destruction, the "cannibal"
suggestions, the roiling imagistic intensity in general—tells

us quite directly that the real subject is that imaginative
power which generates from itself, in this book or any other,
the many forms of which art is prolific. That such a subject
ought to have ended in wonder is a response that comes
naturally to the reader. And in many ways, despite the carnage and the horror, *The Last of the Mohicans* has a terrifying wonder at its foundation, the wonder which dreams even
at their worst can evoke. But this is wonder out of control,
wonder transformed into a kind of sickening awe at the
fecundity of disorder here exhibited, a fecundity to which
the only answer is a violence equally prodigious. Hence the
twist of the book's plot: the demonic Magua who rules the
wilderness is from the start a shadowy emanation of the mind
inventing it all—responsible for it all, and yet apparently
captivated by it all at the same time. In this sense, Cora
Munro's subliminal attraction to the Huron is less a racial
slander than a fitting symbol of the author's hidden attachments. Here lies a part of Cooper's own demonic pleasure;
here we find that delight in disorder which, rationalist as
he may have proclaimed himself, continually linked wonder
and violence throughout Cooper's career.

And yet for all of this the novel ends in a comic self-
mockery which folds back on its own obsessions, transforming them as so much else has been transformed, and leaving
us—the dirges for Uncas and Cora notwithstanding—in a
world where health seems oddly recovered. For the crisis of
the many alterations here comes in those last chapters in
which Natty appears as a "bear"—his totem in *The Pioneers,*
as I have suggested—and Chingachgook, who in the stylized
close will call himself "a blazed pine, in a clearing of the pale-
faces" (p. 442), grins forth from behind the totemic mask of
what must have been an exceptionally large beaver. As
Cooper's critics have observed, and his own epigraphs from
A Midsummer Night's Dream hint, the pattern in these later
movements of his art came in part from Shakespeare;[33] yet
the startling comic implications here have not been fully
noted. Natty's assumption of the bear carries out with per-

verse literalness the main image-pattern of the story, for this costuming gives us one thing inside another—a character "swallowed" by a "beast" of the wild ground. But Natty dons his costume, as do Chingachgook, Gamut, and Heyward, as a means of wise survival; it is as if, like the emblem of death painted on Chingachgook from the start, such things protect the characters from what they wear and fear at once. And it is in this way that the shifting appearances of the end, consciously manipulated by an author perhaps now waking from his dream, indeed become comic. One endures here by assuming what would destroy one's life. This was also, we may note in passing, the very principle which underlay Cooper's lasting call for a sharp attention to the given world.

Cooper assumed the wilderness in *The Last of the Mohicans* in much the same spirit, though he did so by an expense of feeling rather than a movement of mind. In the chaos conventionally identified with that domain—"the waste of the creation," Judge Cooper had called the forest—he located the landscape of his own creative wildness. That trait appalled and even revolted him, as this novel demonstrates on any number of fronts. Yet by its end Cooper could take all the images merely as images, and could testify to his own survival by having the innocent "Apollo" of his fantasy, David Gamut, emerge unscathed from the "moment of tumult" (p. 404) which composes the whole discomposed tale. Wandering in a land of dreams dreamt around him rather than by him, Gamut is Cooper's comic, self-deprecatory replacement in the tale; though Cooper also invented Magua and the shadows who attend him, the singer absolves the author of his own complicity in what has occurred. Gamut, too, has been the victim of history; he, too, is a wondering soul cast into a universe of force which finally cannot touch him. If his life is chaos, his spirit is submission, order, and art. And what more would Cooper wish to claim for himself?

Notes

Chapter One

1. *A Guide in the Wilderness,* ed. James Fenimore Cooper (Cooperstown: Freeman's Journal, 1965), p. 9.

2. Ibid.

3. Ibid., p. 11.

4. Ibid., pp. 11–12; 7; 8–9.

5. For the will, see Henry W. Boynton, *James Fenimore Cooper* (New York: The Century Co., 1931), pp. 13–14.

6. *A Guide,* Introduction by James Fenimore Cooper, p. viii.

7. My summary of these facts is heavily indebted to the work of James Franklin Beard, especially in his headnotes and footnotes in *The Letters and Journals of James Fenimore Cooper,* 6 vols. (Cambridge: Harvard University Press, 1960–68). For the sake of keeping notation in the present book as brief as possible, I have limited references to the *Letters and Journals* largely to those cases in which material actually is quoted in my text. For a conveniently compact statement of Cooper's "difficulties," see Beard's Afterword to *The Last of the Mohicans* (New York: New American Library, 1962), and his Historical Introduction to *The Pioneers* (Albany: State University of New York Press, 1980), esp. pp. xxx–xxxii.

8. See *Letters and Journals,* 1: 8–9, for two cases of Cooper's rather offhand attitude toward money.

9. Ibid., 1: 103.

10. Ibid., 1: 104.

11. Beard speaks of the illness, ibid., 1: 84.

12. Unless otherwise noted, I quote Cooper's novels from the Darley edition, issued in 32 vols. by W. A. Townsend (New York, 1859–61). Most page references will be given in my text.

13. Beard suggests the economic motive for *Precaution, Letters and Journals,* 1: 24.

14. This blaming of the ancestors is a startling touch; see Cooper's similar figure of speech in his report of a horserace for Charles K. Gardner's *The Patriot,* reprinted in *Letters and Journals:* "the men of the North looked as blank and solemn, as if they had all lost their fathers, and on examining into their affairs, had found they were not only dead but bankrupt" (1: 100).

15. *The Pioneers,* ed. James F. Beard, Lance Schachterle, and Kenneth M. Andersen, Jr. (Albany: State University of New York Press, 1980), p. 3; this is from the first preface to Cooper's third novel.

16. This Spanish tale has, one should note in passing, a tone remarkably like that of C. B. Brown's fiction. Little could be farther from Brown, on the other hand, than the voice of Cooper's main story.

17. *The Travelling Bachelor; or, Notions of the Americans,* 2 vols. in 1 (New York: Stringer and Townsend, 1852), 1: 154.

18. Cooper himself refers to Jay in his Darley Introduction; for other sources, see Tremaine McDowell, "The Identity of Harvey Birch," *American Literature* 2 (1930): 109–20; James H. Pickering, "Shube Merrit: Freebooter of the Neutral Ground," *New York Folklore Quarterly* 21 (1965): 31–39; Pickering, "Enoch Crosby, Secret Agent of the Neutral Ground: His Own Story," *New York History* 47 (1966): 61–73; and Warren S. Walker, "The Prototype of Harvey Birch," *New York History* 37 (1956): 399–413.

19. *Letters and Journals,* 1: 48.

20. Three exceptions in *Precaution* are the Spanish incident, the gun accident which wounds Pendennyss, and the late scene in the Napoleonic wars.

21. Marius Bewley, *The Eccentric Design* (New York: Columbia University Press, 1963), p. 79, comments on the parallel between Cooper and Birch.

22. *The American Democrat,* ed. George Dekker and Larry Johnston (Baltimore: Penguin Books, 1969), p. 70: "A long absence from home, has, in a certain degree, put the writer in the situation of a foreigner in his own country; a situation probably much better for noting peculiarities, than that of one who never left it." Cooper already had written a decade earlier, of course, *Notions of the Americans*—supposedly authored by an actual "foreigner" adrift in the United States.

23. *Letters and Journals,* 1: 125; see Beard's comment on Cooper's health, 1: 85.

24. Ibid., 1: 125.

25. Ibid., 2: 61, 75.

26. Ibid., 1: 159, 161.

27. Ibid., 1: 160; the dinner was given by the American minister, and the American guests gathered together before the others arrived.

28. Ibid., 1: 200, 196.

29. Ibid., 1: 161.

30. Ibid., 1: 203.

31. Ibid., 2: 16.

32. Ibid., 1: 163.

33. Ibid., 1: 359.

34. Ibid., 2: 76.

35. Ibid., 2: 32–33.

36. Ibid., 1: 354–55.

37. Ibid.

38. Ibid., 2: 4.

Chapter Two

1. Fred Somkin, *Unquiet Eagle: Memory and Desire in the Idea of American Freedom, 1815–1860* (Ithaca: Cornell University Press, 1967), p. 148, quoting an address by Horace Holley at Transylvania University, 1825.

2. John T. Flanagan, *James Hall: Literary Pioneer of the Ohio Valley* (Minneapolis: University of Minnesota Press, 1941), pp. 42-43.

3. Somkin, *Unquiet Eagle,* pp. 159n, 152-53.

4. Ibid., pp. 153-54.

5. Ibid., p. 155; on the "anxiety," see pp. 4-9. See also Wesley Frank Craven, *The Legend of the Founding Fathers* (Ithaca: Cornell University Press, 1965).

6. My interpretation of Lafayette's visit relies substantially on Somkin's insights, *Unquiet Eagle,* pp. 131-74.

7. *The Travelling Bachelor; or, Notions of the Americans* 2 vols. in 1 (New York: Stringer and Townsend, 1852), 1: 38-39.

8. Edgar Ewing Brandon, ed., *Lafayette, Guest of the Nation,* 3 vols. (Oxford, Ohio: Oxford Historical Press, 1950-57), 1: 191.

9. The writer of the newspaper account commented, as Cooper did in his quoted toast, on the "massive and almost impregnable walls" of the fort—and noted in an aside his regret that "only one or two officers of the navy" were in attendance at the affair, a point which a loyal ex-navy man like Cooper might be likely to notice and lament (Brandon, *Lafayette,* 1: 190, 191).

10. James F. Beard, ed., *The Letters and Journals of James Fenimore Cooper,* 6 vols. (Cambridge: Harvard University Press, 1960-68), 1: 114-19, reprints the account; see *Notions of the Americans,* 1: 177-87, for Cooper's later "fictional" report.

11. *Letters and Journals,* 1: 117-19; the newspapers are quoted from Brandon, *Lafayette,* 1: 204.

12. Somkin, *Unquiet Eagle,* pp. 145-46.

13. James Fenimore Cooper, ed., *Correspondence of James Fenimore-Cooper,* 2 vols. (New Haven: Yale University Press, 1922), 1: 100.

14. *Letters and Journals,* 1: 163.

15. Ibid., 1: 153.

16. Ibid., 1: 184; compare this signature, though, to that at the end of Cooper's letter to Mary Jay, ibid., 1: 211.

17. Stephen Railton, *Fenimore Cooper: A Study of His Life and Imagination* (Princeton: Princeton University Press, 1978), p. 130, suggests Lafayette's role as a substitute father; I think this misses some of the tension visible in their relationship, especially the tension traceable to the national backgrounds of the two men.

18. Cooper's letter to F. Alph. de Syon in September, 1825 (*Letters and Journals,* 1: 125-26), refers to some unnamed project to which he has been asked to contribute; de Syon was an associate of Lafayette during the tour, but it is not clear that the project had anything to do with Lafayette.

19. Ibid., 1: 242.

20. John Jay provided some of the materials for *The Spy,* as I noted in the previous chapter; Lord Stanley is said to have suggested to Cooper that he should set a new novel on the upper Hudson; *The Wept of Wish-Ton-Wish* is dedicated to one "J.R.C.," who is credited with supplying the materials for the tale.

21. *Letters and Journals,* 1: 243.

22. *Correspondence,* 1: 151.

23. *Letters and Journals,* 1: 243.

24. *Correspondence,* 1: 119.

25. *Letters and Journals,* 1: 258; see *Notions* itself, 1: x: "The writer has not

the smallest doubt that many orthodox unbelievers will listen to what he has said of America in this work, with incredulous ears."

26. *Letters and Journals,* 1: 257.

27. *Correspondence,* 1: 151.

28. *Letters and Journals,* 1: 228.

29. Ibid.

30. Cooper did not, of course, invent the particular form he finally used; the transatlantic "letter" had been used in many polemical works in the previous fifty years.

31. "America," *The New Monthly Magazine and Literary Journal* 32 (1831): 299, 308.

32. See Beard's comment, *Letters and Journals,* 1: 147.

33. Ibid., 1: 263.

34. The last of Cooper's defenses came in *The Towns of Manhattan:* "It is now just three-and-twenty years since, that, in another work, we ventured to predict the great fortunes that were in reserve for this American mart, giving some of the reasons that then occurred to us that had a tendency to produce such a result. These predictions drew down upon us sneers, not to say derision, in certain quarters, where nothing that shadows forth the growing power of this republic is ever received with favor. The intervening period has more than fulfilled our expectations." If this was aimed at the English, in part at least, Cooper hardly could make new predictions now about America for American readers. Thus he offered these words near the end: "Nevertheless, the community will live on [through any turmoils], suffer, and be deluded: it may even fancy itself almost within reach of perfection, but it will live on to be disappointed." See *New York,* ed. Dixon Ryan Fox (New York: William Farquhar Payson, 1930), pp. 11, 58.

35. *Notions,* 1: 252; this is Cadwallader's comment.

36. Ibid., 1: 60–61, contains a brief view of a typical New England landscape; this is cursory, however, compared to the Mohawk scene.

37. Ibid., 1: 254.

38. Ibid., 1: 246.

39. Ibid., 1: 248.

40. Ibid., 1: 249.

41. *The Spy,* Darley ed., p. 428.

42. *Notions,* 1: 250.

43. Ibid., 1: 251.

44. See ibid., 1: 242.

45. Ibid., 1: 251, 252.

46. *Letters from an American Farmer,* ed. Warren Barton Blake (New York: E. P. Dutton, 1957), p. 85.

47. *Notions,* 1: 252.

48. *The Deerslayer,* Household ed. (Boston: Houghton, Mifflin, n.d.), p. xxxiii.

49. *The Pioneers,* ed. James F. Beard, Lance Schachterle, and Kenneth M. Andersen, Jr. (Albany: State University of New York Press, 1980), pp. 235–36.

50. H. Daniel Peck, *A World by Itself: The Pastoral Moment in Cooper's Fiction* (New Haven: Yale University Press, 1977), argues generally for the first point I allude to; the second point is D. H. Lawrence's, *Studies in Classic American Literature* (New York: Viking Press, 1964), pp. 47–63.

51. Marius Bewley, *The Eccentric Design* (New York: Columbia University Press, 1963), p. 75.

52. *The Pathfinder,* ed. Richard Dilworth Rust (Albany: State University of New York Press, 1981), p. 33g.

53. The latter terms are Natty's in particular, though they and others related to them are used by other characters as well.

54. See *The Pathfinder,* p. 59.

55. All quotations in the preceding paragraph and this one come from chapter 21. I have thought it unnecessary to give specific page references.

56. *Notions,* 1: 105.

57. When the panther threatens her in *The Pioneers,* Elizabeth also tries to pray: "Her hands were clasped in the attitude of prayer, but her eyes were still drawn to her terrible enemy" (p. 309).

58. Mabel has admitted earlier that, as "a girl from the towns," she is "a little disposed to see danger where there is none" (p. 91). Unless otherwise noted, the quotations in this paragraph of my text, and the preceding one, come from chapter 21 of *The Pathfinder.*

59. *The Works of Edgar Allan Poe,* ed. E. C. Stedman and G. E. Woodberry (New York: Colonial Co., 1903), 7: 8.

60. *Eccentric Design,* pp. 76–77.

61. *The Pioneers,* p. 292.

Chapter Three

1. James F. Beard, ed., *The Letters and Journals of James Fenimore Cooper,* 6 vols. (Cambridge: Harvard University Press, 1960–68), 4: 237-38; see also, 4: 78.

2. *The Pioneers,* ed. James F. Beard, Lance Schachterle, and Kenneth M. Andersen, Jr. (Albany: State University of New York Press, 1980), p. 31.

3. *The Pioneers,* Preface, p. 3.

4. Ibid., p. 4.

5. Ibid., Introduction, p. 10.

6. *The Travelling Bachelor; or, Notions of the Americans,* 2 vols. in 1 (New York: Stringer and Townsend, 1852), 1: 254.

7. *Letters and Journals,* 2: 69.

8. Ibid., 2: 59.

9. Ibid., 2: 60.

10. Ibid., 4: 274.

11. Ibid., 4: 73.

12. Ibid., 4: 254; 260; 259.

13. *The Chronicles of Cooperstown* (Cooperstown: H. & E. Phinney, 1838), p. 26.

14. *Letters and Journals,* 4: 73.

15. *The Pioneers,* Introduction, p. 6.

16. Ibid.; ironically, Cooper later summarized Ambrose Jordan's assertion of just this point, and then refuted it—see *Letters and Journals,* 4: 253.

17. *The Pioneers,* Introduction, pp. 9, 8; Introduction [1851], p. 11.

18. *Studies in Classic American Literature* (New York: Viking Press, 1964), p. 55. See Beard's astute comments about "the solid-seeming world of the book," pp. xxiv–xxv.

19. *Letters and Journals,* 1: 85.

20. "The sale of the Prairie shall be a leasehold for fourteen years—it must be a pretty good Prairie too, that such a thorough tiller, as you, wont work the substance from, in that time" (to Carey and Lea; *Letters and Journals,* 1: 131); "Your idea has been followed, and I have got to work on a nautico-lake-savage romance" (to Richard Bentley, regarding *The Pathfinder; Letters and Journals,* 3: 393).

21. *Letters and Journals,* 1: 131.

22. *The Pictorial Mode: Space and Time in the Art of Bryant, Irving, and Cooper* (Lexington: University of Kentucky Press, 1972). Blake Nevius, *Cooper's Landscapes: An Essay on the Picturesque Vision* (Berkeley: University of California Press, 1976), and H. Daniel Peck, *A World by Itself: The Pastoral Moment in Cooper's Fiction* (New Haven: Yale University Press, 1977), also have much to say about Cooper's "pictorialism."

23. *James Fenimore Cooper* (Stanford: Stanford University Press, 1967), p. 30.

24. Part of the "adult" quality here comes from the very moralism of Cooper's tone, something his opening descriptions wholly lack.

25. *Studies in Classic American Literature,* p. 55.

26. Beard's Historical Introduction, esp. pp. xxxiv–xxxviii, discusses the theme of "dispossession" in the novel.

27. For other instances, see pp. 248, 252, 301, 392, and 424.

28. The contrast between Jones's "jolly" song in the Bold Dragoon and Chingachgook's mournful one is worth special note in this regard.

29. Leslie Fiedler's view of Natty as a child himself, and the hero of other children, in *Love and Death in the American Novel* (New York: Dell Publishing Co., 1966) is one version of the misreading; a far more astonishing one, however, occurs in John P. McWilliams, *Political Justice in a Republic: James Fenimore Cooper's America* (Berkeley: University of California Press, 1972), which espouses the cause of social control—and thus the very ends of Richard.

30. *The American Democrat,* ed. George Dekker and Larry Johnston (Baltimore: Penguin Books, 1969), p. 75.

31. *Much Ado about Nothing,* III, iii, 8–9.

32. So is Hiram Doolittle: see pp. 46, 47, 179, 289, 311, 335, and 354–55.

33. See the tags for chaps. 33 (p. 358), 34 (p. 373), and 29 (p. 316).

34. Edwin Fussell, *Frontier: American Literature and the American West* (Princeton: Princeton University Press, 1965), has many good things to say about the novel; but he misses the bitter note in this last of Natty's statements by clipping his quotation of it (see p. 39).

35. See pp. 23, 24: "I would fain establish a right, Natty, to the honour of this death;"—this last phrase being, by the way, a stunning one—"and surely if the hit in the neck be mine, it is enough; for the shot in the heart was unnecessary—what we call an act of supererogation, Leather-stocking." And, "I am out-voted—over-ruled, as we say on the bench."

36. Stephen Railton, *Fenimore Cooper: A Study of His Life and Imagination* (Princeton: Princeton University Press, 1978), pp. 106–10, pursues the particularly knotty problem of Hannah Cooper and Elizabeth Temple.

37. Fussell's treatment of Thoreau in *Frontier,* pp. 191–212, is particularly suggestive on this issue.

38. Peck consciously bases his own analysis on Lawrence, as well as the theories of Gaston Bachelard. He gives a good account of one aspect of Cooper's art, but does not finally suggest Cooper's real complexity.

39. *The Crater; or, Vulcan's Peak,* ed. Thomas Philbrick (Cambridge: Harvard University Press, 1962), p. 230: "that glorious implement of civilization, the American axe."

40. See *Letters from an American Farmer,* ed. Warren Barton Blake (New York, E. P. Dutton, 1957), esp. pp. 42–43: "Such is our progress, such is the march of the Europeans toward the interior parts of this continent. In all societies there are off-casts; this impure part serves as our precursors or pioneers."

41. As a founding member of the American Bible Society in 1816, Cooper was involved in the effort to convert American Indians to Christianity, an orthodox endeavor clearly undercut in the magnificent resurgence of Chingachgook's paganism. See the intriguing letter from a white woman printed in the ABS *Third Annual Report* (for 1819), reprinted in *Annual Reports of the American Bible Society* (New York: Daniel Fanshaw, 1838), pp. 85–86; among other things, the woman tells of an old Indian chief who is nearing death: "'Me old,' said he, 'me soon *lie down,*' spreading his hand with a low horizontal motion; then raising his eyes to heaven, and extending his hand towards me with devout expression... 'but me shall meet *with Jesus!*'" (p. 86). This is precisely opposite to Cooper's scene.

42. Cooper is trying, however, to indicate Oliver's "hysterical" state of mind here (p. 405).

Chapter Four

1. James Arthur Frost, *Life on the Upper Susquehanna, 1783–1860* (New York: Columbia University Press, 1951), pp. 8–13.

2. Ibid., pp. 98–99, gives figures for the population of Cooperstown and other villages nearby, noting that the early growth had peaked in the 1830s. The present population of Otsego County (1980) is, in fact, about what it was at the time of Cooper's death. In *The Chronicles of Cooperstown,* Cooper at several points notes the progressive decline in the rate of growth—attributing it to, among other causes, "the mania for western emigration" (*The Chronicles of Cooperstown* [Cooperstown: H. & E. Phinney, 1838], p. 78).

3. *A Guide in the Wilderness,* ed. James Fenimore Cooper (Cooperstown: Freeman's Journal, 1965), pp. 46–50.

4. *The Pioneers,* ed. James F. Beard, Lance Schachterle, and Kenneth M. Andersen, Jr. (Albany: State University of New York Press, 1980), Introduction, pp. 7, 8.

5. *Chronicles,* p. 68; see Andrew Nelson, "James Cooper and George Croghan," *Philological Quarterly* 20 (1941): 69–73, which, however, overstates some issues. For Croghan himself, see Nicholas B. Wainwright, *George Croghan, Wilderness Diplomat* (Chapel Hill: University of North Carolina Press, 1959).

6. Ralph Birdsall, *The Story of Cooperstown* (New York: Charles Scribner's Sons, 1925), pp. 180–84.

7. Birdsall, in ibid., pp. 163–73, sketches Nash's character. In the novel, the Reverend Grant lives on the outskirts of the village; his daughter's embarrassed references to their poverty suggest another kind of marginality.

8. Ibid., pp. 9–11.

9. This comes from Henry Clarke Wright's *Human Life* (1849), as excerpted in Louis C. Jones, ed., *Growing Up in the Cooper Country* (Syracuse: Syracuse University Press, 1965), p. 112.

10. Jones, *Cooper Country,* p. 112; see also Wright's tale of "Huldah," the storyteller, pp. 109–10.

11. *The Wept of Wish-Ton-Wish,* Darley ed., p. 55.

12. Mark calls himself "a submissive sojourner in the wilderness of the world" (p. 35).

13. In the final sentence of this passage, the text reads "curled" where I have "curl[s]." There is no literal cottage present on the scene; so, unless Cooper is using "as" with the force of "like" (thereby making "curled" a past participle rather than an indicative), the change I have made seems necessary to the sense.

14. Ringe, *James Fenimore Cooper* (New York: Twayne Publishers, 1962), p. 52.

15. "Thus it is that high civilization, a state of infant existence, and positive barbarity, are often brought so near each other within the borders of this Republic. The traveller who has passed the night in an inn that would not disgrace the oldest country in Europe, may be compelled to dine in the shantee of a hunter; the smooth and gravelled road sometimes ends in an impassable swamp; the spires of the town are often hid by the branches of a tangled forest, and the canal leads to a seemingly barren and unprofitable mountain. He that does not return to see what another year may bring forth, commonly bears away from these scenes recollections that conduce to error. To see America with the eyes of truth, it is necessary to look often..." (p. 243). Cooper's general point, however, is somewhat undercut by the catalog of disproportions and incompletions which introduces it. Dr. Ergot, the silly European who deduces everything he "sees" in the colony, is Cooper's dramatic version of the Old World attitude assaulted in the passage just quoted. In my final chapter, I discuss at some length this same general issue.

16. The last page of the novel tells us that the title derives from young Ruth's gravestone; Content (p. 417) refers to her as "the wept of my household." Actually, "Wish-Ton-Wish," which Cooper defines as an Indian term for the mournful whippoorwill—see also *The Last of the Mohicans,* Darley ed., p. 288—was first reported by Z. M. Pike as the Caddo term for the prairie dog; see Donald Jackson, ed., *The Journals of Zebulon Montgomery Pike,* 2 vols. (Norman: University of Oklahoma Press, 1966), 1: 338–39.

17. Cooper's use of the word "devoted" in this case echoes, ironically, Mark's earlier declaration that he will "cheerfully devote to the howling wilderness, ease, offspring, and, should it be the will of Providence, life itself!" (p. 18). See also: "the devoted hamlet" (p. 325) and "these devoted Colonies" (p. 414).

18. The "hints" to which I refer have to do with the surmise of Louisa Grant

(derived, nicely, from Jones) that Edwards is the illegitimate son of a white man and an Indian woman (*The Pioneers*, p. 304).

19. Most of Cooper's tags in the book come from Shakespeare, and most of these come from the tragedies or the problem plays; the spectral theme in the early chapters thus is underscored by four tags from *Hamlet* regarding the ghost (chaps. 9–12), while three others (chaps. 15, 16, 24) come from *Macbeth*. *Cymbeline, The Merchant of Venice, Troilus and Cressida, King Lear, Coriolanus,* and *The Winter's Tale* provide others (respectively, for chaps. 13, 27; 29, 31; 23; 2; 5, 6; and 7, 19, 21). It is worth noting here that Cooper's tags, though they often point toward specific actions in a given chapter, also usually emphasize theme, atmosphere, and—as in the preponderance of them in this book—genre.

20. *The Travelling Bachelor; or, Notions of the Americans,* 2 vols. in 1 (New York: Stringer and Townsend, 1852), 1: 125. This is, of course, the point made by Cooper himself in the passage quoted in n. 15 above.

Chapter Five

1. James F. Beard, ed., *The Letters and Journals of James Fenimore Cooper,* 6 vols. (Cambridge: Harvard University Press, 1960–68), 1: 396.

2. *Pages and Pictures, from the Writings of James Fenimore Cooper,* ed. Susan Fenimore Cooper (Secaucus, N. J.: Castle Books, 1980), pp. 244–45.

3. *Pages and Pictures,* p. 291.

4. *Gleanings in Europe: France,* ed. Robert E. Spiller (New York: Oxford University Press, 1928), p. 5.

5. *James Fenimore Cooper* (Stanford: Stanford University Press, 1967), pp. 70–71; the planning of the book actually began earlier.

6. *Letters and Journals,* 1: 271.

7. Ibid., 1: 284; see also, ibid., 1: 291. In my final chapter, I discuss the earlier appearance of the "spectral" theme in Cooper.

8. Ibid., 1: 337. The whole passage from which I quote is so long that it suggests some special attraction in the experience.

9. *The Travelling Bachelor; or, Notions of the Americans,* 2 vols. in 1 (New York: Stringer and Townsend, 1852), 1: 245. We also may note here the bloody "end" that comes at the middle of *The Last of the Mohicans;* after the battle at Fort William Henry, Cooper likewise gestures toward the reviving landscape— chilled by a return of winter—while he brings his characters once more into the ruined scene.

10. *Letters and Journals,* 1: 295, 312–14. See also, 1: 296, 340.

11. In his American tales published before *The Wept of Wish-Ton-Wish,* nonetheless, Cooper had insistently introduced "ruins": the deserted clearing visited by Frances Wharton in *The Spy;* Birch's house and the "Locusts" in the same book, each leveled by the war; Natty's cabin in *The Pioneers;* Fort William Henry in *The Last of the Mohicans,* as well as the old fort in the forest visited by Natty and his companions. Since fire is the agent of ruin in so many of these cases—as in *The Wept of Wish-Ton-Wish* and partly in *Wyandotté* itself—we should recall that Cooper's own house in Cooperstown, "Fenimore," burned in 1817, perhaps as the result of arson.

12. See *The Pioneers*, ed. James F. Beard, Lance Schachterle, and Kenneth M. Andersen, Jr. (Albany: State University of New York Press, 1980), pp. 65–66.

13. On Cooper's sympathy for Nick, see the epigraph on the title page, and the passage beginning "Let not the self-styled Christians of civilized society affect horror at this instance of savage justice..." (pp. 488–89). In *The Last of the Mohicans*, Magua's violence is in part explained by the fact that Colonel Munro has inflicted on him the same punishment inflicted on Nick by Captain Willoughby. But Nick's desire for revenge is handled by Cooper with far more insight, even while it leads to a more radical consequence.

14. Her reminder may tell the reader something of Hugh's "failure" in the army.

15. Maud has executed several sketches of Bob, but her lack of "exaggerated sentiments" makes the concealment of those drawings unthinkable (see p. 284). The miniature of her natural mother allows for more indirection and subtlety; Bob first takes it, for instance, as a self-portrait.

16. Stephen Railton is right in calling our attention to the twisting together of war and family in the novel; but he surely goes too far in suggesting that Nick's murder of Willoughby profoundly enables the love between Bob and Maud. See Railton's *Fenimore Cooper: A Study of His Life and Imagination* (Princeton: Princeton University Press, 1978), esp. pp. 237–38.

17. See p. 83.

18. "They Say" is Cooper's brief chapter in *The American Democrat* on the floating lies of public opinion.

19. *James Fenimore Cooper*, p. 38.

20. *Political Justice in a Republic* (Berkeley: University of California Press, 1972), pp. 82–83.

21. Cooper's actual chapter "On Language" in *The American Democrat* is negligible here; I refer instead to his attempt throughout the book to define his various topics exactly, as well as his opinion that "Men are the constant dupes of names, while their happiness and well-being mainly depend on things....Life is made up of positive things, the existence of which it is not only folly, but which it is often unsafe to deny." See *The American Democrat*, ed. George Dekker and Larry Johnston (Baltimore: Penguin Books, 1969), pp. 236–37.

22. Penguin ed., p. 158.

23. Penguin ed., p. 71.

Chapter Six

1. Though Richard Jones mentions a "beaver-dam meadow" near Templeton (see *The Pioneers*, ed. James F. Beard, Lance Schachterle, and Kenneth M. Andersen, Jr. [Albany: State University of New York Press, 1980] p. 110), Cooper clearly derived the main idea for his setting in *Wyandotté* from Grant's *Memoirs of an American Lady*. See James Grant Wilson's edition, 2 vols. in 1 (New York: Dodd, Mead, 1909), 2: 138–39. Perhaps more important than the physical setting is the "sylvan" fantasy Mrs. Grant entertained for the forest patent secured by her father, a fantasy broken by the Revolution; here would seem to lie the germ of Cooper's plot for his novel.

2. See *Wyandotté*, Darley ed., pp. 513–14.

3. *The American Democrat,* ed. George Dekker and Larry Johnston (Baltimore: Penguin Books, 1969), p. 157; see also p. 70, Cooper's Introduction, where the "fulsome, false and meretricious eulogiums" of the contemporary political scene in America are condemned.

4. Grant's view of the Revolution was that it was caused by such demagogues; she also had little liking for the Yankees—for "Obadiah or Zephaniah, from Hampshire or Connecticut, who came in without knocking; sat down without invitation; and lighted their pipe without ceremony; then talked of buying land; and, finally, began a discourse on politics, which would have done honor to Praise God Barebones, or any of the members of his parliament" (2: 147–48).

5. *The Sea-Lions,* Darley ed., p. 8; Cooper's European trilogy might be cited here as the first instance in which he clearly announced the kind of purpose I am speaking of.

6. Leslie Fiedler's comment in *Love and Death in the American Novel* (New York: Dell Publishing Co., 1966), p. 180, is typical: "[Cooper's] talent for invective and his moral intelligence were greater than his psychological insight or poetic skill, and his collected works are monumental in their cumulative dullness. Particularly unreadable are the novels of his later years, when his invective had turned to hysteria and his intelligence was stifled by his piety." In what I have said about *The Sea-Lions,* however, I am not referring to the "trinitarian" question; the universe of the book speaks powerfully of God's presence—as does *The Crater's* scene—but it hardly can be made to "argue" for a particular institutional or dogmatic position.

7. *The Crater; or, Vulcan's Peak,* ed. Thomas Philbrick (Cambridge: Harvard University Press, 1962), p. 9.

8. *The American Democrat,* Penguin ed., pp. 156–57; also, p. 70.

9. See p. 442, which runs parallel to the passages in *The American Democrat* referred to in my previous note.

10. I will speak about this connection in the book's allegory in a later section of the chapter; for one link not discussed there, see Cooper's (and Philbrick's) note, pp. 297–98.

11. The settings of the two novels also have a certain similarity: Willoughby's "knoll" is an island in the middle of the beaver lake.

12. Richard Poirier's comments on a wider pattern of replacement and destruction in American writing, *A World Elsewhere: The Place of Style in American Literature* (New York: Oxford University Press, 1966), may suggest that Cooper's practice, however intensely personal it was, had a larger national significance. See, too, Poirier's comment on Cooper's handling of dialogue, p. 33.

13. As in a sense he did; his work at the Châlet, as Philbrick notes (p. xiii), must have given him innumerable hints about the slow labor of farming, especially on "new" ground.

Chapter Seven

1. The seven novels are the three others already discussed, plus the four remaining Leatherstocking tales. By including the two "Home" novels and the three Littlepage books, one might claim that a full dozen of Cooper's later books took *The Pioneers* as their "source" in important ways.

2. *The Travelling Bachelor; or, Notions of the Americans,* 2 vols. in 1 (New York: Stringer and Townsend, 1852), 1: 248.

3. Ibid., 1: 244–45.

4. Witness Cooper's complaint about the "collision" in Brockden Brown's *Edgar Huntly* (1799): "the cave scene...contains an American, a savage, a wild cat, and a tomahawk, in a conjunction that never did, nor ever will occur." See the original preface, in *The Spy,* ed. J. E. Morpurgo (London: Oxford University Press, 1968), p. 1. Compare this indictment with Bret Harte's of Cooper himself in "Muck-a-Muck," *Condensed Novels* (Boston: James R. Osgood, 1871), pp. 36–37:

> It was toward the close of a bright October day. The last rays of the setting sun were reflected from one of those sylvan lakes peculiar to the Sierras of California. On the right the curling smoke of an Indian village rose between the columns of the lofty pines, while to the left the log cottage of Judge Tompkins, embowered in buckeyes, completed the enchanting picture.
>
> Although the exterior of the cottage was humble and unpretentious, and in keeping with the wildness of the landscape, its interior gave evidence of the cultivation and refinement of its inmates. An aquarium, containing goldfishes, stood on a marble centre-table at one end of the apartment, while a magnificent grand piano occupied the other. The floor was covered with a yielding tapestry carpet, and the walls were adorned with paintings from the pencils of Van Dyke, Rubens, Tintoretto, Michael Angelo, and the productions of the more modern Turner, Kensett, Church, and Bierstadt. Although Judge Tompkins had chosen the frontiers of civilization as his home, it was impossible for him to entirely forego the habits and tastes of his former life. He was seated in a luxurious arm-chair, writing at a mahogany *écritoire,* while his daughter, a lovely young girl of seventeen summers, plied her crochet-needle on an ottoman beside him. A bright fire of pine logs flickered and flamed on the ample hearth.

And, for it is too good to resist further quotation, these other passages:

> Putting on a white crape bonnet, and carefully drawing a pair of lemon-colored gloves over her taper fingers, [Genevra Tompkins] seized her parasol and plunged into the depths of the pine forest. (p. 42)
>
> Genevra had not proceeded many miles before a weariness seized upon her fragile limbs, and she would fain seat herself upon the trunk of a prostrate pine, which she previously dusted with her handkerchief. The sun was just sinking below the horizon, and the scene was one of gorgeous and sylvan beauty. "How beautiful is Nature!" murmured the innocent girl, as, reclining gracefully against the root of the tree, she gathered up her skirts and tied a handkerchief around her throat. But a low growl interrupted her meditation. Starting to her feet, her eyes met a sight which froze her blood with terror.
>
> The only outlet to the forest was the narrow path, barely wide enough for a single person, hemmed in by trees and rocks, which she had just traversed. Down this path, in Indian file, came a monstrous grizzly, closely followed by a California lion, a wild-cat, and a buffalo, the rear being brought up by a wild Spanish bull. The mouths of the three first animals were distended with frightful significance; the horns of the last were lowered as ominously. As Genevra was preparing to faint, she heard a low voice behind her.
>
> "Eternally dog-gone my skin ef this ain't the puttiest chance yet."

At the same moment, a long, shining barrel dropped lightly from behind her, and rested over her shoulder.

Genevra shuddered.

"Dern ye—don't move!"

Genevra became motionless.

The crack of a rifle rang through the woods. Three frightful yells were heard, and two sullen roars. Five animals bounded into the air and five lifeless bodies lay upon the plain. The well-aimed bullet had done its work. Entering the open throat of the grizzly, it had traversed his body only to enter the throat of the California lion, and in like manner the catamount, until it passed through into the respective foreheads of the bull and the buffalo, and finally fell flattened from the rocky hillside.

Genevra turned quickly. "My preserver!" she shrieked, and fell into the arms of Natty Bumpo, the celebrated Pike Ranger of Donner Lake. (pp. 43–45)

5. See Thomas Philbrick's comments on Melville in his edition of *The Crater* (Cambridge: Harvard University Press, 1962), p. x; also, Cooper's own use of the term "Indians," p. 233.

6. H. Daniel Peck's observations about "centers" in Cooper are quite pertinent here; see *A World by Itself: The Pastoral Moment in Cooper's Fiction* (New Haven: Yale University Press, 1977), esp. pp. 91–92.

7. *Pages and Pictures, from the Writings of James Fenimore Cooper,* ed. Susan Fenimore Cooper (Secaucus, N.J.: Castle Books, 1980), p. 250.

8. Douglas Grant, "The Emergence of an American Literature," in *The United States: A Companion to American Studies,* ed. Dennis Welland (London: Methuen & Co., 1974), p. 317. Compare E. E. Hale, Jr., "American Scenery in Cooper's Novels," *Sewanee Review* 18 (1910): 329: "The forest is always there, vast and interminable, stretching its gloomy extent over uncounted leagues of mountain and valley, unbroken save for accidental clearings by wind or fire or rarely by the settler's axe, by lake or stream, impenetrable save for the runs of the deer or the water-course, or the long and difficult trails of the Indian."

9. Morton L. Ross, "Cooper's *The Pioneers* and the Ethnographic Impulse," *American Studies* 16 (1975): 29–39, is especially good on the actual "local characters" on whom Cooper drew. In "Cooper's *The Pioneers:* Origins and Structure," *PMLA* 79 (1964): 579–93, Thomas Philbrick suggests that we should not overestimate Natty's centrality in the book.

10. See pp. 29, 31.

11. Like the Huron whose eyes are gleaming out from the cover of the woods at the end of chapter 2 (p. 32), Magua can merge with the wilderness effortlessly. I shall later discuss a larger pattern of imagery in which this smaller one fits.

12. Thomas Philbrick, "*The Last of the Mohicans* and the Sounds of Discord," *American Literature* 43 (1971): 29, calculates that "blood" and "bloody" are used "at least ninety-five times" in the novel.

13. Peck, *A World by Itself,* pp. 129–30, argues persuasively that Tamenund serves an equally "mythic" purpose late in the book.

14. Philbrick, "*The Last of the Mohicans* and the Sounds of Discord," pp. 35–36, suggests that the eye as a guide to the wilderness of this tale gives way to the ear—for the forest is a place of "discord" as well as darkness. But Cooper is up to something else in the passage just quoted; Natty's slow reaction to the sounds tells

us in particular of his alienation from the woods. Peck, *A World by Itself,* p. 113, overlooks this early emphasis when he remarks that Natty demonstrates "a cold and unfailing efficiency" in the opening chapters, an efficiency marked by "usually acute perception."

15. Cooper's forcing of such images on the attention of his generally "civil" audience is, of course, another instance of "collision." Witness the "charm" which the polite heroine Mabel Dunham finds drawing her eyes, with intense fascination, to the "unequivocally butchered corpses" on the field before her (*The Pathfinder,* ed. Richard Dilworth Rust [Albany: State University of New York Press, 1981], p. 342).

16. E. E. Hale, Jr., made the latter point in the passage quoted in n. 6 above. Peck's general stress on lakes and streams in *A World by Itself* is also instructive here.

17. Cooper and his family had been learning French in preparation for their European voyage; but his use of the language here, especially because of its soft and musical sound, is more than an exercise—it introduces in yet another way that forcing together of opposites which I am discussing.

18. *Cooper's Landscapes: An Essay on the Picturesque Vision* (Berkeley: University of California Press, 1976), pp. 8–9.

19. Ibid., pp. 11–13.

20. The party is eating a hurried meal during Natty's speech; he uses his "broken fork" to point here and there into the night while talking (p. 69). This is hardly a set piece.

21. Perhaps the best expression of this theme in all of Cooper's works comes in the following sentence: "[Hutter] looked about him in silence for quite a minute, examining the sky, the lake, and the belt of forest which inclosed it, as it might be hermetically, like one consulting their signs." *The Deerslayer,* Household ed. (Boston: Houghton, Mifflin, n.d.), p. 71. So, too, Natty himself is a "hermetic" reader of the world.

22. And the genteel scarf is, paradoxically, as coarse as a "fish net" compared to the "little spots" in the river which Natty mentions.

23. The long line of Cooper's "deliberative" characters, beginning with Frances Wharton in *The Spy,* includes Mabel Dunham, Ned Myers, Miles Wallingford, Corny Littlepage, Mark Woolston, and Roswell Gardiner—as well as Duncan Heyward. In most of these cases a similarly "civil" intent operates.

24. See his chart, in *A World by Itself,* p. 135; Philbrick, "*The Last of the Mohicans* and the Sounds of Discord," argues for a thoroughgoing, and indeed intensifying, sense of chaos in the book.

25. The deaths of the child and its mother, which touch off the massacre, are archetypal rather than specific; we have never seen these characters before, and they remain "victims" pure and simple.

26. Another phrase in the passage quoted above—"gliding before the eye"—is also suggestive. "Glide" is used at many points in the book, often giving motion a dreamlike, floating quality: "At the next instant the form of Chingachgook appeared from the bushes, looking like a spectre in its paint, and glided across the path in swift pursuit" (p. 52); Magua and his men at one point are likened to "a band of gliding spectres" (p. 359); while at the moment of his death Magua's own form "glide[s] past the fringe of shrubbery...in its rapid flight to destruction" (p. 428).

27. James F. Beard, ed., *The Letters and Journals of James Fenimore Cooper,* 6 vols. (Cambridge: Harvard University Press, 1960–68), 1: 131.

28. *Pages and Pictures,* pp. 147–49. Philbrick, "*The Last of the Mohicans* and the Sounds of Discord," pp. 27–28, corrects some of Susan's errors as to chronology: Cooper suffered from his fever in June of 1825, and then again in September. Stephen Railton, who is especially interested in the unconscious as an element in Cooper's imagination, proposes to read chapter 12 of the novel as a revelation of Cooper's most serious inner conflict—"his ambivalent unconscious attitude toward the figure of his father." That the fight scene in this twelfth chapter shows us Uncas poised above Chingachgook and Magua, longing to help his father but unable to strike his father's opponent because the two fighters seem to merge with each other, is indeed an intriguing point, and Railton's reading of the scene is persuasive. Yet one notes as well that this kind of "fused" imagery, as Railton does not notice, is found throughout the tale. As I will suggest shortly, the larger pattern cannot be read as having any specific psychological content; the transformations in the fight scene are as dreamlike as the many other changes in the book. But see Railton's *Fenimore Cooper: A Study of His Life and Imagination* (Princeton: Princeton University Press, 1978), pp. 34–36.

29. As I noted earlier, even in *Precaution* Cooper had shown a Gothic predilection. But *Lionel Lincoln* was in fact his first serious exploitation of this mode.

30. As quoted by James Grossman, *James Fenimore Cooper* (Stanford: Stanford University Press, 1967), p. 43.

31. David Gamut's pious comments on the action might be adduced, however, as one means by which Cooper gives to the tale a certain choral order; certainly some of Gamut's religious conceptions may be taken as interpretative "clues"— see Philbrick, "*The Last of the Mohicans* and the Sounds of Discord," pp. 36–37.

32. *Pages and Pictures,* p. 146.

33. See Philbrick, "*The Last of the Mohicans* and the Sounds of Discord," pp. 32–34, where other opinions are cited. We may note that the tragic citations at the end of *The Pioneers*—from *King Lear* and *Timon of Athens*—serve to deepen the action as much as those in this book serve to lighten it.

Index

Adams, John, 45
Adventure: inwardness of, 63–74; in
 Notions of the Americans, 50;
 prominence of, in JFC, 6, 25, 59,
 64; and realism, 69
Afloat and Ashore (1844), 71–72
"America" (1831), 51
America and Europe, contrasts be-
 tween, 31, 34–35, 36, 49, 52, 60,
 67–68, 157–58, 169. *See also*
 American "simplicity"
American Democrat, The (1838): and
 JFC's "opinions," 177; JFC's pose
 as "foreigner" in, 29; JFC's title
 for, 181; language in, 179–81; on
 law, 100; on truth and falsehood,
 185, 192; virtue of simplicity in,
 35
American "simplicity," 34–35, 44
"Angevine" (JFC's farm), 18
Anti-Rentism, 203
Aristocracy of merit, 23, 32, 34
Attention, need for, in JFC's works,
 5, 63–64, 67, 69, 127, 195–96,
 242, 246, 248

Beard, James Franklin, 4, 19, 37
Betts, Bob *(The Crater)*, 194–97
Bewley, Marius, 2, 5, 64, 71
Birch, Harvey *(The Spy)*: doubleness
 in character of, 174–75; JFC's
 relation to, 28–29; and landscape,
 58–59; and Natty Bumppo, 27, 29,
 34, 73; secretiveness of, 23; "sel-

fishness" of, 175; as self-reliant
 American, 34
Bird, Robert Montgomery, 7
Border: JFC's "turn" toward, 25; lore
 of, 123–24; as metaphor, for JFC,
 5–7; naive view of, 3, 27; and
 violence, 24. *See also* Conversion;
 Forest vs. clearing; Orthodoxy
Bradford, William, *Of Plymouth
 Plantation*, 14
Brother Jonathan, 77–78
Brown, Charles Brockden, 239
Bryant, William Cullen, 211
Bumppo, Natty (Leatherstocking tales):
 "all creation" speech of, 71, 74,
 90–91, 93–94, 206, 212, 228, 236;
 in "bear" costume, 247; "benediction" of, 159; vs. Billy Kirby, 89,
 109, 110–12; cabin of, 91–92, 112–
 14; conscience of, 107; deepening
 character of, 222; disappearance of,
 115; dogs of, 91; vs. Elizabeth
 Temple, 90–91, 115; as evocation
 of nature, 88–89, 105, 108; as
 "forlorn" figure, 73; on "Glenn's,"
 233–36, 246; heroism of, 222;
 iconography of, 89; imperceptivity
 of, 228; JFC and, 29, 62, 88, 105,
 107, 117, 207; and the law, 102–3,
 106–7, 209; on "the Leap," 236–38;
 as "lubber," 63–66; lyricism of,
 236; vs. Magua, 226–27; melancholy of, 93; vs. Oliver Edwards,
 93–94, 115; opposition of, to

265

166, 167–68; paradox as formal device in, 155–56, 178; and *The Pioneers*, 130, 156, 159; plot of, subordinated to setting, 172–73; Poe on, 70–71; possible misreading of, 186–87; public purpose of, 183–84, 187; Revolution in, 155, 161, 166, 167–68, 173–74, 177–80; ruins in, 172; setting of, 154–55, 172; settlement and "creation" in, 163; silence in, 168; social fictions in, 170–71;

space in, 155–56, 169, 170–73, 218; syncopated plot of, 171–72; truth-telling and, 182–86, 192; union of critical and romantic purposes in, 177–78; violence in, 155, 171; "war of words" in, 168; and *The Wept of Wish-Ton-Wish*, 130, 155, 160; writing of, 154

Yale University, 21, 123